Culpable

'This book should be read right across the trade union movement, particularly by those at the top of their organisations. It shows exactly what a trade union should do. From representing its members, to warning ministers before something goes wrong and then campaigning alongside the public when it does go wrong. The FBU took Grenfell into the labour movement and worked with the community to fight for justice. That's what trade unionism is all about and the FBU deserves credit for placing this on record in this manner.'

—Tony Kearns, Senior Deputy General Secretary of
the Communication Workers Union

'It should come as no surprise that it is Paul Hampton and the FBU that have produced this monumental study. They are to be heartily commended for doing so. *Culpable* is a searing indictment of the death and destruction neo-liberalism has wreaked and which the FBU has long stood against.'

—Gregor Gall, Visiting Professor of Industrial Relations,
University of Leeds

'In this harrowing chronicle of the Grenfell fire, Hampton frames the frantic moments of heroism and exhaustion of that night within a calm, detailed account of the FBU's fire safety advocacy over the decades leading up to that tragic event. For all the FBU's clear-sighted insistence that deregulation in public services threatened public safety, Hampton shows how this advice was - and has continued to be - marginalised and ignored by governments and industry alike.'

—Daniel Blackburn, Director of the International Centre
for Trade Union Rights

'If anyone still doubts that 72 people lost their lives in the Grenfell Tower fire because successive governments deliberately took away safety measures in the name of cheapness and profit, this lucid, carefully researched, luminously written book by the Fire Brigades Union's thoroughly professional research officer Paul Hampton will put them straight.'

—Francis Beckett, journalist and contemporary historian

'With compelling detail, *Culpable* lays the blame squarely at the door of successive government policies of deregulation of laws intended to protect lives. It clearly lays out how the interests of corporate profits were placed ahead of resident safety, ignoring numerous warnings of the dangers from the FBU, residents and many other experts.'

—Tessa Wright, Professor of Employment Relations,
Queen Mary University of London

Culpable

Deregulation, Austerity and the Causes of the Grenfell Tower Fire

Paul Hampton

Foreword by Steve Wright

PLUTO PRESS

First published 2025 by Pluto Press
New Wing, Somerset House, Strand, London WC2R 1LA
and Pluto Press, Inc.
1930 Village Center Circle, 3-834, Las Vegas, NV 89134

www.plutobooks.com

Culpable is published with the support of the Fire Brigades Union

British Library Cataloguing in Publication Data
A catalogue record for this book is available from the British Library

ISBN 978 0 7453 5102 5 Paperback
ISBN 978 0 7453 5104 9 PDF
ISBN 978 0 7453 5103 2 EPUB

This book is printed on paper suitable for recycling and made from fully managed and sustained forest sources. Logging, pulping and manufacturing processes are expected to conform to the environmental standards of the country of origin.

Typeset by Stanford DTP Services, Northampton, England

Simultaneously printed in the United Kingdom and United States of America

EU GPSR Authorised Representative
LOGOS EUROPE, 9 rue Nicolas Poussin, 17000, LA ROCHELLE, France
Email: Contact@logoseurope.eu

Contents

Foreword

The Grenfell Tower fire was a preventable tragedy. First and foremost, our thoughts and solidarity are with the bereaved, survivors and residents who continue to campaign for justice and change in memory of the 72 lives lost and to prevent a repeat of this tragedy.

The overwhelming majority of firefighters who attended the Grenfell Tower fire were and still are Fire Brigades Union (FBU) members. The union is proud of their efforts to save lives and rescue residents trapped in an impossible situation. The FBU will represent and support our members, who have been profoundly affected by the tragedy.

The FBU warned for years about the risks in people's homes. The union's officials told ministers, MPs, councillors and chief fire officers about the damage caused by deregulation, austerity and fragmentation. The FBU warned the Westminster government decades before the Grenfell Tower fire about the risks of flammable cladding.

The FBU has worked tirelessly for more than eight years since the Grenfell Tower fire to secure justice for Grenfell. The union supported the community through campaigning, financial donations and solidarity. The FBU was a core participant in the public inquiry. The union nationally and locally has lobbied ministers and politicians.

The FBU will not rest until there is justice for Grenfell. The union and its members will learn lessons from the fire. The FBU supports the Grenfell community in its campaign to hold the landlords, contractors and politicians responsible to account. The union will always fight for a resilient, well-resourced and professional fire and rescue service. Our goal is safe homes for all.

The FBU, which represents the vast majority of firefighters and emergency control staff across the UK, produces this book as a record of the union's efforts to secure public safety over many decades. The union will use the book to educate our members, the labour movement and the public, now and in future, so the Grenfell Tower fire will never be forgotten.

Steve Wright, FBU general secretary

Acknowledgements

This book, like everything the FBU does, is the result of collective effort. It is the product of eight years of serious work since the Grenfell Tower fire, standing on the shoulders of more than a century of FBU organising, campaigning and publishing.

The FBU's Grenfell Tower work until 2025 was led by general secretary Matt Wrack. His immense contribution is reflected in these pages. Head office officials Dave Green, Mark Rowe, Riccardo La Torre, Tam McFarlane, Ben Selby and Andy Dark played important roles. The FBU research and policy department, including Elizabeth Molinari, Craig Lloyd, Rhian Jones, Mary Wedgwood, Amy Gardener, Helen Whittle and Tillie Muir, helped in numerous ways. Steve White made an enormous contribution, as a key FBU official and then expert adviser. Other FBU head office staff provided crucial support.

The FBU's London region has represented members every day since the fire and continues to do so. This includes an unprecedented number of police and inquiry interviews, LFB meetings and personal cases. Other FBU officials also provided valuable representation at interviews. Protecting the health and welfare of members has been paramount. Many FBU officials and members are still deeply affected by the fire and its aftermath. They asked not to be individually named here, which of course we have respected. The FBU's legal team for the public inquiry from Thompsons Solicitors, consisting of Gerard Stilliard and Harry Thompson, as well as counsel Martin Seaward, Nick Toms and John Hendy, gave irreplaceable advice and support.

The book was commissioned and authorised by the FBU's executive council. At the time the book went to press, its members were: Colin Brown, Jim Quinn, Tony Curry, Pete Smith, Andrew Fox-Hewitt, Adam Taylor, Andrew Scattergood, Gareth Tovey, Jamie Newell, David Shek, Joe Weir, Chris Wycherley and Val Hampshire. Ian Murray was FBU president. Steve Wright was general secretary. FBU officials across the UK have represented members, joined the silent walks and campaigned to get justice for Grenfell.

The book quotes some historical texts and contemporary testimony in which speakers have used the term 'fireman'. The correct term is firefighter, which has been used by the FBU and the profession for many decades.

The FBU is grateful to Pluto Press for publishing the book. David Castle, Jonila Krasniqi, Melanie Patrick, James Kelly, Robert Webb, Dave Stanford and Hamish Ironside provided valuable advice, as well as editorial, design and marketing support.

The book is dedicated to the Grenfell community, particularly the bereaved, survivors and residents affected by the fire. It is also written to honour firefighters everywhere who put themselves at risk so that communities are kept safe.

Abbreviations

AC	assistant commissioner
ACM	aluminium composite material
ADB	Approved Document B
ADSU	automatic distress signal unit
Appliance	fire engine
BA	breathing apparatus
BAECP	breathing apparatus entry control point
BARIE	breathing apparatus radio interface equipment
BBA	British Board of Agrément
BRAC	Building Regulations Advisory Committee
BRE	Building Research Establishment
BSI	British Standards Institution
BSR	bereaved, survivors and residents
CM	crew manager
CRO	control room officer
CU	command unit
DAC	deputy assistant commissioner
DCLG	Department for Communities and Local Government
EDBA	extended duration breathing apparatus
FBU	Fire Brigades Union
FF	firefighter
Fire Safety Order	Regulatory Reform (Fire Safety) Order 2005
FRS	Fire and Rescue Service
FSG	fire survival guidance
GM	group manager
GRA 3.2	Generic Risk Assessment 3.2
HMICFRS	His Majesty's Inspectorate of Constabulary and Fire and Rescue Services
HSE	Health and Safety Executive
IC	incident commander
LFB	London Fire Brigade

LGA	Local Government Association
MHCLG	Ministry of Housing, Communities and Local Government
NFCC	National Fire Chiefs Council
NHBC	National House Building Council
PDA	pre-determined attendance
RBKC	Royal Borough of Kensington and Chelsea
SM	station manager
TIC	thermal imaging camera
TMO	tenant management organisation
VISION	mobilisation system used in control
WM	watch manager

Introduction

The Grenfell Tower fire was the most appalling tragedy of recent times. It was a crime and an atrocity. On 14 June 2017, 72 people died and several hundred lost their homes and most precious possessions forever. A whole community faced trauma, displacement and devastation. It was the worst domestic fire in terms of fire deaths within living memory in the UK. The Fire Brigades Union (FBU) offers our condolences to the community for their loss.

The FBU is appalled that eight years since the Grenfell Tower fire, there is still no justice for the bereaved, survivors and residents. Firefighters share the community's anger that those immediately responsible for putting combustible cladding and insulation on this high rise residential building – the manufacturers who made and sold the materials, the architects and fire safety assessors, the tenant management organisation, leading councillors and the construction firms that carried out the refurbishment – have not been held to account.

The fact that this inexcusable incident happened in one of the richest boroughs in the capital city of one of the richest countries in the world, only increases the horror with which Grenfell should be viewed. The Grenfell Tower fire was foreseeable and predicted by residents and fire professionals. The FBU will not rest until those who are culpable for the fire are brought to justice.

THE FBU'S UNIQUE CONTRIBUTION

The FBU has produced this book because the organisation brings a unique and original perspective on the fire, its causes and how to prevent another tragedy.

First, the FBU is the trade union that represents the vast majority of wholetime (full-time) and retained (part-time) firefighters and control staff across the UK. Almost all the firefighters who intervened on the night of the Grenfell Tower fire were FBU members.

The union is immensely proud of their efforts to save lives and rescue people in such a terrible situation.

Second, the FBU has a long history of fighting for improvements in public safety. Before Grenfell Tower was built and during the entire period that the building was occupied, the FBU campaigned for legislation to keep people safe in their homes and workplaces. The union fought against attempts to water down safety regulations by ministers, chief fire officers and corporate lobbyists. The FBU also warned about flammable cladding and other hazards in high rise residential buildings, to prevent such a fire from occurring.

Third, the FBU participated in the public Grenfell Tower Inquiry (GTI) and other government and fire service investigations, to better understand what went wrong and learn lessons. FBU officials represented nearly 700 firefighters and emergency control staff who gave witness statements to police and for the inquiry. The FBU supported nearly a hundred firefighters and emergency control staff who gave oral testimony. The FBU collectively submitted seven witness statements, 23 written submissions and other correspondence. The FBU also worked with Grenfell community organisations and other campaigners, briefed our members, ministers, MPs, the London Fire Brigade (LFB) and other bodies, and spoke to national and local media about the fire.

The FBU believes that the terrible loss of life at Grenfell Tower was ultimately caused by political decisions made at the highest level. For at least 40 years, policies relating to housing, local government, the fire and rescue service, research and other areas have been driven by the deregulation agenda, which includes privatisation, outsourcing and contracting out.

This process has seen the replacement of regulations laid down and enforced by the state with systems of self-supervision, where business interests have taken priority. This can be seen across all areas of policy relevant to the fire at Grenfell Tower: research and testing of construction materials, risk assessment, inspection, enforcement, setting standards and systems of decision making.

Deregulation has been the dominant political ideology of most politicians in central government for decades. But it has also been fostered by the direct lobbying of private business interests. Ultimately this agenda has been driven by the profiteering of private businesses. Corporate interests have been prioritised over and above the needs of citizens. In the case of Grenfell Tower, it meant disregarding the needs of people living in social housing.

THIS BOOK

Deregulation and the FBU's interventions to uphold safety are the themes that run through this book.

Chapter 1 explains the context, setting out the situation when Grenfell Tower was built in the early 1970s. At the time, there were a range of public and private bodies responsible for safety. The FBU campaigned to improve the patchwork of regulation, guidance and research, to provide a more robust safety regime. The Fire Precautions Act originally included high rise flats, but this was removed by Conservative politicians during its passage. This was a missed opportunity as Grenfell Tower was about to be built.

Chapter 2 explains how the Conservative governments of Margaret Thatcher unleashed deregulation on all aspects of British society. This was extended by John Major's administration. The period 1979–97 saw deregulation driven by Cabinet committees and special units, intruding into all aspects of building safety and concocting attempts to weaken the fire safety regime. The FBU opposed the 1980 Green Paper, which proposed austerity and deregulation within the fire and rescue service. During the following years, the FBU opposed ministers' attempts to water down the Fire Precautions Act. In 1985, the FBU opposed the weakening of building regulations and the part-privatisation of building control. During the 1980s and 1990s, the FBU prominently opposed privatisation, deregulation and contracting out, including water, council homes and other public services, as well as threats to the fire and rescue service and the Fire Service College.

Chapter 3 explores how the deregulation continued under Tony Blair's New Labour governments, under the guise of 'better' deregulation. During this period, building safety was further weakened and private approved inspection significantly expanded. Through the Fire and Rescue Services Act 2004, the Regulatory Reform (Fire Safety) Order 2005 and other means, every aspect of fire risk management, intervention, prevention and fire protection were fragmented. The FBU was the most prominent voice opposing the deregulation of fire governance and fire safety by the Blair governments. The union was deliberately marginalised for doing so.

Chapter 4 explains how the Conservative-led governments of David Cameron and Theresa May accelerated deregulation, imposing tight restrictions on new safety laws through the 'one in, one out' policy and other rules, dismantling old ones through the Red Tape Challenge and privatising much of what was left. They also imposed austerity, cutting public services to ribbons. This hyper-deregulation agenda only paused because of the Grenfell Tower fire, as well as their self-imposed difficulties with implementing Brexit. The FBU was foremost among those in the fire sector that fought this deregulation. The FBU opposed privatisation of the fire and rescue service via mutualisation, the sale of the Fire Service College and the attempt to privatise the London control room. The FBU was also the most prominent voice against austerity, arguing for investment, national standards and an independent fire inspectorate.

Chapter 5 examines high rise building safety in more depth. It shows how early warnings about flammable cladding in the 1990s were ignored by ministers and the construction industry. After the Garnock Court fire in 1999, the FBU warned the Westminster parliamentary investigation in writing and with testimony about the risks of flammable cladding. Instead, the building regulations and Approved Document B guidance were further weakened and rendered incoherent, making room for more cladding. Even reports by the privatised BRE sent to government about real fires and deaths in high rise buildings were disregarded. In light of deaths at a high rise incident in Hertfordshire in 2005, the FBU asked for a review of stay put. After further fires and deaths, including firefighter fatalities, the FBU warned DCLG about high rise building safety.

Chapter 6 shows how modernisation, a euphemism for deregulation, damaged the fire and rescue service. After the turn of the century, the Westminster government only took advice from chief fire officers, who implemented fragmentation and austerity cuts. Ministerial oversight was minimal, especially after the inspectorate in England was scrapped. Guidance on high rise firefighting was ineffective. The new regime meant savage reductions in the number of firefighters and far slower response times. In London, this involved the privatisation of fire appliances, training, the aborted sell off of its control room, and other attacks on the workforce. The FBU worked with others in the sector, such as the APPG on Fire and Rescue, the Fire Sector Federation and other professionals to warn of the risks and the weaknesses of the Fire Safety Order, including with fire risk assessors and enforcement.

Chapter 7 explains how the refurbishment of Grenfell Tower destroyed its fire safety protections and paved the way for the fire. The failures of cladding and insulation manufacturers, private building contractors and public bodies before the fire are drawn into sharp relief. Flat doors, stair doors, the smoke ventilation system, the dry riser and the lifts all had major flaws. The needs of vulnerable residents were neglected. Alarmingly, despite Grenfell residents giving numerous warnings of these fire safety failings, none of those responsible for the building listened and acted on their complaints.

Chapter 8 analyses events on the night of the Grenfell Tower fire. It shows that firefighters were faced with an impossible situation within half an hour of the fire starting, with almost all fire safety measures failing to protect residents. Firefighters embarked on a tremendous effort to control the fire and to rescue the residents. The chapter rejects claims that firefighters and emergency control staff were at fault for not evacuating the building sooner. They did their professional best in the circumstances. The blame lies with those who made the building unsafe before the fire.

Chapter 9 looks at responses to the Grenfell Tower fire, mostly by the Westminster governments, through new regulation and guidance. Despite some measures, such as the cladding ban and new laws, the deregulation drive has persisted. Private provision for testing, certification and building control continue. Enforcement remains weak. The fire and rescue service has not received the necessary investment from central government. The chapter critically reviews the work of the Grenfell Tower Inquiry, acknowledging its value but pointing to weaknesses in its findings and recommendations. It describes campaigns by the FBU and others to secure justice for Grenfell.

Chapter 10 reflects on the situation eight years on from the fire, when thousands of homes are still clad with flammable materials and tens of thousands of people are still not safe in their homes. The fire safety regime established by central government failed and must be changed fundamentally. The FBU proposes a transformative programme for fire safety, as part of the union's ongoing campaign to ensure justice for Grenfell and safe homes for all. This requires investment in the fire and rescue service, national standards and consultation with the FBU, the voice of the frontline.

The FBU warned and campaigned on the many of the key issues that led to the Grenfell Tower fire. No other organisation had such a track record in trying to prevent such a disaster. The firefighters' side of the story deserves to be heard.

THE CAMPAIGN CONTINUES

The Grenfell Tower inquiry published its Phase 2 report in 2024. The Westminster government has accepted the report and apologised for past failures. The inquiry made some recommendations the FBU can agree with, but others the union believes need careful scrutiny. The recommendations do not go far enough to transform and revitalise the publicly owned, publicly accountable fire and rescue service.

The inquiry report is likely to set the fire safety agenda for many years to come. It will affect every single emergency fire control, every single fire station, training department, fire safety department, all across the UK. Eventually, the police may bring prosecutions. The Westminster government and other administrations across the UK will make their responses, and the FBU will support genuine positive measures to improve public safety.

The Grenfell Tower fire took place in the capital, but it was not just a London matter and not just a matter for the London Fire Brigade. The FBU said from the beginning that such a fire could have happened in other parts of the UK. Almost every fire and rescue service has some high rise residential buildings on their ground, but the problems are of course even wider. In the aftermath of Grenfell, we discovered that the same cladding is in place on buildings across many parts of the UK in homes, workplaces, hospitals and schools.

The building safety crisis is wider than simply cladding. Hundreds of thousands of people today are stuck in homes with major fire safety problems. Hundreds of thousands of people live in accommodation with failings in compartmentation, in windows and fire doors, and in other basic standards required by law.

Residents and leaseholders are still paying tens of thousands of pounds for remediation work. They are paying thousands of pounds for so-called waking watches, which five years ago the Westminster government and its friends in the National Fire Chiefs Council promised would be a temporary measure.

The fundamental principle is the right of everyone to live in safe homes. Governments at Westminster and millionaire businesses have taken a basic element of human dignity – the right to a decent home – away from thousands and thousands of working class people across the UK. The FBU stands in solidarity with the cladding campaigners, the housing activists and the safety specialists in the fight for remedy. The FBU along with other progressive organisations will have to fight to ensure that those who caused the damage are made to pay for it. Not the residents nor the workers, but from the wealthy and their profits.

1

Housing as a social service

The Grenfell Tower fire on 14 June 2017 led to the deaths of 72 residents and the devastation of a whole community.

Grenfell Tower was part of the Lancaster West Estate in North Kensington, London. It was a residential block of 25 storeys, including the basement and ground floor, rising to level 23. At the time of the fire, there were 123 flats, home to more than 300 people. Grenfell Tower was designed in the late 1960s. Building work began in 1972 and was completed in 1974. Between 2012 and 2016, the building was extensively refurbished.[1]

Grenfell Tower was built at the end of the sustained post-war mass housing boom, which transformed the housing landscape of many UK cities. The building was owned by the Royal Borough of Kensington and Chelsea (RBKC). From 1996 until the fire, it was managed by the Kensington and Chelsea tenant management organisation (TMO).

This chapter describes the post-war context at the time Grenfell Tower was built. It sets out the main building regulations and guidance, particularly those applying to high rise residential buildings. It also examines fire legislation and some incidents that informed safety at the time Grenfell Tower was built.

SOCIAL HOUSING

Grenfell Tower was part of the large social housing stock in London. Social housing is 'rented housing provided at rents below market levels, by local authorities or housing associations, to people who can demonstrate that they are in housing need'.[2]

Social housing is one of three main forms of tenure, along with private renting and home ownership. After the Second World War, home ownership rose steadily, becoming the dominant form of tenure. Social renting rose over the post-war boom, peaking at almost a third of all housing at the time Grenfell Tower was ready for habitation.[3]

The importance of social housing was well captured by Labour MP Aneurin Bevan. He argued that 'one of the reasons why modern nations have not been able to solve their housing problems is that they have looked upon houses as commodities to be bought and sold and not as a social service to be provided'.[4]

Between 1945 and 1975, around 440,000 high rise flats – defined as flats in blocks of five or more storeys – were built in the UK, housing or rehousing approximately one and a half million people. The vast majority of high rise residential buildings were in inner city areas.[5]

After the Second World War, successive Westminster governments made the level of housing completions a major political priority. Initially, all new housing was built by local authorities and private building was rigorously controlled. In the 1940s almost all council housing was built in large, suburban estates in 'cottage' houses. In 1954, the Conservative government relaxed controls on private building and the following year announced that the bulk of new housing needs could now be met by the private sector.

In 1956, ministers replaced the previous site subsidy, that was paid per dwelling, by a much smaller one paid per acre as well as a new storey height subsidy. Flats in blocks of four, five and six storeys qualified for very large increments to the basic house subsidy, wherever they were built. Above six storeys, the subsidy rose by a fixed increment for each additional storey. This encouraged the mass building of high rise residential buildings, commissioned by local authorities but built mostly by private companies. The funding lasted until 1967. The Labour government's Housing Subsidies Act gradually discouraged high rise building.[6]

Grenfell Tower was built at the end of this post-war drive for high rise residential social housing. It is important to recognise the social vectors, such as class and ethnicity that intersected at the block when it was built. Social theorist Ida Danewid captured some of those contradictions:

> When Grenfell Tower was built in 1974, the surrounding area in Ladbroke Grove was known as one of the most degraded places in London. The harsh conditions of the piggeries in the nineteenth century, the slums of the 1930s and the race riots of 1958 had earned the area a notorious reputation … Populated by the poorest of the English working class and people of Irish, Jewish and Spanish descent, after 1948 and Empire Windrush, Ladbroke Grove also became home to the Afro-Caribbean immigrants excluded from living elsewhere, alongside a sizeable Moroccan community. While Grenfell quickly became known as the 'Moroccan Tower' – a result of its large number of Moroccan immigrant residents – it was, like the street that runs south of the building, originally named after Field Marshal Lord Grenfell, a senior British Army officer who served in various colonial campaigns in Africa, including the Zulu and Kaffir wars. A strange coincidence it might seem, but, as we shall see, it is deeply revealing of how racial and colonial logics continue to structure global cities like London.[7]

BUILDING SAFETY

The Second World War exposed the weaknesses of such a fragmented system of regulation and guidance covering building safety. An FBU pamphlet, *Freedom from Fire* (1943) articulated the kind of building safety regime needed in the post-war world:

> The introduction of a new building law designed to reduce the possibility of fire outbreaks by laying down minimum standards in the construction of buildings and the materials used which must be incorporated into all local building regulations, and providing for consultation of competent fire service officers in the consideration of plans for the reconstruction or alteration of existing buildings.[8]

Shortly before Grenfell Tower was designed and constructed, building safety arrangements had changed significantly, towards tighter and more prescriptive regulation.

In 1966, national building regulations came into force in England and Wales.[9] The Building Regulations 1965 replaced around 1,400 local by-laws and were prescriptive. They set out in great technical detail a rigid set of rules with which it was necessary to comply. The Building Regulations 1976 consisted of an A5 publication of 306 pages, with 44 pages devoted to fire safety.[10]

The Building Regulations required that for buildings taller than 50 ft (15 m) the external wall should 'not include any combustible material' and that 'any cladding on any external wall should have a surface complying with the requirements for Class 0'.[11]

The Building Regulations Advisory Committee (BRAC) was constituted in 1962. BRAC was the statutory advisory body that ministers consulted on proposals to change building laws and guidance. It was a non-departmental public body and a designated scientific advisory committee.

London had its own building legislation, made up of the London Building Acts 1930 to 1939, as well as the London Building (Constructional) By-laws. Section 20 of the London Building Acts (Amendment) Act 1939 imposed additional fire safety requirements depending on the height of a building, including an 80-foot (24-metre) height limit for fire safety reasons. Section 34 required that the means of escape from fire had to be satisfactory. After 1965, these regulations were overseen and enforced by specialists from the Greater London Council (GLC).

The modern building control system in England and Wales was introduced in 1966. It was based on achieving minimum standards of design and building work in the construction of domestic and industrial buildings. The regulations were regarded as 'mandatory or non-negotiable, based on prescribed design standards and measurements that developers were expected to follow'. They provided 'little flexibility for interpretation and surveyor discretion, and did not encourage applicants for building-control consent to have recourse to alternative guidance or design possibilities'. Unfortunately, the building-control system was soon subject to 'criticism for stifling innovation in design, adding to development costs, and contributing to the construction of a bland built environment'.[12]

In 1966, the Westminster government established the Agrément Board to provide an independent, authoritative source of data on the performance of building products and their suitability for use.[13]

The British Standards Institution (BSI) was the recognised UK national standards body, established by Royal Charter and partly sponsored by central government. During this period, the BSI introduced test methods to assess fire propagation properties (BS 476-6) and flame spread across the surface (BS 476–7). These tests determined whether products met the national Class 0 classification.[14]

In 1972, the Building Research Establishment (BRE) was created, when three separate laboratories – the Building Research Station, Fire Research Station and Forest Products Research Laboratory came under common management. This was the government research facility. At its peak in 1975, BRE employed 1,350 staff.[15]

The National House Builders Council (NHBC), set up as a not-for-profit organisation, ran an approved house builder register and warranty scheme, to carry out inspection and certification.[16]

Although both the Building Regulations and the London laws permitted some cladding on the external walls of buildings, the Grenfell Tower public inquiry found that the regulations were robust:

> There was no room for doubt about what constituted the 'surface' for the purposes of the external cladding requirements, and specific thicknesses and descriptions were prescribed for external cladding so that there was no ambiguity about what type of cladding was permitted and what was not. As we will see, that clarity was lost in later guidance …[17]

HIGH RISE RESIDENTIAL SAFETY

After the Second World War, the Westminster government published the *Post-War Building Studies*, a collection of technical reports intended as the basis for codes or regulations applicable to new buildings more than 100 feet (30 metres) high. Key recommendations in these reports included:

Limiting the use of combustible materials
Limiting the number of people using a staircase
Recommending two independent escape routes for every part of a building
Limiting the height of single-staircase buildings to 42 feet (under 13 metres)
Promoting self-closing doors.[18]

Fire safety in high rise residential buildings was codified by a BSI code of practice published in 1962. Its recommendations applied to blocks of flats or maisonettes having any floor more than 80 feet (24 metres) above the ground. The height was selected as a basis for the recommendations because dwellings above that height were beyond the reach of rescue or firefighting from a mobile ladder outside the building. The code articulated a version of what became known as the 'stay put' policy:

> The assumption should no longer be made that buildings must be evacuated if a fire occurs and high residential buildings should, therefore, be designed so that the occupants of floors above a dwelling which is on fire, may, if they choose, remain safely on their own floor.[19]

In 1971, the BSI published a revised code of practice for flats and maisonettes, with specific 'stay put' advice to residents. It expounded on the limits of fire service intervention, compartmentation and evacuation:

> Owing to the high degree of compartmentation provided in dwellings in modern blocks, the spread of fire and smoke from one dwelling to another and the need to evacuate the occupants of adjoining dwellings are unusual. The occupants should be safe if they remain where they are. Nevertheless, the possibility that individuals may seek to leave the building cannot be overlooked and provision should therefore be made for the occupant of any dwelling to do so by his own unaided efforts, using adequately protected escape routes within the building without outside assistance …

> It is no longer assumed that when a fire occurs in a block it is necessary to evacuate the whole block, whole floors or even dwellings adjacent to the fire. In an emergency, however, the occupants of dwellings would generally first try to escape from a fire by the most obvious route in order to reach safety before being cut off by smoke and hot gases. Where escape routes are adequately protected, safety may be reached within the building, or in the open air clear of the building, by the occupants' own unaided efforts and without reliance on rescue by the fire service.[20]

By the time Grenfell Tower was finished, the risks of fire in high rise residential buildings, including multiple fire deaths, were known to building safety researchers and politicians. In 1975, a BRE report warned of 'the remote possibility of a catastrophic fire with high loss of life, which would distort the statistical picture, and cause considerable public alarm and disquiet'.[21]

Another BRE paper warned that 'because there is a lack of appreciation by the building profession of the design and construction requirements for dependable fire protection provisions, high life-risk situations must exist in such buildings'.[22]

THE FIRE AND RESCUE SERVICE

The Second World War was the catalyst for a more centralised fire and rescue service, overseen from Whitehall, but still locally governed through fire authorities and boards. The FBU set out its vision, even while the fighting continued:

> The essential requirements for an efficient post-war fire service:
>
> 1. A general community fire extinction service freely available to citizens of town and country alike.
> 2. The introduction of a comprehensive Fire Prevention Act, binding all property owners to observe certain standard fire prevention regulations, and giving the fire service powers to inspect all such places to ensure that the provisions of the Act are not violated.[23]

In February 1945, the FBU convened a public conference on fire protection in London, involving ministers, chief fire officers, fire engineers, councillors and others with a stake in the industry. Jack Grahl, FBU national officer opined that 'it would seem to me to be an excellent thing if from this conference we could get some form of Fire Prevention Advisory Committee which could operate in a purely advisory capacity ...'[24]

The post-war fire sector was governed by the Fire Services Act 1947. Public safety was assured by national standards of fire cover, which proscribed strict numbers of fire engines and response times for higher risk locations. The act established a system based on minimum staffing levels for fire brigades (known as 'establishments'), which meant local fire authorities could not reduce fire cover without the permission of ministers.

The act created the Central Fire Brigades Advisory Council (CFBAC) as the statutory stakeholder body to provide ministers with expert fire advice. The CFBAC was chaired by the fire minister and included representatives from the Home Office, Association of Metropolitan Authorities, Association of County Councils, the FBU, Chief Fire Officers Association (CFOA), London Fire Brigade, Institution of Fire Engineers, Fire Research Station and Scottish Home and Health Department.

The act placed a statutory duty on fire brigades to give advice 'on request' on fire prevention matters, but inspections of high rise residential buildings by firefighters were not required.

During the 1950s, the fire and rescue service was consolidated. However it did not stand still, with improvements to national standards of fire cover and the development of fire safety measures, of prevention and protection. The CFBAC established a fire prevention sub-committee to advance fire safety provision. At the FBU's conference in May 1960, the union discussed a visionary policy for the fire and rescue service, *A Service for the Sixties*. FBU general secretary John Horner explained its purpose:

> The service ought to be engaged on the following line of development: The abandonment of routine chores which now occupy the largest proportion of a fireman's duty period; their replacement by fire inspections, public educational duties on fire hazards, the

> extension of fire prevention duties to the lower ranks, in conjunction with expanded fire prevention departments which, taking over responsibilities under the new Factories Act, should control all public security measures concerned with fire dangers as a whole.[25]

However, as the FBU repeatedly observed, it was often only in response to tragic incidents involving multiple fatalities that fire safety legislation was introduced, starting with factories and offices, then hotels and other higher-risk premises.[26]

In 1961, the FBU successfully moved a motion at the Trades Union Congress (TUC) on protection against fire. Conservative home secretary Rab Butler wrote to the TUC to thank the trade unions for the proposals, promising the government would be taking legislation forward. The FBU threw its weight behind national fire prevention week, organised by the Fire Protection Association (FPA).[27]

In 1962, Conservative home secretary Henry Brooke established an interdepartmental committee of officials to assess the adequacy of existing fire prevention legislation. The committee concluded that it was not appropriate nor practicable for the government to compel the owners of dwellings to protect their property against damage by fire. Instead, this was left to voluntary arrangements between owners and insurance companies. However, the committee found that the law relating to fire precautions in certain kinds of residential accommodation and in places of public entertainment was inadequate.[28] In 1964, a draft Fire Precautions Bill was produced, which formed the starting point for subsequent legislation.[29]

In 1965, FBU conference carried policy on strengthening fire safety in high rise and other multi-occupancy dwellings. New FBU general secretary Terry Parry told the conference, 'we think the law should be strengthened where multi-occupied blocks are concerned'. The resolution stated:

> The Fire Brigades Union considers it essential in the national interest that the functions of fire brigades be greatly extended in the field of promoting and enforcing improved fire safety

> measures in all industrial and commercial premises and all places of public assembly. Additionally, they should also be concerned with the direct promotion of schemes to improve fire safety measures in domestic premises, chiefly by advice and instruction but should be required to approve and enforce standards in premises of multiple occupancy.[30]

In 1966 Labour home secretary Roy Jenkins announced a committee of inquiry into the fire service, chaired by industrialist Ronald Holroyd. The FBU made two submissions and disseminated the inquiry's findings. In 1968, the FBU's first submission, *Backing Britain's Fire Service*, argued that:

> The very first steps which should be taken in the field of fire prevention measures are:
>
> (a) bring all existing legislation dealing with fire safety measures into one all embracing Act,
> (b) produce national codes of practice, and
> (c) strengthen enforcement powers of fire brigades in relation to legislation dealing with fire safety.[31]

The FBU's second submission, *Without a Chance* (1969), made several important recommendations:

> Firstly … the fire service should be the inspecting agency in all matters relating to fire hazards … because they are the skilled people. Secondly, the local authority should be an enforcement agency … they prosecute if necessary … Thirdly, that there should be more statutory powers relating to the prevention of fire. Fourthly, that powers of entry should be given to the fire service in order to carry out spot checks … Consideration should be given to the employment of properly trained firemen on more positive fire prevention duties.'[32]

In May 1970, Holroyd published his *Report of the Departmental Committee on the Fire Service.* Key recommendations included common national codes of practice to standardise essential fire prevention requirements, with flexibility for enforcing authorities to apply them. Fire prevention and building safety measures were also proposed:

> Only men with operational firefighting experience and knowledge and experience of fire should be used for enforcing fire prevention legislation in premises when they have been occupied. We recommend that fire authorities, using their fire brigades for this purpose, should be responsible for enforcing all such legislation ...
>
> We recommend that it should be the mandatory duty of the building regulations authority in England and Wales and in Scotland, where it is not also the fire authority, to consult the fire authority before approving plans of new or altered buildings, so that the fire brigade's views may be taken into account.[33]

Although firefighters already had some statutory powers from factories and offices legislation, these were restricted to certain types of premises. The amount of work involved was never properly resourced by central government. The split in responsibilities between fire services and building control highlighted by the Holroyd report was never satisfactorily resolved.

FIRE PRECAUTIONS ACT – A MISSED OPPORTUNITY?

The passage of the Fire Precautions Act is a stark demonstration of missed opportunities to improve fire safety. Had high rise flats been designated or regulated in some form by the Fire Precautions Act, this would have improved fire safety at Grenfell Tower from the beginning.

The Fire Precautions Act was introduced after the Conservative party under Edward Heath won the general election in 1970. The draft bill, circulated in July 1970, included the requirement that blocks of flats and maisonettes over two storeys high should have a fire certificate. The government estimated that there were 45,000 blocks of flats owned by local authorities in England and Wales at the time. However, it failed to implement this measure.[34]

At least two steps backwards were taken in the course of the bill's passage. First, flats were excluded from the list of premises planned for mandatory fire certification. Instead it was left to the discretion of the fire authority, in consultation with the building authority, to decide whether particular premises should be required to have a fire certificate. Home Office minister Richard Sharples spelt this out at the second reading in November 1970, stating that high rise blocks of flats, 'will not be subject to the designation procedure, but a special procedure'. The new law left the question whether a fire certificate is required in a particular case 'to the discretion of the fire authority in consultation with the housing authority'.[35]

Second, the designation of flats received another blow after environment minister Paul Channon wrote to Sharples with 'official' concerns. He argued that it would be 'important to consider carefully … the rate at which existing local authority flats are to be brought within the fire certificate procedure of the new Bill, and also the standards which are to be imposed under this procedure'.[36]

Sharples accepted that a rapid rate of application and 'the imposition of very high standards' could result in 'very considerable expenditure', making sizeable inroads into authorities' housing budgets. He mentioned a new code of practice for fire precautions in new flats that would call for a secondary means of escape in all but a few types of three- and four-storey and some higher flats. Sharples' reply to Channon included the observation that 'there may well be cases, (although I cannot think they will often arise in council owned property) where the risk of fire is more acceptable than the risk of homelessness'.[37]

The Fire Precautions Act received royal assent on 27 May 1971, although it was not until the following year that premises requiring a fire certificate were designated. The Home Office circular on the new act stressed that a different procedure applied to flats. The Home Office and the Ministry of Housing and Local Government (from 1970 part of the Department of the Environment) stymied the potential for designating high rise residential buildings for the purposes of certification and enforcement action by fire authorities. A Home Office note sent to the CFBAC stated that flats and tenements were premises that would be considered under the act in the future.[38]

The FBU welcomed the Fire Precautions Act. In 1971, Terry Parry told the TUC to support the new law, while calling on the

Westminster government 'to speedily introduce enabling legislation to strengthen fire safety greatly, especially in hotels and hostel-type premises and in places of entertainment and public assembly'. In 1972, the FBU's *Firefighter* magazine described implementing and extending fire prevention legislation as its most pressing priority, alongside firefighters' pay and the consolidation of larger fire brigades.[39]

TRAGEDIES AND THEIR LESSONS

The post-war period saw a litany of fire safety and building failures. These were often followed by inquiries, which drew conclusions and made recommendations for change. Probably the most high profile and relevant to the Grenfell Tower fire were Ronan Point and Summerland.

On 16 May 1968, a gas explosion in a flat in Ronan Point, in the London Borough of Newham, led to the collapse of part of the 23-storey block. Four people were killed and another resident later died in hospital. The Labour government commissioned an inquiry led by Hugh Griffiths QC. One of its recommendations was that the minister of housing and local government must accept responsibility for seeing that the British Standards and Codes of Practice referred to in the regulations were kept up to date.[40]

In response to Griffiths' recommendations, the Ministry of Housing and Local Government asked local authorities to appraise all their blocks over six storeys in height and built of large pre-cast concrete panels. Yet the wider design and fire risk failings persisted with Ronan Point itself and other buildings like it.[41]

On 2 August 1973 the Summerland leisure centre fire on the Isle of Man killed fifty people and injured eighty. The Summerland fire commission chaired by judge Joseph Cantley concluded that no-one – neither clients nor authorities nor architects – ever stood back and looked at the Summerland project as a whole. Summerland's owners were criticised for the absence of an evacuation procedure. The commission found that Oroglas cladding did not play the primary role in the spread of fire in Summerland. However, the void behind the combustible wall 'may well have been the biggest single structural contribution to the disaster of the fire'. It made recommendations on project management, inspection and testing.[42]

After the investigation, Terry Parry praised Lord Cantley's report into the incident. Parry underlined 'the vital importance of someone being in charge from the outset of designing a building of this kind, for that person to be named, to take the major decisions and to be known to be taking those decisions'. He also highlighted the need for 'firm, close liaison from the commencement of a project right through until occupancy between fire officers, architects, building surveyors, planners and all other interested parties'.[43]

Central government had a robust system to assess tragedies and learn lessons, through the CFBAC. On 4 February 1975 a man died on the balcony of his 13th floor flat after a fire at Longlents House in the London Borough of Brent. The inquest coroner called for changes to the regulations in high rise blocks. Labour home secretary Roy Jenkins asked the CFBAC to investigate the incident.

The CFBAC concluded that occupants of flats needed to be more fully aware of the need to keep exit routes free from fire hazards and obstructions, as well as know what to do in the event of fire. The committee recommended strengthening guidance in the code of practice. The CFBAC also suggested reviewing arrangements for the training and equipping of fire brigades to deal with fires in high rise buildings.[44]

As a result of the CFBAC report, advice to residents was improved by an amendment to the BSI code of practice in 1978. This advised that, if a fire was evident or reported elsewhere than in a resident's own flat, residents would normally be safe to stay in their flat. They were advised to close doors and windows, but to leave at once, closing doors behind them, if smoke or heat entered the flat before doors and windows could be closed.[45]

When residents started moving into Grenfell Tower, there was at least a national framework of oversight for high rise safety, and some moves to improve it. There were of course still weaknesses with the system, and an opportunity was missed to designate high rise flats under the Fire Precautions Act. In the succeeding decades that system was dismantled through deregulation, replaced by a light touch and hands off approach that paved the way for subsequent disasters.

2
Thatcher's deregulation unleashed

The general election on 3 May 1979 was a watershed. The Conservative party, led by Margaret Thatcher, represented an abrupt, decisive and unprecedented break with the past.[1] Thatcher was re-elected in 1983 and 1987, until succeeded by John Major from 1990 to 1997. Successive Thatcherite governments aimed to impose their agenda of privatisation, deregulation and contracting out of public services.

The FBU understood the threat posed by the Thatcher government. In July 1979, the *Firefighter* magazine cover featured a large picture of the new prime minister, with the banner headline, 'Wrecker – We name the woman who is destroying the economy'. It added, 'She Cuts, We Bleed'.[2] Another *Firefighter* editorial signalled a clear message to Thatcher, 'Cut out the cuts', warning of the impacts of reduced fire budgets and the threat of shelving fire safety legislation.[3]

THATCHER'S DEREGULATION

In May 1979, Thatcher used the first Queen's Speech of the new parliament to articulate her new approach. She said:

> Our policies will be founded on a firm belief in the need to promote profits and profitability … We shall therefore make a start in extending the role of free enterprise by reducing the size of the public sector – it needs reducing – and by making economies in public spending …[4]

Ministers and senior civil servants assembled to map out their strategy. John Hoskyns, new head of the No. 10 policy unit, authored a paper proposing to 'review scope for, and stimulate, private sector competition to supply public sector services (e.g. transport, refuse collection, housing and maintenance)'.[5] Before the election, Hoskyns had co-authored the *Stepping Stones* report for Thatcher's inner circle, which had bluntly demanded 'deregulating the private sector'.[6]

In July 1979, Thatcher made a speech to the Conservative summer school on 'The Renewal of Britain', in which she pledged:

> We will remove some of the regulations and red-tape which have accumulated to such an extent that some who might otherwise have been working to create wealth and employment gave up in despair. But though leadership can inspire, no government, by itself, can supply the vital spark which has been removed from this nation.[7]

Chancellor of the exchequer Geoffrey Howe chaired a ministerial steering group (known as MISC 14), whose priorities included to 'cut the red tape' and 'let the market economy serve the people'. It instigated an interdepartmental review of the building regulations.[8]

After re-election in 1983, the Thatcher government's deregulation agenda accelerated. John Redwood, Thatcher's policy adviser, drafted a paper on deregulation. He argued:

> Our first conclusions are that the government is still tied up in too many areas it should not be in. It is regulating too many things; administering too complex a system of taxes and benefits; overlapping with local authority activities; and retaining some functions which could pass easily to the private sector.[9]

Thatcher convened a meeting on administrative and legislative burdens with senior ministers and advisers. The record of the meeting stated: 'The prime minister said she was very disappointed at the progress of this exercise.'[10]

During 1985, Lord David Young of Graffham convened a cabinet group on deregulation, known as MISC 114. The committee was composed of key ministers and senior civil servants. The committee met seven times, took papers on reducing building regulations and fire regulations. The final meeting was chaired by Thatcher.[11]

The outcome was the White Paper, published by Lord Young on 16 July 1985, entitled *Lifting the Burden*.[12] It signalled the acceleration of the deregulation agenda, heralding forthcoming changes to the building regulations, building control and a review of the Fire Precautions Act. The White Paper stated:

> Deregulation means two things. First, freeing markets and increasing the opportunities for competition. Second, lifting administrative and legislative burdens which take time, energy and resources from fundamental business activity … Deregulation has been a continuing priority of the government since 1979 and much has already been achieved.[13]

A young Tony Blair, Labour's Treasury spokesperson, challenged whether the White Paper was 'about subordinating vital protections for the consumers and employees in the interests of ideological obsession with deregulation'. He warned that 'any loss of standards … in fire regulations or health and safety regulations would be a wholly unacceptable and wrong price to pay'.[14]

Young wrote to Thatcher, describing *Lifting the Burden* as 'a beginning rather than an end to our efforts'. He argued that 'there is still a long way to go domestically' and envisaged a second White Paper on deregulation in the new year.[15] A new ministerial group on deregulation, known as MISC 121, was established as a result.[16] Thatcher announced the intention to speed up deregulation during the Queen's Speech at Westminster. She said:

> The Gracious Speech continues our reforming approach with a considerable programme of legislation. It provides for measures to promote employment, especially among young people; measures to extend enterprise and increase competition by more privatisation and deregulation; measures to ensure that the social services are effectively managed and soundly financed; measures to strengthen the accountability of local government …[17]

In 1986, the Westminster government established an advisory panel on deregulation, appointing a range of business people. Lord Young, now secretary of state for employment, told the House of

Lords the panel 'has been set up to provide advice to the Enterprise and Deregulation Unit on the impact of regulations on business'.[18] The Department of Employment launched a booklet *Cutting Red Tape*, complete with cartoons on the 'maze' of regulations, business people tripping over, getting strangled or having their hands tied by red tape.[19] David Trippier, undersecretary of state for employment, told parliament how the government drove deregulation:

> There is the small central task force on deregulation, known as the Enterprise and Deregulation Unit, based at the Department of Employment and including staff on secondment from other departments or the private sector; there are the deregulation units in all departments reporting direct to a minister with responsibility for reducing burdens on business; and there is a new system to assess the cost to business of complying with new regulatory proposals.[20]

After the Conservatives won the 1987 general election, the deregulation drive transferred to the Department of Trade and Industry (DTI), where Lord Young and Francis Maude were leading ministers. Maude made clear the continued priority of deregulation:

> The government are committed to reducing the burdens on business – particularly small businesses – from legislative and administrative regulation. Prime responsibility for that task lies with individual departments, but work is co-ordinated by the enterprise and deregulation unit, now located in the Department of Trade and Industry. We aim to ensure that regulation which is unnecessary is avoided or removed; that essential regulation is made less burdensome; and that proper account of the cost to business is taken in all relevant policy decisions.[21]

BUILDING SAFETY DEREGULATED

The Thatcher government pressed ahead to implement wholesale changes to building regulation.[22] In June 1979, environment secretary Michael Heseltine told the Institute of Housing conference, 'I am looking at this because I am determined that the construction of housing and of all other buildings shall be freed of petty, unnecessary and bureaucratic restrictions.'[23]

Behind the scenes, ministers resolved to review the building regulations and planning procedures, including local authority building control, the Building Regulations Advisory Committee (BRAC) and Building Research Establishment (BRE).[24]

In December 1979, Heseltine launched an attack on the national building regulations at the National House Building Council (NHBC) conference. He argued that any new system of building regulation would have to have 'maximum self-regulation, minimum government interference', be totally self-financing, and simple in operation. He advocated the reduction of the building regulations to 'a minimum number of functional requirements and performance standards set out in subordinate legislation along with procedural matters'. The formal requirement of 'deemed to satisfy' should cease in favour of more informal arrangements involving approved codes of practice and technical requirements. Heseltine questioned the system of building control and suggested a system of nationally approved professional 'certifiers' as an alternative to local authority building control.[25]

In 1981, ministers published a command paper, *The Future of Building Control in England and Wales*. It stated that 'the present detailed form of the [Building] Regulations is inflexible for many purposes, inhibits innovation, and imposes unnecessary costs'. Heseltine said it was intended 'to give the industry and the building professions new freedom to regulate their own affairs within the framework of national standards of design and construction'. The command paper claimed that 'the present system of building control ... is more cumbersome and bureaucratic than it need be'. It explained the government would press on with proposals for private approved inspectors, despite significant dissent.[26]

In July 1983, the Housing and Building Control Bill was debated in parliament. Labour MPs opposed the part-privatisation of building control, warning of the risks to public safety. Gerald Kaufman called the bill 'a curious mixture of legislative provision for institutionalised negligence coupled with the most tortuous bureaucracy created to eliminate bureaucracy'. John Fraser warned:

> There are grave dangers in allowing the building industry to collude with a private enforcement service which, at the end of the day, depends for its profits on whether it continues its services ... The developer can choose to go to the local authority under some circumstances and can pick his building inspector under other circumstances. I am opposed to the pick and choose philosophy in the proposed system of the privatisation of building control.[27]

The FBU opposed the part-privatisation of building control and supported other trade unions in the sector resisting these moves. The FBU stated:

> The government's plan to hand building control over to the private sector is tantamount to inviting another Summerland disaster, according to the National and Local Government Officers Association (NALGO) ... The union has launched a campaign against the proposal in the new Housing and Building Control Bill to allow builders to opt out of local authority control. Under the slogan 'This Bill will kill', NALGO is campaigning to highlight the dangers to the public if the government's proposals become law ... [including] the possible loss of 4,000 building control officers' jobs.[28]

The Thatcher government promoted deregulation of building safety through the Agrément Board. In 1979, environment ministers asked civil servants to undertake a quick review 'of the scope for increasing the marketability of agrément certificates' and 'to explore with the British Standards Institution the feasibility of implementing the group's recommendation that the agrément function be transferred to that body'. The review concluded that the Agrément Board should remain independent.[29]

Ministers considered a possible relationship between the agrément system and their new proposals for building control. Housing minister John Stanley told parliament that agrément certificates could be given a role in the new system of building regulations, particularly in the approved documents. The newly christened British Board of Agrément (BBA) welcomed these proposals.[30]

During the first Thatcher administration, the Building Research Establishment (BRE) underwent significant disruption, which would ultimately lead to its privatisation. In 1980, the P-E Consulting Group was appointed to investigate the financial arrangements of the BRE.[31] The Thatcher government examined 26 government establishments employing over 33,000 staff, including the BRE.[32]

Privately, Heseltine wrote to the review team about 'general enabling legislation in the field of privatisation', specifically raising his wish to change the status of the BRE. Labour MP Tam Dalyell asked Heseltine in parliament 'what consultations he is having with the representatives of the building industry on the proposed privatisation of the Building Research Establishment at Watford'. The reply claimed ministers were 'still considering the options for the future status of the Building Research Establishment'.[33]

By 1984, the Housing and Building Control Act was on the statute book.[34] The Building Act 1984 also came into force. It laid down primary legislation for building regulations in England and Wales.

A year later, the Building Regulations 1985 came into operation. The regulations no longer contained full technical details and were cut from more than 300 pages to 25 pages. The 'functional requirements' for fire safety were set out in Part B of Schedule 1. Part B1 Means of escape had its own mandatory rules from which there was no other way of complying. (It also referred specifically to the British Standard Code of Practice CP3, Chapter IV, Part 1: 1971 on flats and maisonettes).[35]

The Building (Inner London) Regulations 1985 brought London into the national building regulations for the first time, just before the abolition of the Greater London Council (GLC).[36] The FBU opposed the Westminster government's plan to abolish the GLC, which had responsibility for both the fire and rescue service in the capital and building safety. The FBU joined the Democracy for London Campaign, warning that the abolition of the GLC would adversely affect public services.[37]

In 1985, the *Burdens on Business* report attacked red tape, advocated self-certification instead of building control. It proposed to reduce and simplify the building regulations, especially the detailed requirements on fire precautions.[38]

Lord Young chaired the Cabinet's deregulation committee (MISC 114). The committee discussed a Department of the Environment paper, *Action Document: Building Control*, which floated the possibility of abolishing the building regulations altogether. It stated:

> The next stage which will start this year is to review the requirements of the regulations, to see how far they can be reduced or dropped altogether ... The simplest and quickest way to achieve de-regulation would be to cease altogether to regulate some aspects covered at present by regulations. Candidates for dropping under this radical option might be the regulations covering ... safety of stairways ...
>
> The option of abolishing the regulations altogether and relying on insurance would, if it could be fully implemented save the staff and resources devoted to building control in local authorities ... Ministers should be asked to consider a more radical alternative of abandoning the regulations in their present form and 'privatising' the setting of requirements by relying on the insurance industry.[39]

Although ministers did not proceed with these drastic steps, they continued their deregulatory drive. Environment secretary Patrick Jenkin pledged that the new building regulations would be 'subject to continuing review to ensure that they comply fully with the principles for minimising regulatory controls set out in the Government's White Paper *Lifting the Burden*'.[40]

The government pressed ahead with private approved inspectors. The Building (Approved Inspectors etc.) Regulations 1985 set out the detailed procedures for operating the system of private certification, to provide developers with an alternative option to local authority supervision. Ministers approved the National House Building Council's subsidiary company, NHBC Building Control Services Ltd, as the inspector to supervise the erection of dwellings of up to four storeys (or three storeys and a basement). The

NHBC's insurance scheme, applying to all dwellings it inspected in this capacity, was also approved.[41]

In 1986, the Department of the Environment commissioned a report on the role and operations of the BRE by Peter Harrop and Henry Chilver. Their report recommended that BRE should be run more as a business, earning income from all its customers and with a target of earning income from non-government sources.[42]

Environment secretary Nicholas Ridley welcomed the recommendations made by the study:

> BRE's primary role should be to act as contractor for government, working on health and safety in buildings, the performance of buildings, standards and codes of practice on construction and the pursuit of national policies on the construction and use of buildings ... Government research conducted as part of its sponsorship of the construction industry should be more concerned than at present with fostering competitiveness and less with performance standards and research of this kind should be carried out mainly through research associations on a cost-sharing basis with industry.[43]

After the Conservative general election victory in 1987, Ridley returned to the status of BRE. Ridley announced that BRE was a candidate for executive agency status within the Department of the Environment. He argued that 'the proposal to designate BRE as an executive agency ... will extend BRE's ability to compete for commissions from both the public and private sectors'. In 1990, BRE become an executive agency. Ministers claimed that it would provide BRE with 'new freedoms and will improve its ability to serve the needs of Government, the construction industry and building users'.[44]

BRE chief executive Roger Courtney noted that by the time BRE was given executive status, staffing had more than halved from its peak in 1975 to just 654 in 1989. Courtney argued that 'the Harrop-Chilver report had clearly paved the way for BRE becoming such an agency'. The move to executive agency status was 'the final stage in BRE's transition from a centrally funded organisation concerned essentially with scientific research to one which provided a range of professional services, including research, for a variety of customers within and outside government'.[45]

ATTEMPTS TO DEREGULATE FIRE SAFETY

The fire and rescue service was the target for central government deregulation during the Thatcher administrations. Within the first year of Thatcher's government, deregulatory pressure began to be applied to matters of fire safety, especially the Fire Precautions Act. In 1980, a major assault launched on the fire and rescue service, when the Home Office published its 400-page, *Review of Fire Policy*. In the polite language of the day, it advocated cuts: 'there may be over provision which may enable judicious reductions to be made which would not result in an unacceptable increase in property loss or casualties'.[46]

The *Review of Fire Policy* was particularly critical of fire prevention and the Fire Precautions Act. It claimed that 'developing fire prevention legislation had placed a significant financial burden on both the public and private sectors of the economy'. The review acknowledged that residents of 'multi-storey, multi-occupied, domestic residential buildings' faced additional risks from fire, including from the actions of neighbours and 'circumstances where they have no capability to secure their own protection'.[47]

The review recognised that 'tenants on the upper floors of high blocks of flats' were more seriously at risk in the event of fire than the occupants of an ordinary house and that 'that the removal of the controls would result in a reduction in standards and lead to the recurrence, albeit infrequently, of multiple fatality fires'. However it noted the Fire Precautions Act had not thus far been applied to high rise residential buildings and opposed extending the law to such higher risk premises.[48]

The *Review of Fire Policy* contained a chilling passage on the effects of reducing the building regulations:

> While it might thus be concluded that large multi-death fires could become more frequent if there was a significant reduction in the provisions of the Building Regulations, it ought to be remembered that, just as the benefits of any additional controls would

> be slow to emerge because of the rate of increase in buildings, the effect of any reduction in standards would be equally long term. It could well be some years before any significant multi-death fire occurred as a result of reduction in building controls ...[49]

Ministers also published *Future Fire Policy*, a Green Paper consultative document. It proposed 'an adequate level of fire protection to be provided as economically as possible'.[50]

FBU general secretary Ken Cameron warned Thatcher that the union would meet any firefighter redundancies with strike action. The FBU launched its alternative to the government's Green Paper at the TUC. National officer Mike Fordham warned it was 'a direct attack on the standards of fire safety'.[51] The FBU's booklet, *Fire Safety – A Public Issue*, set out its objections. The review followed a political philosophy of 'cut irrespective of consequence':

> The review suggested a fundamental change in the way that the Fire Precautions Act 1971 was applied. Instead of all designated premises requiring fire certificates, fire authorities would be empowered to be selective, so that only the 'more serious cases' would still require certificates. The FBU vehemently argued that 'fire certificates are the only means of regulating standards in premises and the only means of the fire prevention inspectors being able to monitor an occupier's continuing compliance with those standards'.[52]

The FBU alternative was to expand the scope and powers of the Fire Precautions Act, legislation to increase the use of sprinkler systems and more resources for fire inspectors.

In 1981, the consultation proposed that the CFBAC agreed to establish a joint committee on standards of fire cover. It spent three years deliberating over whether to reduce the provisions to protect public safety.

In 1982, Brandon Rhys Williams, the Conservative MP for Kensington asked the home secretary if he would consider 'amending the Fire Precautions Act 1971 to include multi-occupied residential buildings among those requiring fire certificates'. Whitelaw replied that because the Housing Act 1980 had imposed a duty on local authorities to require adequate means of escape from fire in houses in multiple occupation of three storeys or more, he did not 'consider that further legislation is warranted at the present time'.[53]

FBU officers' rep Frank Clayton warned of the consequences of introducing self-certifying system of 'responsible persons', instead of fire certification and inspection in the Fire Precautions Act. Clayton argued:

> The system proposes that a person called 'a responsible person' should by means of observance of a code of practice that compliance with that code will become a requirement in order that the premises can be considered satisfactory. The complete onus for compliance becomes the forte of the 'responsible person' who will have been given time limits to meet the standards … Are the Review Committee seriously suggesting that a system which relies upon the trust to be given to individual 'responsible persons' could work efficiently, I very much doubt it … I urge the FBU to vigorously oppose the self-certification principle contained in this document and to negotiate for a more effective and satisfactory system of fire law enforcement to protect life and property to the highest possible standard.[54]

The Thatcher government's second term saw a major escalation in efforts to deregulate the fire and rescue service. Leon Brittan took over as home secretary. The assault on fire safety gathered pace inside central government. Within Downing Street, policy advisers were pushing to include fire regulations in the burdens exercise. One adviser urged the prime minister to 'ask Leon Brittan to report on whether the fire regulations are too costly a burden bearing in mind the obvious sensitivities …'[55]

In 1984, Brittan told the Chief and Assistant Chief Fire Officers Association (CACFOA) presidential dinner: 'We have a duty to the community generally to ensure that the fire service is as cost effective as it can be … Each year, therefore, auditors are asked to pay special attention to securing better value for money in specific areas. Next year the fire service will be one of those'.[56]

Shortly afterwards, the *Report of the Joint Committee on Standards of Fire Cover* was published. It noted the 'considerable boom in high-rise building during the 1960s' and concluded that there was no case for lowering existing standards, including those for high risk premises (renamed 'special risks') such as tower blocks that required a pre-determined attendance. The FBU described the report as 'a victory for the union and other bodies on that committee who fought against a concerted campaign by the Home Office representatives to reduce standards'. The union pointed to a range of incidents, where these standards meant firefighters had made a professional intervention to save lives and rescue people, because they had the resources available to do so.[57]

In 1985, Lord Young's deregulatory drive saw fire precautions come under scrutiny as a 'burden' on business'. Young's, *Lifting the Burden* White Paper lauded the desire to replace the certification requirements of the Fire Precautions Act 1971, even claiming this would 'reduce administrative burdens on the fire service'.[58]

Brittan published a consultative document entitled *A Review of the Fire Precautions Act 1971*. It included proposals for 'a modified system of fire precautions controls which would replace the fire certification arrangements of the current system with a statutory duty on the owners-occupiers of premises put to a designated use to achieve and maintain a reasonable standard of fire safety'. The consultation document made clear however that any changes would not involve increased staffing or increased expenditure levels by fire authorities.[59]

The FBU made a robust response to the review. National officer Dave Matthews unpicked the proposals:

> The government is intent, as it sees it, on lifting the burden of fire prevention from industry which we know will lead to an increase, not only in fire losses and damages, but also deaths from fire ... The document on the whole very clearly shows the proposals have been designed in such a manner so as to provide for a new method of applying fire prevention measures, using the self-regulation practices, aided by flexibility of fire authorities in monitoring standards ... The proposed reliance on the willingness and public duty of the responsible person to carry out his responsibilities without enforcement is worrying ... [The FBU] cannot agree to a set of proposals which in our opinion will lower the standards and effective control of fire protection

> legislation, and simultaneously create a situation within the service that will, in our opinion, inevitably lead to a reduction in fire prevention staffing levels in fire brigades.[60]

Home Office minister Giles Shaw rebuffed representations that some hostels and houses in multiple occupation should be designated under the Fire Precautions Act, thereby requiring a fire certificate. He said 'it has been so far decided that it would be wrong to contemplate any new designations while the Act is being reviewed'.[61]

Behind the scenes, Lord Young continued to warn about 'the costs to and burdens on business imposed by the current Fire Precautions Act and how these may be affected by any new proposals'.[62]

In 1986, the Audit Commission published its first occasional paper, entitled *Value for Money in the Fire Service*. The FBU's conference condemned the report, 'as an attempt to reduce the fire service effectiveness as a public service at the expense of public safety'. It warned that the government was 'placing the public at greater risk from fire in the interest of saving money'. The FBU criticised the decision of the Home Office to set up the working party on the back of the Audit Commission report and committed the union to 'use every means at their disposal to fight any detrimental proposals that ensue'.[63]

Deregulation of the fire and rescue service loomed, despite vociferous opposition from the FBU. Michael Simmonds from the Adam Smith Institute published *The Burning Question*, essentially a manifesto for privatisation. It stated:

> Private enterprise can provide fire services as cheaply and as efficiently as those provided by the public sector ... The government should encourage local authorities to consider incorporating their fire brigades into companies which, although they would be owned (at least to begin with) by the local authority, would have an identity separate from the council. This will enable a more business-like relationship to be maintained and make it easier for potential competitors to compete fairly.[64]

In 1988, the DTI's Enterprise and Deregulation Unit appointed the architects Bickerdike Allen Partners to review the interaction of building and fire legislation. Their report, *Fire and Building Regulation: A Review* was published in 1990. It claimed a 'widespread favourable appreciation of the 1985 Building Regulations as having effectively lifted some burdens from business'. The report proposed giving the fire inspection role to building control officers, 'leaving the door open' to the privatisation of fire prevention through the wider use of private approved inspectors.[65]

The terms of reference were loaded towards deregulation, asking whether fire legislation placed 'burdens on business'. The consultants argued that for new and materially altered buildings, there was 'a case for putting all the constructional aspects of fire safety into a final certificate of compliance issued by the building control officer'. Given safeguards, they believed that 'within the context of construction technology in general it should be possible for the building control profession to deal successfully with most matters normally encountered in the course of enforcing part B of the Building Regulations'. The consultants also emphasised the role of private sector fire consultants and the 'for advice growing market'.[66]

In 1990, FBU conference held a brief but hard-hitting debate on the Bickerdike Allen report. Delegates instructed the executive council to 'resist any attempts to undermine or diminish the role of the fire service in fire safety matters and mount a political and public campaign to achieve this end'. Ted Kibbler told the conference, 'I have never read such a vicious and biased anti-fire service document'. He warned that 'private inspectors would be able to insist that a fire authority issue a fire certificate to a building they have not approved'. Ian Shaw said the officers' national committee thought it was 'the most dangerous document in relation to fire safety that has been published'. Delegates warned that if implemented, it could slash jobs and open the service to privatisation.[67]

Officers' rep Glyn Evans explained in *Firefighter* magazine the deregulatory drive behind the report:

> The review was the result of an initiative by the Enterprise and Deregulation Unit of the DTI. This unit was specifically set up to reduce the burden upon industry by removing or replacing

> any legislation or regulations which had the effect of hampering business start up, growth or expansion. It is not likely therefore, that such a unit will be overly concerned with maintenance or improvement of safety standards, but only their likely detrimental effect on business growth potential.[68]

MAJOR'S DEREGULATION

John Major replaced Thatcher as prime minister in 1990. His governments continued with the deregulation agenda. John Redwood, undersecretary of state for trade and industry told parliament that the government had 'a strong programme of deregulatory work', in which 'removing or reducing burdens on business is vital to successful enterprise policies'.[69]

The Major government launched a major deregulation drive, which would take in aspects of building safety and fire safety. Michael Heseltine, secretary of state for trade and industry introduced the Deregulation and Contracting Out Act. He argued that 'businesses feel that they are swamped with red tape' and that the new law would provide 'an order-making power to allow the amendment or repeal of outdated or unnecessarily burdensome legislation'.[70]

Heseltine appointed a deregulation task force, chaired by former minister Francis Maude, who had lost his seat in 1992 and worked for consultants Morgan Stanley. Its terms of reference were:

> To help the President of the Board of Trade promote deregulation which will enhance the competitiveness of United Kingdom business and the effectiveness of the voluntary sector. To advise him on action for government departments and associated bodies or agencies to take to remove unnecessary regulation or to reduce the burden of necessary regulation. This will include domestic, European and international regulation enforced in the United Kingdom.[71]

The taskforce included representatives from Bovis Construction and Ove Arup, as well as Michael Fallon (management consultant) and Archie Norman (Asda). Both would later become Conservative MPs, and in Fallon's case, a business minister promoting deregulation in the years before the Grenfell Tower fire. Labour MP Jim Cunningham quipped: 'Will the minister explain why there are more ex-Tory Members of Parliament on the deregulation task force than small business men.'[72] Heseltine argued:

> Deregulation is central to improving United Kingdom competitiveness. Unnecessary requirements stand in the way of market entry, innovation, investment and jobs. We have a programme of repealing or amending more than 1,000 regulations and we are on target to deliver nearly 500 by the end of the year.[73]

Deregulation also affected residents of Grenfell Tower directly. In 1991, the Lancaster West Estate received a government grant to develop a tenant management organisation. The TMO management agreement received approval from the Secretary of State. On 28 February 1996, RBKC entered into an agreement with the TMO, contracting out the management of Grenfell Tower and the surrounding neighbourhood.[74]

BUILDING SAFETY DAMAGED

Under Major's administration, building control faced renewed demands for deregulation, driven by the work of the government's industry-led taskforces. In 1994, the DTI published a booklet, *Deregulation – Cutting Red Tape*, which stated:

> New initiatives to encourage more inspectors to come forward in the private sector and so to provide the benefits to be derived from increased competition in the building control service. Steps will also be undertaken to improve the operation and clarity of the regulations on approved inspectors.[75]

Months later, the Major government published *Fire Safety Legislation and Enforcement: Report of the Interdepartmental Review*. It recommended an enhanced role for private approved inspectors: 'There is no reason why the enhanced role for building control authorities should not be exercised by approved inspectors ...

Increased self-compliance in building control is a goal worth pursuing when the necessary codes and standards are in place.'[76]

The FBU vigorously fought the proposals. Firefighter Glyn Davies told the TUC Congress:

> The current deregulation drive is not only damaging to workers. It has potentially disastrous implications for the general public ... Self-regulation downgrading of the status of primary fire safety legislation, a blurring of responsibilities between the Health and Safety Executive, fire brigades and building control officers – none of these will enhance the safety of the public.[77]

The Deregulation Task Force report threatened building safety law:

> Anyone who wants to comply with the Building Regulations by a route other than that set out in the Approved Documents must prove to the building inspector that their alternative is compliant. We think that this burden of proof should be reversed. The current legal status of approved documents should be changed so that businesses can develop innovative ways of complying with the regulations without having to prove that they are not breaking the law. They should provide a safe haven, not a straitjacket.[78]

In 1995, the FBU was invited by the Building Regulations Division of the Department of the Environment to contribute to a review of fires in large single-storey uncompartmented buildings. The FBU hosted a meeting on the matter and proposed a central forum to tackle the issues.[79]

The FBU made a formal submission to central government, published in a pamphlet, *A Fighting Chance* (1995). It explained that when firefighters respond to an incident, 'something or someone has already failed and a chain of unforeseen events with unknown consequences and risk factors has been created'. Firefighters dealing with such incidents have to assume 'what can go wrong, will go wrong and will go wrong at the worst possible moment' and 'any system that relies upon the human factor to be reliable is itself inherently unreliable'. The pamphlet emphasised the importance of Part B of the Building Regulations, and drew attention to the importance of fire resistance, the risks from combustible materials and compartmentation. The FBU proposed an interdepartmental working party to examine the whole question of the appropriate levels of fire safety measures in buildings.[80]

During 1996, environment minister James Clappison expanded the private approved inspector scheme in at least three significant respects. First, NHBC Building Control Services Ltd, until then the only approved inspector, was henceforth allowed to control developments containing dwellings of any height as well as those containing mixed uses.[81]

Second, ministers made the Construction Industry Council Approved Inspectors Register (CICAIR) a designated body for approved inspectors. This power had previously been restricted to ministers. The Construction Industry Council (CIC), was established in 1988, originally as the Building Industry Council.[82]

Third, further corporate approved inspectors were appointed. A Department of the Environment circular notified local authorities that BRCS (Building Control) Ltd, Butler and Young Associates Building Control and Fire Safety Consultants Ltd and TPS Special Services Ltd could act as approved inspectors.[83]

The Major administration brought the process of deregulation to a final conclusion by privatising BRE just before it left office. In 1993, the government published a White Paper on science, technology and engineering, *Realising our Potential*. It announced that all government research establishments would be reviewed by the Cabinet Office Efficiency Unit. The review recommended privatisation of some of BRE's functions. As Roger Courtney put it, 'BRE was thus being considered for privatisation for a period of some three years before the process actually commenced'.[84]

In 1995, environment secretary John Gummer announced:

> I wish, however, to see BRE's expertise more directed towards stimulating innovation in construction and to helping industry improve its performance and competitiveness. I believe that closer links between BRE and industry will be achieved more effectively if BRE were in the private sector. I therefore intend to commission consultants later this month to advise me on the

> relative advantages and disadvantages of the options for transferring BRE to the private sector.[85]

By 1996, Gummer determined that his preferred option was 'to privatise BRE through a competitive sale'.[86] A team from the existing BRE management proposed a takeover by their own body, the Foundation for the Built Environment. The sale was completed on 19 March 1997. BRE was henceforth a private sector body, owned by the Foundation for the Built Environment.[87]

Threats to fire safety

The Major administrations continued the deregulation zeal of the Thatcher governments, with the fire and rescue service constantly in the spotlight. In 1993, the Home Office published, *A Review of the Fire Precautions Act*, by consultants Edmundson and Hubbard. The report acknowledged 'a widely held view that the [Fire Precautions] Act has been successful in its primary objective in that there have been no major losses of life in premises certified under the Act'. However it concluded that 'the 1971 Fire Precautions Act does not provide the most suitable legislative means of ensuring fire safety in the 1990s and beyond'. It speculated about a 'totally deregulated environment'. It explicitly stated that deregulation was the motivation for the review, even though this might conflict with public safety:

> The review was carried out with the government's deregulation initiative in mind, while admitting that the legislative means by which desired safety goals are achieved and the aim of reducing burdens on business do not always sit easily together. A possible self-compliant approach to fire safety discussed in this report may go some way to reduce burdens, although the extent to which these are acceptable will depend upon the respective weights given to the importance of maintaining existing levels of fire safety and the desire to reduce burdens on business.[88]

In 1993, a DTI construction task force reported on fire safety legislation. Its report was never published officially, but a series of recommendations from it appeared in a government booklet, *Deregulation Task Forces Proposals for Reform*. These included consolidating the 'valuable elements' of the Building Regulations and the Fire Precautions Act into 'a revised set of Building Regulations under the control of the Department of the Environment'. It added: 'All regulatory provisions must be economically tested before adoption, with cost proportional to benefit.'[89]

In 1994, Heseltine, announced that a government committee involving the Home Office, Department of the Environment and Health and Safety Executive (HSE) would review the operation and effectiveness of fire safety legislation. Heseltine told parliament that the review was triggered by the prime minister's last progress meeting on deregulation, the need to eliminate duplication between enforcement agencies and 'in response to concerns of business such as those of the deregulation task force for the construction industry'.

The FBU published a booklet, *Cutting the Lifeline*. It stated bluntly: 'We believe that if the members of the fire service are considered good enough to rescue people from fires, to fight fires and occasionally in doing so to lay down their lives then they are eminently good enough to have a say in fire safety legislation and its enforcement within the UK.'[90]

The Major government made drastic proposals to diminish the Fire Precautions Act:

> There are gaps and overlaps in current fire safety legislation, which has developed in a piecemeal fashion. Simplification is both possible and desirable, without lessening levels of public or workplace safety ... General fire precautions, process fire precautions and other aspects of health and safety should all be brought within the same legislative framework under the umbrella of the HSWA [Health and Safety at Work Act] ...
>
> Fire certification under the FPA 1971 is imprecisely targeted and does not allow sensible modernisation of fire precautions. It should be discontinued on the current basis. A simpler and less costly form of certification for certain types of premises where

> there is a high life risk should, however, be retained for reasons of public confidence.'[91]

Heseltine told parliament that 'the report puts forward a number of proposals which the review team believes would reduce burdens on business'. The report was put out for consultation.[92]

The FBU published another booklet, *Who Will Pick Up the Pieces?*, containing the union's response to the government's interdepartmental review of fire safety legislation and enforcement. The FBU strongly opposed the proposal to subsume the Fire Precautions Act into the Health and Safety at Work Act, thus giving fire safety secondary status, and instead advocated a new Fire Safety Bill for the UK, with the Home Office as policy department, and the fire service as the enforcing authority.[93]

The FBU kept up the pressure on central government to withdraw its flawed proposals, including an early day motion opposing deregulation, which garnered more than a hundred signatures.[94] In May 1996, ministers conceded that fire safety enforcement should rest principally with fire authorities. The FBU celebrated the outcome as a victory following a three-year campaign.[95]

But the attacks continued. In 1995, the Audit Commission published its report, *In the Line of Fire*, as part of its drive for value for money. Work on the report was carried out by management consultants Ernst and Young. The report recognised the increasing demands on fire and rescue services were not matched with appropriate funding, and the insufficient emphasis placed on fire safety. However it proposed a range of attacks on national standards of fire cover and on firefighters' conditions of service in order to fund the required changes.[96]

In 1996, Tom Sackville told parliament in response to the Audit Commission's recommendation, national standards of fire cover would be reviewed by the CFBAC.[97]

The Department of the Environment issued a consultation paper aimed at reducing the number of Local Acts containing fire safety provisions. The FBU submitted its objections.[98]

As part of the FBU's efforts to push back the government's plans on deregulation, the union launched a concerted campaign on fire safety. On 1 March 1996, the FBU sponsored a forum at Westminster, entitled *Fire Safety in the 21st Century*. The event was chaired by Labour MP John Heppell and hosted by Ian McCartney, Labour's shadow minister for employment. Glyn Evans, speaking for the FBU, launched the draft Fire Safety Bill, aiming to consolidate at least 54 other fire statutes into one, coherent new law.[99]

John Heppell moved this fire safety text as a private members' bill in the House of Commons. He argued:

> My Bill is also progressive and forward-looking. It incorporates many new recommendations that were made as a result of the 1993 Home Office review of the Fire Precautions Act 1971. My Bill supports the Government's view announced in May 1996 that fire safety should in general be treated separately in legislation and that its enforcement should rest principally with fire authorities. Indeed, one of the main intentions of the Bill is to create a one-stop shop for fire safety ...
>
> I make no apology for the fact that the Bill is drafted by firefighters and I hope that hon. Members will accept that firefighters are the best people to talk about fire safety. The Bill enjoys the support of all the fire service organisations represented by the Central Fire Brigades Advisory Council for England and Wales, which advises the Home Office on all matters relating to the fire service.
>
> Finally, I repeat that firefighters are the experts on fire safety. Let us put responsibility with the fire service, which is where the majority of the general public already think it lies. Let us make sure that the people who go into fires when we are coming out of them are protected. Let us make sure that we have decent fire safety legislation for the twenty-first century.[100]

The Major government opposed the FBU's Fire Safety Bill. Sadly, the campaign ran out of parliamentary time, with the general election looming. However the FBU continued to hold up its guard against the threat of deregulation. Writing in the union's *Firefighter* magazine, Ian McCartney warned of what was at stake at the election:

The Tory strategy is not new: for 17 years we have had persistent deregulation in pursuit of the Thatcherite dream ... What they didn't tell their party conference was that a secret cabinet committee had already met and drawn up covert plans to privatise key emergency services if they win the next election.[101]

3

Blair's 'better deregulation' unchecked

After 18 years of Conservative governments, 1997 was a potential turning point year, when the self-styled 'New Labour' government led by Tony Blair came to power. The party was re-elected again in 2001 and 2005. For 13 years, Labour governments led by Blair, and later Gordon Brown, set the parameters of policy.

The spectre of deregulation did not disappear. It deepened under the rubric of 'better' regulation.[1] This continuity was well captured by Peter Mandelson's comment, 'We are all Thatcherites now'.[2] Charting the furtherance of deregulation under Labour is crucial for understanding what happened to building safety and fire safety during these years.

BLAIR'S DEREGULATION

Labour's 1997 general election manifesto promised 'the protection of business from undue burdens'. It spoke of efficient and fair regulation across a range of industries.[3] David Clark, the new Cabinet Office minister, articulated within weeks the continuation of deregulation. He stated: 'Our aim is to create the economic conditions in which business can flourish. We want to modernise government for business – particularly small firms – and citizens. That is why we have undertaken to cut unnecessary red tape and not to impose burdensome new regulations.'[4]

Clark told parliament that the Deregulation Unit had been 'renamed the Better Regulation Unit to reflect our priority to get regulation right'. It remained within the Cabinet Office, with around 40 civil servants, almost half of whom had worked for the previous administration. He said:

> The government is committed to ensuring that regulations are simple, helpful and fair both to business, particularly small firms, and to the citizen ... As we made clear in our manifesto, we are committed not to impose unnecessary burdens on business. I am also appointing a revitalised Task Force and will work with them to lift regulatory burdens wherever appropriate.[5]

The Deregulation Task Force became the Better Regulation Task Force.[6] The government introduced Regulatory Impact Assessments. Blair announced that no proposal for regulation with an impact on business, charities or the voluntary sector should be considered by ministers without carrying out an impact assessment.[7] The Better Regulation Unit became the Regulatory Impact Unit. Cabinet Office minister Graham Stringer described it as 'a whole new approach to cutting government red tape'.[8]

Blair chaired the Panel for Regulatory Accountability, which met for the first time on 15 December 1999, 'with the remit to modernise the regulatory system, simplify existing regulation and ease regulatory pressures on business and the public sector'. The prime minister appointed a Minister for Regulatory Reform in each government department 'to oversee a programme of measures to reduce regulatory burdens'. Lord Larry Whitty was appointed for the Department of the Environment, Transport and the Regions and Mike O'Brien for the Home Office.[9]

The centrepiece of the Blair government's deregulatory drive during its first term was the Regulatory Reform Act 2001. In 1999, Lord Charles Falconer of Thoroton announced a consultation on extending 'the scope of the deregulation order-making process'. At the Regulatory Reform Bill's second reading in the House of Lords, Falconer stated:

> The [Regulatory Reform] Bill will provide a major tool for this and future governments to reform entire regulatory regimes and to tackle unnecessary, overlapping, over-complex and over-burdensome legislation. It builds on the acknowledged strengths of the deregulation order-making procedure, including the rigorous parliamentary scrutiny of proposed orders, and

> provides additional safeguards. It facilitates reducing the burden of regulation.[10]

The Regulatory Reform Act 2001 came into force just before the general election. The Labour Party manifesto in 2001 committed to continuing the deregulation agenda. It stated: 'Regulation should be introduced, where it is necessary, in a light-touch way. We will cut back the red tape associated with regulation, examine opportunities to put time limits on regulations, deregulate by secondary legislation, and offer help to small firms.'[11]

In 2001, Blair announced the formation of the Office of Public Services Reform, to support government departments in carrying forward the reform of public services.[12] Blair summed up the approach taken by the New Labour administration in a pamphlet, *Reforming Public Services: Principles into Practice*. The pamphlet promoted the New Labour mantra of 'what matters is what works'. It set out four 'principles' to achieve 'customer-focused public services'. The deregulatory theme was spelt out:

> More flexibility is required for public service organisations and their staff to achieve the diversity of service provision needed to respond to the wide range of customer aspirations. This means challenging restrictive practices and reducing red tape; greater and more flexible incentives and rewards for good performance; strong leadership and management; and high quality training and development ... An element of contestability between alternative suppliers can also drive up standards and empower customers locked into a poor service from their traditional supplier.[13]

Blair argued that governments had 'too often been ready to introduce new regulations, without removing old, redundant ones'. He pledged 'the removal of needless bureaucratic rules' and railed against 'excess regulation'. He highlighted the Cabinet Office's Regulatory Impact Unit and another Regulatory Reform Action Plan, listing 250 actions to 'remove regulatory burdens and red tape'. Worse, Blair made an explicit argument for the privatisation of public services:

> Alternative providers can also help drive up performance across the service as a whole, even where the individual citizen does not gain a wider choice as a result. Widening the market to create more suppliers of public services (contestability) can improve the quality of management and value for money. In the private sector as much as half of all productivity gains come from new entrants to the market, as opposed to incremental improvements from existing companies.[14]

In 2004, Chancellor Gordon Brown commissioned Philip Hampton, chair of Sainsbury, with a remit to make proposals to reduce regulatory 'burdens on business' across all major national regulators and local authorities. Hampton's final report (2005) recommended:

> Entrenching the principle of risk assessment throughout the regulatory system, so that the burden of enforcement falls most on highest-risk businesses, and least on those with the best records of compliance ... making much more use of advice ... substantially reducing the need for form filling ... The review estimates ... its proposals could reduce the need for inspections by up to a third, which means around one million fewer inspections ...[15]

Gordon Brown embraced the policy trajectory towards 'a new, risk-based approach to regulation to break down barriers holding enterprise back'. The new regime would entail 'no unjustifiable inspection, form-filling or requirement for information ... the risk based approach targets the necessary few'. This new approach would 'help move us a million miles away from the old belief that business, unregulated, will invariably act irresponsibly'. Brown summed up the new approach with a pithy formulation: 'Not just a light touch but a limited touch.'[16]

In 2005, the Better Regulation Task Force published another report, *Less is More*, on reducing burdens, at the behest of the prime minister. It came to two key conclusions:

> The United Kingdom can considerably reduce the regulatory burden on business by adopting the successful Dutch approach

> to reducing administrative costs ... We need a 'one in, one out' approach to new regulation, which forces departments to prioritise between new regulations and to simplify and remove existing regulations.[17]

This report laid out a detailed description of the 'one in, one out' approach to regulation. It stated:

> 'one in, one out' is an easily understood description of the way we want people who are involved in putting administrative burdens on others to think and to behave ... Regulatory bodies need to work out which are the most important regulations, which we can do without and which ones can be removed from the regulatory basket. 'one in, one out' emphasises that choices have to be made. If ministers do want new laws they will need to prioritise and drop other proposals – thus stemming the flow, or repeal existing laws – thus reducing the stock.[18]

The centrepiece of Blair's third term deregulation was the Legislative and Regulatory Reform Act 2006, which would implement the Hampton recommendations and replace the Regulatory Reform Act 2001. The act was specifically designed 'to enable provision to be made for the purpose of removing or reducing burdens resulting from legislation and promoting regulatory principles'.

The bill defined 'burden' as any of (a) a financial cost; (b) an administrative inconvenience; (c) an obstacle to efficiency, productivity or profitability; or (d) a sanction, criminal or otherwise, which affects the carrying on of any lawful activity.

BUILDING SAFETY UNDER 'BETTER' REGULATION

In Blair's first administration, John Prescott was secretary of state for the environment, transport and the regions (DETR), with overall responsibility for the Building Regulations, guidance, building control and building safety research. In Blair's second administration, Stephen Byers was secretary of state for transport, local government and the regions (DTLR). In May 2002, DTLR was broken up and John Prescott's Office of the Deputy Prime

Minister (ODPM) took over its building safety functions. The pivotal minister was Nick Raynsford, who held key responsibility for the Building Regulations, guidance, building control and building safety research between 1997 and 2005.

Raynsford made his deregulatory approach clear from the beginning. First, he took a hands off approach to the Building Research Establishment (BRE). When asked about BRE's operations, he bluntly stated: 'The Building Research Establishment was privatised in March 1997; the department therefore no longer has responsibility for its operations.'[19] Henceforth, ministers were not held to account by parliament for the activities of BRE.

In 1998, Raynsford announced his intention to make regulations to amend the Building Regulations, so that applications from corporate bodies seeking approved inspector status would be made to a designated body, rather than to the secretary of state. The Construction Industry Council (CIC), which already anointed individuals seeking approved inspector status, would be designated for corporate bodies as well. At the same time, Raynsford approved the application from RBC Ltd to become a corporate approved inspector. The rationale was clearly deregulatory. Raynsford asserted:

> Wider competition between approved inspectors and local authority building control should be a stimulus to greater efficiency and higher standards of service to the customer. To help bring about this result, I am working to devolve the setting of charges for local authority building control to individual local authorities.[20]

Raynsford brushed off complaints about private approved inspectors, despite admitting that his department 'currently conducts no formal monitoring of private contractors providing building control services'.[21] Labour MP Brian White, formerly chair of the Local Government Association planning committee, raised the issue of the conflict of interests faced by the National House Building Council (NHBC), the first private approved inspector but who also ran the NHBC Buildmark warranty scheme. As White put it:

> The NHBC gives quality awards to various builders. Despite its denials, I have a letter from a major builder saying that the NHBC tells the builders when the inspection will take place, and how to get round it ... There should be a distinct split between the inspection role and the provision of warranties. One company should not do both.

Raynsford's response was to parrot the NHBC's assurance that it would introduce 'management reforms [to] help to make the NHBC services more transparent, more impartial and more responsive to consumer concerns'.[22]

In 1999, Raynsford announced the publication of building control performance standards, produced by the industry steering group. However the 'eleven standards for the good conduct of building control' were not statutory, but voluntary. Raynsford reiterated the primacy of deregulation. He told MPs: 'Competition between local authority building control departments and approved inspectors is an important spur to efficiency, and beneficial to the builders and developers who are the immediate clients for the building control service.'[23]

The New Labour government's deregulatory approach was also evident in its handling of the British Board of Agrément (BBA). In 1998, like BRAC, it was subjected to the financial management and policy review of non-departmental public bodies. Raynsford said the review would 'assess the extent to which the Board's functions are necessary for the achievement of the government's policies, and whether these functions should continue to be carried out as at present, privatised, contracted out or transferred to another body to ensure best value'.[24] Raynsford announced his conclusions from the BBA review:

> I propose to invite the council to amend the company's memorandum and articles of association so that the secretary of state for the environment, transport and the regions can relinquish many of the powers he currently has. The BBA will retain its existing status as a company limited by guarantee under the Companies Act.

> In order to emphasise the importance to government of the BBA, I propose that the secretary of state should be represented on its ruling council, and, in order to protect previous investments of public funds, that he retains controls over the disposal of the company or its assets, through specific clawback provisions. Other commercial and organisational issues should, rightly, be passed to the BBA council to decide. The secretary of state will cease to make appointments to the council, but will be consulted upon them.[25]

Ministers during Blair's second administration continued to cover for private approved inspectors and to extend their reach. In 2001, Labour MP Andrew Dismore challenged ministers on complaints about the work of approved building inspectors. The minister Alan Whitehead replied that he had received 'a small number of complaints', but gave a ringing endorsement to the NHBC. He said:

> NHBC Building Control Services Ltd carries out building control on about half the new homes built for sale in England and Wales and on a substantial number of new homes built by registered social landlords ... I have no evidence that the quality of building control service provided by NHBC Building Control Services Ltd is in general different from that provided in the new homes sector by local authorities.[26]

Dismore pressed the issue again, only for Whitehead to claim: 'This competitive situation is widely regarded as a stimulus to better, more efficient building control services.'[27]

The FBU's single most significant intervention on building safety during this period was in response to the House of Commons Select Committee on Environment, Transport and Regional Affairs investigation in cladding risks, in June 1999. The FBU submitted a memorandum and the union's fire safety adviser Glyn Evans gave testimony to the committee.[28] Evans went on to chair the BSI committee that examined external cladding systems for buildings (see Chapter 5).[29]

The FBU continued to fight for building safety during this period. In 2002, FBU conference carried a resolution brought by

Cornwall, which called on the union's executive council 'to bring forward through the CFBAC 'changes in building regulations to make it a requirement of all new residential builds that domestic sprinkler systems be installed'.

Tony Carvell for the FBU's officer's national committee spoke about the wider importance of building safety measures. He said: 'We are not just talking about domestic sprinklers, we are talking about residential sprinklers ... not just houses, residential care homes, HMOs particularly, blocks of flats. You have heard how much these sprinklers cost and it's peanuts.'[30]

In 2005, the ODPM launched consultation on *Proposals for Amending Part B (Fire Safety) of the Building Regulations*. The FBU made a detailed submission, after organising two well attended national meetings, comprising practitioners who had a fire safety role in their respective fire and rescue authorities. The FBU's submission underlined the union's support for sprinklers in homes:

> As a policy principle the FBU believes that all new dwellings, or buildings being converted to dwellings from another use for the first time, should be fitted throughout with an appropriate fire suppression system, such as residential sprinklers. The fitting of fire suppressions systems should become a fundamental requirement of the Building Regulations, not simply as a compensatory feature for, or trade off with, other fire safety measures.[31]

The FBU also wanted the height criteria changed to 11 metres, reflecting the reach of fire service ladders (this would become pertinent after the Grenfell Tower fire, when ministers came forward with new legislation):

> We have distinct problems with the height criteria of 18m above the fire service vehicle access level, referred to in this paragraph which activates the recommendation for the provision of firefighting shafts, for the following reason. It is based upon ladders that the fire and rescue service no longer use and have not used since the mid 1970s. In Scotland this height criteria has been reduced to 11m in the Technical Standards which support the Building (Scotland) Regulations 2005 to take account of this sit-

> uation and we recommend that the Approved Document follows suit wherever that height is referred to.[32]

The FBU responded bluntly to the ODPM proposal that it was '*minded* to remove the requirement for self-closing devices on doors within dwellings'. The FBU argued: 'The FBU does not and never will support this proposal. We do not support the removal of safety measures on the basis that they may be disabled, ignored, or removed, by those that they are designed to protect.'[33]

The FBU strongly opposed refuges in high rise buildings:

> The FBU is very uncomfortable with the use of refuges and believes that all buildings, other than those which are intended to provide treatment or care, should be designed to ensure that any and all of its potential occupants can evacuate themselves by their own unaided efforts. That is a fundamental principle of means of escape in case of fire and one that we have never abandoned ... As a result we would recommend that there is a far greater use in new buildings of evacuation lifts for non-ambulant disabled persons or a system of progressive horizontal evacuation to an evacuation lift and a move away from refuges.[34]

The consultation document asked with regard to buildings other than dwellings: do you support the proposed change to the guidance on phased evacuation so that, in the first instance, only the fire floor is evacuated? The FBU response was:

> On the basis of the research carried out by Professor David Purser of the Building Research Establishment into the evacuation strategy following the Twin Towers disaster in New York we would support the proposal subject to the following caveat; Paragraph 3.24(c) (Simultaneous evacuation) should be extended to include the following purpose groups; 4 Shop and commercial, and 7(a) Storage and other non-residential.[35]

The consultation did not ask pertinent questions with respect to the external fire spread. The ODPM did suggest that Part B of the

Building Regulations should be reviewed and updated every five years. The union responded:

> The FBU would support such a programme in the absence of anything better. However if the format of the Approved Documents took the format that we have suggested of loose leaf folder linked to an electronic web based updating system it is possible that they could be updated more frequently if necessary. There are attractions to that rather than waiting for a five year period when something can be clearly seen not to be working or that requires tweaking to improve its performance.[36]

FIRE SAFETY UNDER 'BETTER' REGULATION

During the first Labour government under Blair, Jack Straw was home secretary with responsibility for the fire and rescue service. George Howarth was fire minister at the Home Office for the first two years. In July 1999, Mike O'Brien took over as fire minister, until the general election in 2001.

On fire safety matters, the first Blair administration made amendments to the Fire Precautions Act, while proceeding cautiously with plans to overhaul the fire safety regime. In 1997, Howarth told parliament that the government strongly supported the aims of the Fire Safety Bill, sponsored in the previous parliament by Labour MP John Heppell, with backing from the FBU.[37] It proposed consolidating existing legislation and enhancing the powers fire inspectors had to enforce fire safety law. Howarth seemed initially keen to distance the new administration from the previous government's approach:

> I can give this firm commitment: no such deregulation will take place under this government. We consider fire safety, particularly in those respects, to be of the utmost priority and we will ensure that the necessary legislation is in place to protect people in those and all other circumstances in which they might be threatened by fire.[38]

However, Howarth soon announced the publication of a consultation document, *Fire Safety Legislation for the Future*.[39] Howarth told MPs the government had resolved 'to proceed with a thorough overhaul of fire safety legislation along the lines set out in the consultation document'.[40]

The FBU continued to promote a more robust regime for fire safety. In February 1998, Glyn Evans spoke at the Fire Safety Development Group (FSDG) seminar held at Westminster. Evans proposed the creation of a statutory Fire Safety Commission, along the lines of the Health and Safety Commission, as an independent body to advise on fire safety matters. The Fire Safety Commission would be created under the auspices of the Fire Safety Act.[41]

In July, the FSDG held its annual reception on the terrace of the House of Commons. The event was sponsored by the newly formed All-Party Parliamentary Group (APPG) on Fire Safety, chaired by Jim Fitzpatrick, who prior to his election as an MP had served on the FBU executive council. Evans addressed the gathering to propose the creation of a statutory, strategic Fire Safety Commission.[42]

In November, the FBU launched a discussion paper entitled *Safety in Partnership* at the House of Commons. Fire minister George Howarth welcomed the paper and asked Home Office officials to prepare their response for the next full CFBAC meeting. In 1999, FBU conference carried a motion demanding that the executive council 'redouble their efforts to secure the Fire Safety Bill as the primary piece of fire safety legislation, with the fire service the enforcement body for this legislation'.[43] Howarth told MPs:

> The Fire Brigades Union discussion document, *Safety in Partnership*, which sets out proposals for a strategic forum to consider fire safety matters will be considered by the Central Fire Brigades Advisory Council at its meeting on 18 May. I have already made it clear that the concepts of developing policies around shared goals, making sure those policies are inclusive, involving those outside government and becoming more forward and outward looking are absolutely right. This approach also ties in with the Better Regulation Task Force's recent review of enforcement, which suggested that fire safety initiatives should be coordi-

> nated by a national forum representing government regulators and stakeholders.[44]

Nevertheless, the Home Office only agreed to a non-statutory body, the Fire Safety Advisory Board, arguing it had only no parliamentary time to put the body on a statutory footing. The terms of reference were put to the CFBAC. All participants supported the proposals, with the exception of the LGA, who said they were not prepared to attend the new board's meetings. The FBU supported the Fire Safety Advisory Board, arguing that it was 'effectively the Fire Safety Commission by another name'. In 1999, Fordham, Evans and Ken Knight (chair of the CACFOA fire safety board), met with new fire minister Mike O'Brien to discuss the next steps. O'Brien told the meeting he was committed to the Fire Safety Bill, suggesting a possible route to the legislation via the Regulatory Reform Bill. He commended the FBU for the Fire Safety Advisory Board and said it would go ahead.[45]

However, the FBU was frustrated by the lack of progress on the Fire Safety Bill and unhappy with the proposed use of the regulatory reform process:

> We are concerned that a Regulatory Reform Act Order cannot achieve all the aims that the FBU Fire Safety Bill would. The primary reason is that the Regulatory Reform Bill is limited with regard to introducing any new regulatory provisions that do not already exist as it is essentially deregulatory in principle and a number of the FBU's proposals within the Fire Safety Bill are new.[46]

In August 2000, the Fire Safety Advisory Board held its first meeting. The FBU lamented that it was not a statutory body, but was at least an independent part of the CFBAC structure. The membership included most fire stakeholders (including the LGA) and was chaired by Pamela Castle, an environmental law specialist.

O'Brien's turn

In March 2000, O'Brien made a hostile speech to the LGA fire conference, in which he argued for an agenda of 'modernisation' of the fire and rescue service. He criticised the service for 'outdated' practices and insisted that the Fire Service College should look for private sector involvement, under the mantra of 'what matters is what works'. He claimed the CFBAC was 'slow, bureaucratic and … bogged down in detail'.[47]

In 2001, O'Brien told the LGA fire conference of the government's intention to publish a White Paper on fire 'modernisation'.[48] A draft was circulated, including to the FBU. O'Brien also spoke at FBU conference, where he told delegates to expect 'continuing transformation' in the coming years. The White Paper was put on hold because of the general election – but the signal about future 'modernisation' was clear.[49]

In June 2001, the Blair administration also moved responsibility for fire from the Home Office to the newly created Department for Transport, Local Government and the Regions (DTLR).[50] In May 2002, the administration created the Office of the Deputy Prime Minister (ODPM) under John Prescott, with responsibility for the fire and rescue service transferring to this department.[51] Fire ministers included Lord Jeff Rooker, Chris Leslie and Phil Hope.

Blair's second administration introduced retrogressive changes to the fire and rescue service, sweeping away many of the pillars that had made the sector a world class service. It introduced the Fire and Rescue Services Act 2004, the Civil Contingencies Act 2004 and the Regulatory Reform (Fire Safety) Order 2005.

The Bain report

In September 2002, in the wake of the FBU's pay dispute, ministers announced an 'independent review of the fire service', chaired by Professor Sir George Bain.[52] Raynsford spelt out its agenda:

> Modernisation includes full-time firefighters working in the same crew as retained (part-time) firefighters; ending the ban on overtime; allowing management to change, where necessary, the rigid shift system of two days on, two nights on, then four days off in order to provide a better service; giving firefighters some medical training as paramedics, and allowing them to carry resuscitation equipment such as defibrillators; the fire service sharing control rooms between brigades and with other emer-

> gency services, to provide a more efficient response; and taking action to improve the management of sickness in the fire service to reduce the high numbers who retire early through sickness and ill-health.[53]

In December, Prescott published the Bain report, *Reducing Risk, Saving Lives.* It was a spiteful assault on firefighters and the FBU. The report's recommendations to central government included:

> Implement a risk-based approach to fire cover as a matter of urgency ... Amend or remove Section 19 of the 1947 Fire Services Act as soon as possible ... Legislate to put the Fire Service on a new statutory basis ... A new body should replace the Central Fire Brigades Advisory Council (CFBAC) for England and Wales ... The Grey Book should be amended to simplify nationally determined conditions of service to four core areas: pay, total hours, overall ranks and basic leave ... The National Joint Council should be replaced by a smaller body.[54]

Prescott immediately began imposing the Bain proposals. He told parliament that he would repeal Section 19, allowing chief fire officers to cut firefighter jobs without recourse to ministerial approval. In March 2003, Raynsford said removing section 19 was 'consistent with the principle of cutting back on consent regimes and red tape'.[55]

The Fire Safety Advisory Board was scrapped after its thirteenth meeting in 2003, at the behest of fire minister Phil Hope.[56]

Fire and Rescue Services Act 2004

In 2003, Prescott introduced the Fire Services Bill, which gave the Westminster government the powers to impose pay and conditions settlements. By November, the Fire Services Act 2003 came into force, although ministers did not exercise their new powers.[57]

Prescott also published the White Paper, *Our Fire and Rescue Service*, setting out 'our plans to modernise and reform the fire and rescue service in England and Wales'. The White Paper committed the Westminster government to introduce a new bill to set the legal framework for delivering the changes outlined. It also pledged to set up the Practitioners' Forum, led by CACFOA.[58]

The ODPM select committee held an inquiry into the proposals. The FBU submitted a written memorandum and FBU president Ruth Winters, general secretary Andy Gilchrist and assistant general secretary Mike Fordham gave oral testimony. The FBU's memorandum stated:

> The FBU regrets the government's intention to disband the CFBAC and replace it with a number of bodies, from most of which staff representatives are to be excluded. Neither do we understand why the membership of these new bodies needs to be mutually exclusive.
>
> The FBU supports a partnership approach to these new bodies, and believes that the union, as the legitimate voice of the majority of staff should be involved in all aspects of the service including strategy, policy and delivery. Any attempt to exclude the FBU from these important bodies contradicts the government's public commitment to social partnership.[59]

The FBU also criticised the scrapping of national standards of fire cover and the misuse of integrated risk management plans (IRMPs). However the FBU was ignored. By July 2004, the Fire and Rescue Services Act 2004 was on the statute book.[60]

Regional control

Deregulation also meant ministers developed the disastrous regional control project. The Bain report supported amalgamation of controls and the White Paper also promoted a regional approach to fire and rescue. The Mott MacDonald report, commissioned by ministers, called for nine regional control centres to replace the 46 control rooms in England, one control room for Wales (instead of three) and a review of the eight control rooms in Scotland. In 2003, Raynsford announced:

> We are also today publishing Mott MacDonald's most recent study into fire and rescue control rooms, and HM Fire Service Inspectorate's review of the subject. The study reinforced the

> report's conclusions that regional control rooms would significantly enhance national resilience. The government is persuaded by the conclusions of the study and proposes to establish regional control rooms in England ...[61]

In 2004, the FiReControl project commenced.[62] Despite early warnings from the FBU and the House of Commons Select Committee, ministers continued to advocate for regional control rooms.[63] FBU control rep Sharon Peverett captured the implications of regional controls:

> Modernisation is a word used by the government to introduce new practices in the fire and rescue service, which to us who work within the service means one thing – cuts to our jobs, but even more importantly, cuts to the response we can make to the public when we are needed. Remember: firefighting begins with 999.[64]

Fire safety

Ministers also pursued plans to 'reform' fire safety legislation. Lord Falconer promised an Order under the Regulatory Reform Act.[65] In 2002, fire minister Chris Leslie published a consultation document on fire safety law. Leslie motivated the proposals explicitly in deregulatory terms. Businesses would no longer be required to obtain a fire certificate and therefore pay the administration fees to fire authorities to obtain a certificate. He said:

> The government is committed to fire safety and the modernisation of legislation will significantly reduce the burden on businesses throughout the country ... while the reforms will make legislation easier to understand and, most importantly improve fire safety, they will also save business money.[66]

In 2004, the ODPM issued a statement on the Regulatory Reform (Fire Safety) Order saturated with the language of deregulation. It stated:

> The aim of the proposed reform is to reduce burdens on business that are caused by the existence of multiple, overlapping general fire safety regimes ... For employers, the proposals would not impose significant additional burdens since they would recreate requirements which already exist ... The removal of multiple and overlapping fire safety provisions and their replacement with a single fire safety regime would constitute the reduction of a significant burden – as would the removal of the need to apply for fire certificates and the costs associated with the issue of certificates.[67]

The paper proposed the repeal of London Building Acts (Amendment) Act 1939, stating:

> This Act principally imposes burdens on the owner and occupier of certain buildings in Inner London (including warehouses above a certain size and buildings over certain height limits).
>
> Section 20 gives the council power to attach conditions, when approving plans for work on such buildings, for the provision and maintenance of fire alarms, automatic fire detection systems and other fire prevention measures. Section 20(2C) provides that the council may impose additional conditions, in respect of any special fire risk area, for the provision and maintenance of 'proper arrangements' for lessening the danger from fire. Failure to comply with a condition is an offence.[68]

The Order would repeal the Fire Precautions Act 1971, which it said 'imposes various burdens on owners, occupiers and others who have responsibilities in relation to certain premises as well as burdens on fire authorities and other local authorities'.[69]

In the following months, the Regulatory Reform Committee took written evidence and held hearings on the Fire Safety Order. The FBU memorandum warned:

> However, simply placing a duty to enforce the Order without providing either a duty to carry out inspections, or to develop an enforcement programme to do so, is not sufficient in our opinion to preserve the current level of public safety or equal the

current requirements of the Fire Precautions Act 1971 insofar as it relates to the issue of fire certificates. In section 5(3) of the 1971 Act the enforcing authority is under a duty to consider whether or not in the cases of premises which qualify for exemption from holding a fire certificate to grant an exemption and if they do not so agree they must inspect the premises and commence the fire certification process.

The issue of fire certificates or the grant of exemptions from fire certification under the Fire Precautions Act 1971 also gave clear and measurable indication of the enforcement activities of the fire authorities. Once this process is removed then no equivalent measure or indeed target will exist and public confidence in the Order could well be jeopardised. It should be noted that there are no national targets in force or proposed that we are aware of relating to the fire safety enforcement activities of fire and rescue authorities ...[70]

FBU fire safety adviser Glyn Evans gave testimony to the committee, reiterating the union's concerns about scrapping fire certificates. He told MPs:

> When this Order goes through, the Fire Precautions Act 1971 will be repealed and therefore the procedure of issuing fire certificates to buildings will cease, and, whatever one may think of fire certification in terms of it being bureaucratic – and it is – it has been extremely successful and it is well liked by business because it gives them a document which says that their building is safe.

Evans also explained the importance of local acts.

> Those parts of local acts which impact upon the building construction or the method of design and construction of a building are being dealt with through the Buildings Regulations or are dealt with through the review of a part of the Buildings Regulations which has just commenced with the buildings division ... A fundamental tenet of our fire safety law since the eighteenth century has been two-fold: that people should be able to get out

> of a building if it catches fire for any reason; and there should be fire-fighting equipment provided in that building for the occupants to use if it is safe for them to do so, to deal with a small fire before it becomes a big one. Many of the local acts that are listed in the rear of the RRO contain these provisions, but, as I say, they are quite definite provisions ... Our concern hinges on this caveat 'where necessary' ... we would say that it potentially could lead to a lowering of existing standards.[71]

In 2005, after friction with the Regulatory Reform Committee, the government laid the draft Order before parliament.[72] However ministers were unable to get the new law on the statute book before the general election.

Blair's third term

In Blair's third administration, David Miliband became secretary of state for the newly created Department for Communities and Local Government (DCLG). The new department had responsibility for fire and rescue services in England as well as fire safety. After a year, Miliband was replaced by Ruth Kelly. Jim Fitzpatrick was fire minister (May 2005–May 2006), followed by Angela Smith (May 2006–June 2007). The FBU leadership also changed in 2005, with Matt Wrack elected general secretary and Andy Dark as assistant general secretary.

The Regulatory Reform (Fire Safety) Order was made on 7 June 2005. However Fitzpatrick agreed to 'allow business and enforcers more time for preparation', which meant it came into force on 1 October 2006.[73]

However, serious matters remained unresolved. Labour MP Michael Clapham questioned the relationship between fire and building control. Fitzpatrick responded:

> We are carrying out a consultation of a revision of the Building Regulations and Fire Safety Procedural Guidance, a document which sets out protocols for the communication of fire safety information and views between building control bodies, fire and rescue services and applicants for building regulatory approval. We have also developed, in parallel, in consultation with stake-

> holders including the Chief Fire Officers' Association (CFOA), key performance indicators (KPIs) to measure the overall performance of building control bodies.[74]

Clapham also asked what measures were in place to ensure advice from consultants on fire risk assessments under the Regulatory Reform (Fire Safety) Order 2005 was competent, impartial and professional. He questioned why third party accreditation schemes were not in place. Fitzpatrick replied: 'The Regulatory Reform (Fire Safety) Order 2005 does not impose specific requirements about the competence, impartiality or professionalism of consultants employed to undertake a fire risk assessment on behalf of a responsible person.'[75]

Inquiry

In 2005, the ODPM Committee launched an inquiry into the fire and rescue service. It sought to evaluate developments since the 2003 White Paper and the subsequent legislation. The committee specifically sought evidence on the implications of the introduction of regional control centres and on 'civil resilience' as far as it related to the fire and rescue service. The FBU made a detailed written submission, sounding the alarm about cuts and resilience under the new the IRMP process.[76] The FBU also warned of the dangers of running down fire certificates and scrapping of the CFBAC. It underlined concerns about weak enforcement:

> There needs to be clear and strong guidance on the enforcement of the Regulatory Reform (Fire Safety) Order 2005 … to ensure the enforcement activities of fire and rescue authorities are properly carried out. We see little or no evidence that this will in fact be the case or that any targets are being set for them to do so. We have significant concerns over the near-ending in some brigades of the fire certification regime. The running down of this regime pre-dates even the introduction of the Order to the House.[77]

On behalf of the FBU, Matt Wrack, Ruth Winters, control rep Val Salmon and officer's rep Jack Ford gave oral evidence to the

ODPM committee. They raised concerns about the abolition of national standards and the limits of IRMP, which allowed for different levels of response. Wrack illustrated the point with reference to high rise residential fires:

> Since the introduction of local integrated risk management plans there are no national standards. We are concerned that you could end up, and are increasingly ending up, with effectively a postcode lottery. We do not see why, if you have a fire in a tower block in Birmingham, you should get a different standard of response than if you have a fire in a tower block in London. Unfortunately, because of IRMP, at the present time that is perfectly possible.[78]

Winters added that the dissolution of the CFBAC had also hampered the provision of national guidance, fire safety and accountability. Although there were few questions directly on the Fire Safety Order, MPs did raise the issue of prevention. Winters reminded MPs of the FBU's leading role on these matters. She said:

> [The FBU] led on the Fire Safety Bill prior to the fire service dispute which rolled up to the regulatory reform orders and fire safety. We signed up to risk-based fire cover ... all part of the modernisation agenda in the late nineties. Community fire safety – we have set up a joint protocol with the chief fire officers in the late nineties ...[79]

In 2006, Labour MP Celia Barlow secured a Westminster Hall on fire safety. Labour MP David Taylor raised concerns about the scrapping of fire certification. Andrew Dismore, chair of the FBU's parliamentary group, argued: 'The difficulty with guidance notes is that they are not legally enforceable. They do not even have the force of a code of practice, which would be rather more useful than mere guidance notes ... I am concerned that there will be a watering down.'

Fitzpatrick replied on behalf of the government: 'We consulted on making the guidance statutory, but there was no clear majority in favour of that. We consider that statutory guidance that could effectively impose a list of requirements does not fit with the risk-based regime that we are trying to introduce.'[80]

As the Fire Safety Order came into force, Glyn Evans feared 'a slide back into an era of large multi-fatality fire' that had blighted the end of the last decades of the twentieth century.[81]

Another consequence of the deregulatory reforms was the change to arrangements for the fire inspectorate in England. On 1 February 2007, HM Fire Service Inspectorate was abolished. In October, the Chief Fire and Rescue Adviser's Unit was established 'to provide strategic advice and guidance to ministers, civil servants, fire and rescue services in England and other stakeholders (including the devolved administrations), on the structure, organisation and performance of the fire and rescue service.'[82] The Audit Commission developed a performance assessment framework for the fire and rescue service in conjunction with CFOA.[83]

BROWN: 'BETTER REGULATION' CONSOLIDATED

In June 2007, Gordon Brown became the prime minister. Hazel Blears became DCLG secretary of state, with responsibility for the Building Regulations and building safety, along with the fire and rescue services in England. Other relevant ministers included John Healey and Iain Wright. Fire ministers were Parmjit Dhanda (June 2007–October 2008), Sadiq Khan (October 2008–June 2009), Sarah McCarthy-Fry (June 2009) and Shahid Malik (June 2009–May 2010).

One of Brown's first decisions was to move the Better Regulation Executive into the Department for Trade and Industry, to form the Department for Business, Enterprise and Regulatory Reform (BERR). This measure further elevated the regulatory reform programme within central government.

Ministers introduced the Regulatory Enforcement and Sanctions Act 2008. It established the Local Better Regulation Office to keep the burdens of regulation on compliant businesses to a minimum. It also established the Primary Authority principle, enabling businesses to be inspected by one regulator. The act imposed a duty on regulators to review burdens, reduce those found to be unnecessary and unjustifiable, and report on progress annually.[84]

Iain Wright, the building regulations minister, pressed on with the review of building control. In 2008, Wright told BRAC that the review of the building control system was welcome, 'particularly with its emphasis on both improving compliance and reducing burdens'.[85] DCLG launched its *Future of Building Control* consultation. Wright told parliament that the government was consulting on:

> Removing statutory notification stages which will stop builders having to make unnecessary calls to building control and will require local authorities to take a more risk-based approach to their work which will stop unnecessary inspections …
>
> Limiting the use of building notices to ensure local authorities have more up-front information at the start of the project in order for them to direct their limited time and resources at high-risk projects, thus allowing a lighter-touch regime for good builders and low risk projects that are likely to comply …
>
> Continuing to encourage other ways for builders to show compliance in addition to the traditional inspection route – specifically expanding and improving the competent persons schemes (self-certification by registered installers).[86]

In 2009, the tardiness on enforcement was summed up by fire minister Shahid Malik, who told MPs:

> Enforcement of compliance with the building regulations is undertaken by local authorities. There is no central register of enforcement notices served or prosecutions brought. In the main, local authorities aim to resolve issues that arise through inspection of and advice to those undertaking work. Enforcement notices and prosecution are only used as a last resort.[87]

The FBU continued to warn of the weaknesses with the building regime and worked with other fire sector actors to improve the situation. Mike Wood, vice-chair of Passive Fire Protection Federation argued in *Firefighter* magazine that 'firefighters take it on trust that a building they enter will have adequate built-in fire protection, to maintain its stability under fire so people can get out safely and they can get in'. Wood pointed to the situation with the luxury apartment development at Pacific Wharf in London, which was 'a death trap for people living there'. Although private approved building inspectors had passed the flats has having been constructed properly, 'there was no effective fire compartmentation, which could have risked the whole building'.[88]

Under Brown's premiership, ministers continued to promote the deregulatory aspects of the Regulatory Reform (Fire Safety) Order 2005, with ministers keen to emphasise the 'risk-based approach'.[89] MPs questioned ministers about the competence of fire risk assessors. Fire minister Sadiq Khan gave a brisk answer: 'The government have no plans to regulate the work of fire safety risk advisors or assessors.'[90] Khan was asked about fire authorities' enforcement of the Fire Safety Order and whether it was consistent with other 'better regulation' guidance. He responded:

> We have issued guidance on enforcing the provisions of the Regulatory Reform (Fire Safety) Order 2005 to all enforcing authorities, under article 26 of the order. This makes clear that all enforcing authorities are expected to enforce the order in accordance with the principles of the 'Enforcement Concordat' issued by the Cabinet Office.[91]

In 2009, DCLG published its first evaluation of the Fire Safety Order. Although the report mostly presented the legislation as a success, it still highlighted concerns about the responsible persons, risk assessment, the competence of fire risk assessors and enforcement.[92] Nevertheless, Shahid Malik gave the Fire Safety Order a clean bill of health:

> The Fire Safety Order places the responsibility for fire safety in all non-domestic premises, including hostels and halls of residence, in England and Wales, with a 'responsible person' for the premises-usually the employer, owner or occupier. It requires the responsible person for the premises to carry out a fire safety risk assessment and to put in place appropriate fire safety measures to adequately protect lives in the event of a fire. In other types of multi-occupied residential premises, including blocks of

> flats and houses in multiple occupation, the order applies to the common parts of the premises, rather than the individual domestic units themselves. In these premises, the 'responsible person' is likely to be the landlord.[93]

The most graphic deregulatory failure during this period was the FiReControl project, which ministers and chief fire officers continued to promote despite multiple flaws. In 2010, the Communities and Local Government Committee held an inquiry into FiReControl. The FBU submitted a written memorandum outlining the union's opposition. In February, Wrack gave oral testimony to the committee:

> On behalf of the Fire Brigades Union we have opposed the FiReControl project from the start on grounds of its operational usefulness to the fire and rescue service, on the basis of its threat to the efficiency of the fire and rescue service, on the basis of local accountability and on the basis of cost. I have to say that the previous seven years have just confirmed our position more so than when we started out.[94]

Between 1997 and 2010, Labour government's laid waste to the fire and rescue service, affecting every aspect of firefighters' work. Beneath the hyperbole, irreparable destruction had been wrought to the fire safety regime and the resources firefighters could bring to tackle major emergencies. The situation got worse in the following years under the coalition. But no account of the Grenfell Tower fire is complete without reference to the damage done in the first decade of the new century.

CONSERVATIVES PERSIST WITH DEREGULATION

The Conservative Party in opposition took every opportunity to promote deregulation and push it further. In 2007, John Gummer and Zack Goldsmith published *Blueprint for a Green Economy*, for the shadow cabinet. It called for scrapping the Approved Documents and local authority building control:

> We should therefore extend the approach adopted by the Code for Sustainable Homes, abolishing all the current Building Regulations Approved Documents and replacing them with National Building Standards (NBS). These will be the necessary minimum outcome requirements …
>
> A relatively limited number of objective measurements of outputs would replace the complex and detailed prescriptions of the Building Regulations. Planning permissions would automatically be subject to meeting the National Building Standards (NBS). There would no longer be any need for local authority building control departments. This significant reduction in bureaucracy would also encourage innovation because it would be the outputs that mattered.[95]

In 2009, the Conservative Party published *Regulation in the Post-Bureaucratic Age: How to Get Rid of Red Tape and Reform Quangos*, setting the deregulatory agenda for a future government. It stated that ministers would introduce 'a stringent "one in – one out" requirement where any new law must include cuts in old laws which, together, produce a net 5 per cent reduction in the regulatory burden', repeal 'burdensome regulations', and introduce sunset clauses and curbs on the powers of inspectors.[96]

Shortly afterwards, Conservative leader David Cameron gave a speech to Policy Exchange expressing support for deregulation. He appointed Lord David Young to lead a review on health and safety regulation, because of his 'track record of deregulation and cutting bureaucracy'. Cameron said:

> It is clear that what began as a noble intention to protect people from harm has mutated into a stultifying blanket of bureaucracy, suspicion and fear that has saturated our country … For the good of our society, we need to sort out the nonsense of this over-the-top culture of health and safety and compensation … So let me make it clear: yes, the Conservatives will reduce the burden and impact of health and safety legislation in our country and bring some common sense back into compensation.[97]

4

Cameron's deregulation accelerated

The year 2010 marked another defining moment for deregulation. The Conservatives and Liberal-Democrats formed a coalition government at Westminster, which accelerated the deregulation agenda, driving attacks on safety laws and giving the private sector a free hand. This would have disastrous consequences for the residents of Grenfell Tower.

In the coalition government, David Cameron was prime minister, Nick Clegg deputy prime minister and George Osborne chancellor of the exchequer. In the Cabinet Office, the key figures were Francis Maude, Kenneth Clarke and Oliver Letwin. Vince Cable became business secretary, assisted initially by Mark Prisk and Ed Davey. From 2012, Michael Fallon was the other key business minister.

CAMERON'S COALITION: DEREGULATION AT THE CORE

The coalition's programme for government had deregulation at its core. It promised:

> We will cut red tape by introducing a 'one-in, one-out' rule whereby no new regulation is brought in without other regulation being cut by a greater amount … We will impose 'sunset clauses' on regulations and regulators to ensure that the need for each regulation is regularly reviewed … We will support the creation and expansion of mutuals, co-operatives, charities and social enterprises, and enable these groups to have much greater involvement in the running of public services.[1]

The deregulatory drive came right from the top. David Cameron made successive speeches advocating rapid, exhaustive deregulation throughout his administration. The cabinet established a star chamber, the Reducing Regulation Sub-Committee, with the business department and Cabinet Office driving deregulation.[2] Cameron promised the Federation of Small Businesses:

> So this deregulation initiative is serious. We're going to follow it through and we're going to get rid of those regulations, so we are the first government in modern history to have taken away more regulation. We're going to do that at home and we are now increasingly doing it in Europe as well.[3]

Open Public Services

The first strand of the deregulation was to open up more public services to the private sector – the same privatisation agenda that had been promoted by Thatcher. Cameron made a much-trumpeted speech on the Big Society, when he stated:

> We've got to get rid of the centralised bureaucracy that wastes money and undermines morale. And in its place we've got to give professionals much more freedom, and open up public services to new providers like charities, social enterprises and private companies so we get more innovation, diversity and responsiveness to public need.[4]

Cabinet office minister Francis Maude announced the Open Public Services White Paper.[5] Cameron pledged that it would mean 'Less bureaucracy. Less officialdom.' Oliver Letwin told MPs:

> There could not be a more important issue than this ... To unlock innovation, the White Paper commits us to diversity of provision, removing barriers to entry, stimulating entry by new types of provider and unlocking new sources of capital. To ensure that public sector providers can hold their own on a level playing field, the White Paper sets out measures to liberate public sector bodies from red tape. To encourage employee ownership within the public services, the White Paper sets out the measures that we are taking to promote mutualisation and employee co-operatives.[6]

The FBU opposed the White Paper. Matt Wrack warned of the risks in the *Guardian*: 'You cannot build the long-term stability a critical 999 emergency response service needs, especially with regard to training, on the sands of the private sector. No matter how big or how stable a private company looks, it can't be trusted with a 999 service.'[7]

Limiting new regulation: 'one in, one out'

The new government immediately set about stemming the flow of new regulations. Business minister Mark Prisk announced the new 'one in, one out' rule to stem new laws: 'If a minister wishes to bring forward a new regulation, they must show that they have removed a regulation and that that will reduce the overall burden of regulation, ensuring that businesses see a net reduction.'[8]

Business secretary Vince Cable told the British Chambers of Commerce about the rationale:

> The one in, one out rule – the first of its kind anywhere in the world – has begun to turn back the tide since it took effect … Under its provisions, a minister who wants to introduce a new rule which generates costs for business must first identify a corresponding cut in regulation elsewhere with the same value. The process is designed to force departments to exhaust all the alternatives before seeking to legislate …[9]

Despite reporting reductions in the 'burden' of regulation, the administration soon pushed further. Business minister Michael Fallon introduced the 'one in, two out' rule:

> I am announcing today a doubling of the rate at which Whitehall departments must cut the burdens their regulation places on business … From January 2013, the current 'one-in, one-out' constraint … will be replaced with a 'one-in, two-out' rule that whenever a regulation creates costs, twice as much saving must be found by scrapping or simplifying regulation … By the end of the parliament, they will be expected both to have achieved 'one-in, two-out' from January 2013 and to have introduced enough deregulation to balance out the cost of any regulation

they introduced over the last two years. This new approach is intended to ensure that regulation is the last resort for government departments.[10]

Reducing existing regulation: the Red Tape Challenge

The coalition government also attacked the existing stock of regulation.[11] Cameron railed against red tape, launching the Red Tape Challenge:

> There are over 21,000 statutory rules and regulations in force, and I want us to bring that number – and the burden it represents – down. Indeed, I want us to be the first government in modern history to leave office having reduced the overall burden of regulation, rather than increasing it.[12]

Cable told the British Chambers of Commerce:

> The presumption will be clear: regulations will be presumed guilty unless proven innocent ... Every four weeks we will be publishing, on Red Tape Challenge, the regulations that have an impact on a particular area of our lives ... We will then take action. And this time we will presume that you are right; we will assume that the regulations should go. Unless ministers can robustly defend the need to keep an unpopular regulation, departments will get rid of it.[13]

Business minister Ed Davey told parliament, 'in the chancellor's Budget we announced a three-year moratorium on regulations for micros. We have also set up the Red Tape Challenge. We are dealing not just with future regulation but with the stock of regulation, an exercise that was long overdue.'[14]

Cable introduced an Enterprise and Regulatory Reform Act, to further reduce burdens on business: 'The Bill also contains provision for accelerating deregulation. Much is being done at present through the one-in, one-out system to prevent small companies, in particular, from being suffocated by red tape, and we are working with like-minded governments in Europe.'[15]

It was soon followed by further deregulation. Kenneth Clarke said: 'The Deregulation Bill is just the latest offspring of the government's highly ambitious Red Tape Challenge, which has already identified and removed barriers to the growth of our economy to the tune of £212 million each year. There is much more to come.'[16]

Cameron boasted about the results of the Red Tape Challenge to the Federation of Small Businesses: 'This is going to be the first government in modern history that at the end of its parliamentary term has less regulation in place than there was at the beginning. We've now identified those 3,000 regulations that we're going to scrap and we have already got rid of 800 of them.'[17]

Health and safety attacked

The coalition government also took aim at health and safety law. Cameron appointed Lord David Young of Graffham, the arch-deregulator from the Thatcher years, to investigate whether health and safety law was a 'burden on business' and if health and safety law should apply to the emergency services, including firefighters.

Young was crystal clear about his intentions. He told *The Times*: 'I want to exclude all the emergency services from health and safety. Technically speaking, the firemen could say they wouldn't go to a fire because it was too dangerous. We've just got to get sense back into the system.' After meeting FBU officials, Young retreated.[18] His report, *Common Sense, Common Safety*, did not proceed with taking firefighters out of safety law.[19]

In 2012, Cameron launched an extraordinary attack on safety:

> I am determined that we do everything possible to take the brakes off business: cutting taxes; slashing red tape; putting billions into big infrastructure projects; making it much easier for British firms to get out there and trade with the world. And there is something else we are doing: waging war against the excessive health and safety culture that has become an albatross around the neck of British businesses ... So this coalition has a clear New Year's resolution: to kill off the health and safety culture for good.[20]

The Conservative Party fought the 2015 general election on their deregulation record. Their manifesto promised: 'We will cut red tape, boost start-ups and small businesses. This government was the first in post-war history to reduce the burden of regulation. We will cut a further £10 billion of red tape over the next parliament through our Red Tape Challenge and our One-In-Two-Out rule.'[21]

The Conservatives won a 12-seat majority. An Enterprise Bill was announced in the Queen's Speech, to further promote deregulation: 'Extending the government's ambitious target for cutting red tape to cover the activities of more regulators to enable them to contribute to the deregulation target … Extension of the Primary Authority scheme to streamline regulation around the country.'[22]

Cabinet Office minister Matt Hancock pledged to continue with the privatisation agenda: 'The government is committed to supporting the growth of public service mutuals and delivering the manifesto commitment to guarantee the right to mutualise within the public sector.'[23] New business secretary Sajid Javid launched a new cutting red tape programme:

> I am determined to take the brakes off British businesses and set them free from heavy-handed regulators. The government's pledge to cut £10 billion in red tape over the course of this parliament … these reviews will look not only at the rules themselves but the way they are enforced. We want firms to tell us where red tape is holding them back …[24]

A year before the Grenfell Tower fire, Javid accelerated deregulation, announcing at the British Chambers of Commerce conference a new 'one in, three out' process. He said:

> We're also introducing a new rule for government departments. In the last parliament we introduced a policy called 'one in, two out'. It meant that every time a new regulation that cost money to comply with was introduced, the government had to remove or modify existing rules with double the cost to business. For every one pound of regulatory burden we created, two pounds worth had to be removed. Today I can announce that we're upgrading that to 'one in, three out'. If departments want to bring in new

> regulatory costs for things that weren't in our manifesto, they will be expected to find savings worth three times as much.[25]

Austerity

Alongside its deregulation agenda, the Cameron government imposed the worst cuts to public spending in living memory, decimating public services including local government, building safety and the fire and rescue service. They imposed what Clegg called 'savage cuts' to public services, attacks on firefighters' pensions and pay restraint. Austerity fundamentally weakened the social fabric supporting communities across the UK.

The FBU made frequent, explicit public warnings about the consequences of job cuts for national resilience and public safety.[26] Early in the new administration, the FBU warned that ten thousand fire service jobs were under threat from central funding budget cuts. Matt Wrack said:

> This government seems intent on imposing cuts that will wreak havoc within the fire and rescue service and short change both the public and firefighters. These pernicious cuts must be fought to defend public safety. They are not inevitable, but politically driven. The FBU will oppose these draconian attacks on an essential frontline service and robustly defend the key role firefighters play in keeping communities safe. We cannot just meekly roll over and accept this. Neither should the employers. Firefighters are professionals – and we won't stand by and see our service dismantled piecemeal.[27]

On 17 November 2010, the FBU held a mass rally at Westminster, demanding investment not cuts. Two and a half thousand firefighters descended on London to lobby parliament, one of the largest FBU gathering at the time. Lobbies were also held in Edinburgh and Cardiff.[28]

Two years later, FBU members descended on Westminster again, meeting MPs over fire service cuts and firefighter pensions. The union ran advertisements on bonfire night, bluntly warning the public that government cuts cost lives and that if budgets are slashed, people would suffer. Wrack said: 'I make no apology for the need to be hard hitting because these cuts will put safety at risk. We make no apologies for giving that warning.'[29]

In 2013, former chief fire and rescue adviser Ken Knight published an efficiencies review at the request of fire minister Brandon Lewis. The FBU was highly critical of Knight's report, calling it a 'fig leaf' for further cuts to the fire and rescue service. The union emphasised the absence of a national fire risk assessment to fully measure the resilience of the service in the face of multiple hazards, as well as the real impact of cuts on firefighter jobs.[30]

The communities and local government committee conducted a brief investigation of the Knight review, collecting written evidence and some oral testimony. The FBU made a written submission and Wrack gave evidence:

> There are massive cuts being made in our fire and rescue service. You had a number of chief officers here last year and I think they equivocated on this issue. I want to be very clear: those cuts will put public safety at risk, those cuts will put firefighters' safety at risk, they will put lives at risk, they will mean that homes that could have been saved will be lost, and businesses that could have been saved will be lost. That is the point that Ken Knight has completely missed.[31]

On 16 October 2013, firefighters again marched through central London, making demands on ministers on pensions, cuts, jobs and privatisation. The FBU estimated that around half of all firefighters available – those not on shift, about to go on shift or coming off night shift – attended the event.[32]

Austerity really began to bite, after cuts were back loaded in a vain attempt to disguise their severity. The FBU's *Sounding the Alarm* report stated:

> Since the coalition government came to power over 5,000 frontline firefighter jobs have been cut across the UK, threatening national resilience ... The FBU has been accused of 'scaremongering' when our representatives have highlighted the threat these jobs cuts make to national resilience. However even chief officers are now warning that any further reductions to fire and

rescue service funding will compromise our ability to resource the national resilience requirements ... This confirms FBU warnings that cuts are threatening national resilience.[33]

PICKLES AND BUILDING SAFETY DEREGULATION

In Cameron's first administration, Eric Pickles was secretary of state for the Department for Communities and Local Government (DCLG). The department had responsibility for building regulations in England,[34] with all three ministers Liberal-Democrats: Andrew Stunell, Don Foster and Stephen Williams.

Ministers regularly expressed their support for deregulation. In 2010, Pickles articulated his own zeal: 'Today I am asking councils to put localism into action and help us cut back red tape, wrest control away from the bureaucrats, reverse the years of creeping state control and return power to people, communities and councils.'[35]

Pickles announced the Localism Bill. He boasted, 'This is a deregulating Bill ... Councils have been drowning in red tape and rules and paralysed by a culture of centralism.'[36] The legislation swept through parliament and became law within a year.

Pickles told the House of Commons: 'I am proud of my Department's reputation as one of the most deregulating Departments in Whitehall'.[37] He made the same boast at the Confederation of British Industry annual dinner.[38] Pickles reiterated this position at the British Chambers of Commerce annual conference. He told the audience, 'Business has been wrapped up in red tape and regulation for too long. It's time to give you room to breathe. I'm proud of my department's record on deregulating'.[39]

Building regulations and guidance

In 2010, Pickles published a list of what his government regarded as 'unnecessary regulations, ridiculous micromanagement or outdated laws' that they intended to revoke or simplify. It was explicitly linked to the 'one in, one out' rule and 'sunset clauses'. The list included the Building Regulations 2000 and Approved Inspector Regulations 2000. Ministers explicitly intended to 'reduce 18 separate pieces of building regulations into two', in order to 'cut the administrative burdens on both business and local authorities' and 'consult on local fire protection requirements to see if they are still required'.[40]

Stunell organised a rapid consultation. Although the Building Regulations remained the national minimum standard, he promised that the programme of work would be 'deregulatory in nature'. Stunell pledged 'to explore the potential for deregulation and streamlining of the existing provisions'. Ministers also tried to weaken building control. Stunell told parliament that 'as part of this deregulatory element we also need to explore what changes may be needed to the building control system. I believe there is scope to enhance compliance and reduce the burdens on those who use the system'.[41]

DCLG published *Future Changes to the Building Regulations – Next Steps*, reiterating that 'the programme will contain a significant deregulatory workstream'. It also contained a passage that is highly prescient to later events at Grenfell Tower, with regard to the evacuation of vulnerable people from buildings. It stated:

> On a different theme, a number of respondents raised the issue of egress from a building for people with disabilities in the case of fire. It was suggested that the existing provision was unacceptable as it permitted an approach that could leave a person with a disability within a building (albeit within a safe refuge) in the event of a fire evacuation. Whilst the Department has not been presented with any evidence that the approach is, in practice, any less safe, it notes the concern about this provision and will keep the issue under review.[42]

The paper admitted 'the need to raise the levels of compliance' and 'a strong call for increased legal enforcement'. This included increasing in the range of powers available (such as stop notices), an increase in the level of fines and 'measures to encourage local authorities to take more legal action'. It also exposed failings with the part-privatised system of building control:

> Some suggested that building control should be fully privatised, others that it should be returned wholly to local authorities.

> Clearly there are pros and cons to both. A number of suggestions were made about how better to level the playing-field in a mixed public/private building control system. Others suggested that all building control officers should be licensed and subject to external monitoring although there was not a great deal of evidence to justify setting up such a regime.[43]

Despite evidence that the building safety system was failing, Stunell proposed to 'reduce costs and burdens by simplifying or improving processes for both local authorities and approved inspectors'. He promised 'helping incentivise businesses to improve compliance by introducing additional voluntary mechanisms, such as extending the competent person self-certification schemes framework and introducing specialist third-party certification schemes'.[44]

In 2012, Don Foster became communities minister. He continued with deregulation. Foster launched a new coterie of building industry experts, tasked with 'rationalising the entire framework of building regulations, and national and local housing standards'. The terms of reference for the review included the Building Regulations themselves and the Approved Documents.[45]

Most significantly, Foster told the House of Commons that the government would lay regulations 'to repeal unnecessary fire provisions in 23 local Acts'. These changes repealed the London Building Acts (Amendment) Act 1939, Section 20, which dealt with fire safety in tall or large cube buildings and Section 21 with the uniting of buildings.[46]

In 2013, the limitations previously placed on which type or dwellings approved inspectors could undertake their building control functions were removed. This meant private approved inspectors were able to cover all types of building control work.[47]

Communities minister Stephen Williams was asked about the independence of approved inspectors. His response illustrated the government's laissez faire approach. He replied that Inspectors' Code of Conduct was a matter for CICAIR Ltd and 'the government has no plans to change the relevant provisions in the Building Act 1984 or Regulation 9 of the Building (Approved Inspectors etc.) Regulations'.[48]

Pickles bragged of his achievements: 'The Department has made considerable progress in slashing red tape and saving business money ... It is important to recognise the achievements of not only deregulation but better regulation which will provide great benefits to businesses and individual citizens.'[49]

When Pickles gave evidence to the Grenfell Tower Inquiry, he falsely claimed that the building regulations were exempt from deregulation. The inquiry's Phase 2 report did not accept his claims. Instead it found that 'he was personally an ardent supporter of the government's deregulation policy', who supported the deregulatory approach 'including the application of the policies to the Building Regulations'. While he was Secretary of State 'deregulatory considerations appear to have permeated every aspect of the department's development, assessment and implementation of policy'.[50]

Cameron's second administration

In Cameron's second administration, Greg Clark was DCLG secretary of state and James Wharton the minister responsible for the building regulations. The change of personnel did not alter the deregulatory approach on building safety.

Ministers launched a new Cutting Red Tape review, which aimed 'to give housebuilders their say on ineffective rules and heavy-handed enforcement that stop them building homes'. Javid said: 'This review will give housebuilders and smaller construction businesses a powerful voice as part of our £10 billion deregulation drive.'

Housing minister Brandon Lewis promised:

> We are determined to remove barriers faced by housebuilders to ensure we continue to keep Britain building as quickly and safely as possible. We want to hear the views of firms big and small so we can remove unnecessary red tape and help housebuilders do what they do best, building the homes we need.[51]

Cameron's brief second administration did nothing substantial with respect to the Building Regulations or Approved Document B. Wharton told MPs: 'My Department is considering a number of issues related to the Building Regulations and the building control system. We will make an announcement about our plans in due course.'[52]

This period saw growing criticism raised about building control and private approved inspectors, even from Conservative MPs. In 2015, Maria Miller secured a debate in the House of Commons on building control. She drew attention to the potential conflict of interest that some companies provided home warranties and were also approved inspectors She asked rhetorically:

> How do we know that all approved inspectors are doing their jobs to the highest professional standards? Exactly how independent are they? In the 30 years that approved inspectors have been in existence, how many have been struck off for poor performance or over questions of independence? I think we will find that the answer is absolutely none.[53]

By contrast, ministers continued to laud the part-privatised building control regime. Clark told an NHBC gathering:

> The NHBC is a credit to the industry – an example of how standards can be raised and maintained independently of government. Not only does the NHBC certify houses, it also helps insure them – providing warranties on around 80 per cent of all the new homes built in this country: A model of taking direct responsibility that ought to be applied more widely.[54]

In 2016, Gordon Henderson secured a Westminster Hall debate. He told MPs: 'The truth is that the system is simply not working, not least because those charged with regulating building work are not themselves regulated.' Wharton's response expressed the same complacency that pervaded the government's longstanding approach to building safety:

> On the whole, it works well, it delivers the appropriate standards and most homes in this country are built to an extraordinarily good standard, by international comparisons. We should be

> proud of the system we have and of the people who work in and contribute to it, day in, day out.[55]

Behind the scenes, Wharton pushed deregulation towards the outright privatisation of building control. This is clear from the minutes of BRAC meetings during his tenure and from his correspondence. In October 2015, Wharton met with senior civil servants about the building control review. Sarah Morgan, Wharton's assistant private secretary circulated an email summing up the minister's views, which included 'looking further into the option of privatisation'.[56]

Ministers considered drastic deregulation of building safety in the years before the Grenfell Tower fire. In 2015, senior civil servants in the Building Regulations and Energy Performance Division sent Clark and Wharton a memorandum outlining options for more radical reform of the building control system. It stated:

> If ministers wish to take a view on unlocking potentially wider reform to drive efficiency, there are more fundamental questions which we could explore to redraw the boundary between local authorities and Approved Inspectors. This would include enabling Approved Inspectors to undertake more of the types of work currently solely the responsibility of local authorities, through to providing that only Approved Inspectors should undertake compliance checking work.[57]

CAMERON AND FIRE SAFETY DEREGULATION

In Cameron's government, DCLG had responsibility for fire and rescue services in England. Pickles was secretary of state, Bob Neill was initially fire minister, followed by Brandon Lewis and then Penny Mordaunt. The FBU continued to fight for fire safety, despite its exclusion from channels to ministers. The CFOA-run Practitioners' Forum ceased to function and was disbanded.[58]

The new government wasted no time in accelerating the drive to deregulate the fire and rescue service. In 2010, Neill addressed the FIRE conference:

> It has never been more important that we are open to new ideas, to new ways of working and delivery, and to greater flexibility in providing services ... Should we be looking to regulate further? 'No' would be my answer. We must move away from the view that the only way to solve problems is to regulate, neither you nor business need to be bound hand and foot with red tape ...[59]

Neill responded to reports in *The Times* newspaper about fatalities at a high rise fire in Shanghai. He wrote:

> Suggestions that the government is putting fire safety at risk in tall buildings (Fire threat to high-rise blocks, 18 November) by potentially removing provisions for sprinklers are factually wrong ... The government's position is very clear: sprinklers continue to play an important role in protecting people from fire. However, as part of a broader deregulation initiative, we are removing duplicate and unnecessary provisions from primary legislation and an assorted collection of Local Acts to allow individuals, councils and business to get on with their job without unnecessary government meddling – but never where it puts lives at risk.[60]

Neill told MPs:

> We are committed to removing needless bureaucracy and unnecessary burdens contained within existing secondary legislation and other forms of regulation ... New regulatory burdens on businesses are given full consideration through the new one-in-one-out process, which ensures that the costs imposed by new regulations are offset by reductions elsewhere.[61]

In 2011, Neill spoke at the LGA annual fire conference. He told the fire sector 'regulation is therefore a last resort' and expressed his support for the 'one in, one out' rule.[62]

Neill also pledged in parliament that 'the core programme of the Department is deregulatory'. He said:

> All future regulations will be developed in full compliance with the government's one-in, one-out rules meaning that new regulatory burdens we impose on businesses will be given full consideration to ensure that the costs being imposed are offset by reductions in the overall cost of regulation imposed by the Department.[63]

Neill instigated the Fire Futures review. It endorsed privatisation, suggesting on Fire Safety Order enforcement that fire and rescue services 'may wish to delegate some aspects to private sector experts in the longer term'.[64] FBU assistant general secretary Andy Dark said:

> The government suggests that fire and rescue authorities should be required to consider commissioning their fire and rescue service from other providers. The FBU believes these proposals are incoherent and do not provide resilience. The union totally rejects any suggestion that fire authorities, in any guise, should become a commissioning agent, with fire services being delivered by another provider. We reject totally the privatisation of the fire and rescue service.[65]

Fire Service College

The coalition government pushed through the privatisation of the Fire Service College, once a world-renowned institution that previous administrations had allowed to decline. Neill informed MPs that the college would be sold to the private sector.[66] The FBU opposed the privatisation. Officers' rep Jack Ford argued:

> Privatising the Fire Service College will not secure its future. If the recent financial collapse caused by the private sector has taught us anything, it is that nothing is secure in the private sector, which is why the fire service is in the public sector. The Fire Service College is world-renowned with some fantastic facilities. And it does need investment, but selling it off to the private sector is not the answer. The college is a centre of excellence. It's important to the fire service and all the work we do. It's time to think again.[67]

In 2013, new fire minister Brandon Lewis confirmed the sale of the Fire Service College to Capita for £10 million. He told MPs: 'I am particularly pleased that important partners, such as the Chief Fire Officers Association and the Local Government Association, have reacted positively to the sale, and I would like to wish Capita every success in realising their vision for the college.'[68]

Mutualisation as the route to privatisation

In 2011, the Open Public Services White Paper heralded mutuals as vehicles for privatising public services. Cleveland Fire Brigade was the first to explore this avenue. Brigade management registered a Community Interest Company with Companies House.

Local Labour MPs Tom Blenkinsop and Alex Cunningham put ministers on the spot about their plans. In 2012, Bob Neill admitted that Cleveland Fire Brigade had 'discussed their proposals for the establishment of a separate, for-profit community interest company, informally with the department'. However he said DCLG had 'not offered any funding or formal advice on this issue'.[69]

In November 2012, Neil O'Connor, director of fire, resilience and emergencies at DCLG wrote to key stakeholders, asking for views on potential mutualisation in the fire sector. O'Connor referred to the need for legislation 'to enable fire and rescue authorities to contract out their full range of services to mutuals'.[70]

The FBU challenged the whole basis of ministers' proposals: 'The FBU believes that the introduction of mutualisation initiatives into the fire and rescue service would be a landmark decision by any government and would represent a nadir of governmental concern for public safety'.[71]

Fire minister Brandon Lewis wrote to James Duddridge, chair of the Westminster Regulatory Reform Committee, looking for a route to open up fire and rescue. Lewis sought the committee's views 'on our proposals for a Legislative Reform Order that would enable fire and rescue authorities in England to contract out their full range of services to a suitable provider, including a public service mutual'. Lewis wrote:

> Fire and rescue authorities should be able to adopt alternative models for the delivery, under contract, for some or all of their services by a suitable alternative provider e.g. a mutual, social enterprise, or other appointed contractor. Certain provisions in existing legislation preclude some services from being delivered by alternative providers. Cleveland Fire and Rescue Authority are currently exploring the delivery of their services via a mutual social enterprise and the Cabinet Office and the Department are supporting them as a pathfinder for the fire sector. Cleveland would like to be in a position to deliver the full range of their services via a mutual social enterprise in 2014.

Lewis admitted that Cleveland had received 'funding for professional support to help with their mutual process from Mutual Support Programme and Department of Health to help them explore mutualisation'. He added that 'It is intended that the support given to Cleveland Fire and Rescue Authority will provide tools available for other fire and rescue authorities including potential contracting and commercial models.'[72]

Labour MPs Ian Lavery and Dave Anderson savaged the mutualisation proposals on the committee. Duddridge told Lewis that a majority of the committee (seven to five) opposed the mutualisation.[73]

The FBU wrote directly to Duddridge, as well as the All Parliamentary Fire Safety and Rescue Group.[74] Wrack wrote to Lewis following an exchange at the FBU's parliamentary group meeting. Lewis claimed 'it is not the government's intention to roll out privatisation of the fire and rescue service; recent media attention characterising it as such is completely misleading'.[75]

Wrack explained the issues in *Firefighter* magazine:

> The FBU has responded vigorously to a letter from the fire minister Brandon Lewis suggesting the government wants to contract out the entire fire and rescue service. This is outright privatisation and a threat to every single firefighter – and to the standard of service provided to the public. They have made it clear that the mutuals programme in Cleveland is part of these privatisation plans, designed to fragment and atomise our

> service, so the vultures from the private sector can pick over the bones of what's left. They want to privatise so they can make firefighters work longer hours for less pay, making profits that will be funnelled into offshore accounts, avoiding tax and decimating the service to the public. The overwhelming majority of firefighters do not want privatisation, nor is there any public demand for it. The privatisation threat is real and the FBU has warned of it before. The fire minister's letter has drawn outrage from many politicians and Labour's spokesperson John Healey MP has already said that 'Firefighting is a no-go area for privatisation'. The FBU will do everything we can to keep our fire and rescue service as a publicly owned and democratically run service, free from the profiteers who would ruin it.[76]

Lewis was forced to retreat. He denied privatisation was the intention: 'In recent weeks, this canard has emerged from hibernation as it has been suggested that this government is seeking to 'privatise' the fire service. I would like to state for the record that this is completely untrue.'[77]

Lewis claimed that mutualisation had local support in Cleveland, which was strongly rebutted by local FBU officials. Andy Noble, FBU North East executive member reported that 'our members in Cleveland … remain totally opposed to any move which takes the service out of direct local fire authority control and employment'. Noble said Labour councillors who had supported the original proposal should wake up to 'the monstrosity they had created' and put a stop to it before it was too late.[78]

Cleveland FBU members persuaded the Labour group on Redcar and Cleveland council to oppose the mutual. All the Labour MPs in Cleveland opposed it.[79] FBU members in Cleveland were surveyed by the independent YouGov polling organisation to seek their views on the mutual. The chief fire officer's plans were overwhelmingly thrown out by FBU members. Some 97 per cent of those surveyed said that they were fully opposed to the proposals. The same proportion (97%) also said that they thought the fire and rescue service would change for the worse if it were to become a 'for profit' mutual. Wrack said:

> Firefighters have given a clear verdict on these mutualisation plans and it is an outright rejection. This is a huge blow to government plans to privatise the fire and rescue service. Earlier this year, the government was desperately trying to sneak through changes in the law, but were found out by MPs and the FBU. The government has thrown hundreds of thousands of pounds at Cleveland to try and get this through. This is another case where the FBU, working with local MPs and politicians, has managed to turn the tide. Our collective organisation makes the difference. We will now be campaigning to consign these mutual proposals to the scrapheap.[80]

Ultimately, ministers were forced to abandon privatisation. This was a triumph for local FBU members and a massive victory for firefighters elsewhere. Despite political support and central funding, Cameron's government was not able to spread the poison of privatisation deep into the heart of the fire and rescue service.[81] By the time Penny Mordaunt became fire minister, it was clear the department had given up on mutuals in fire.[82]

Fire Safety

In 2013, the Department for Business, Innovation and Skills (BIS) reviewed enforcement of the Regulatory Reform (Fire Safety) Order 2005. The report claimed that the objective of the Fire Safety Order had been to reduce 'burdens on business and overlap of enforcing authorities'. It revealed significant failings with respect to risk assessments.[83] Nevertheless, fire minister Penny Mordaunt was complacent about the light touch approach:

> It is the responsibility of enforcing authorities to satisfy themselves that the responsible person has complied with their duties under the Fire Safety Order 2005. Under the Fire Safety Order, building owners are required to carry out a fire risk assessment of their premises and put in place and maintain adequate and appropriate fire safety measures to ensure that the risk to life in the event of fire is reduced to as low as reasonably practicable. The Order is not prescriptive about what particular safety measures are needed; these are for the building owner to deter-

> mine based on the specific circumstances of their building and the needs of the occupants, including those who may be particularly vulnerable to the risk from fire.[84]

The National Audit Office (NAO) also found serious reductions in prevention and protection services. The numbers of audits and inspections, hours spent on fire safety checks by fire service and hours on campaigns had all reduced by around 30 per cent since the coalition government came to power. The NAO found that 'Evidence from our case studies suggests that some, but not all, authorities had reduced their prevention and protection work in response to funding reductions'. The West Midlands and the London Fire Brigade, in particular, 'mentioned the potential impact of staff reductions on delivering their protection work'.[85]

The FBU fought for public fire safety and firefighter safety. Often incidents of public deaths and injuries also involved firefighter casualties. Firefighters would attempt rescues and get people out of danger. But sometimes victims did not survive and firefighters got hurt. The FBU tried to learn lessons from incidents where casualties had occurred.

In 2011, the FBU wrote to Ken Knight regarding professional standards. The union pointed out delays to operational guidance and failure to commission new projects. The FBU referred to an earlier Health and Safety Executive report, which he said had confirmed that firefighter safety has been compromised by the previous government's 'modernisation' agenda. The union proposed an additional operational guidance project be commissioned to develop response planning based on worst-case planning scenarios'. This was intended to build on the Pathfinder trials, which had developed minimum staffing and equipment needs for a range of incidents, including high rise residential fires.[86]

Wrack gave evidence to the select committee, explaining the failure to assess risks and learn from major incidents. He also emphasised the failure to learn lessons from fires and fire deaths (particularly in the absence of a body such as the CFBAC):

> Our view is that there is evidence that fire services are not learning lessons from earlier tragedies and that we have coroners

> identifying, in some of those cases, that precisely the same point that has been made in a previous coroner's inquest is now being made in a subsequent coroner's inquest. I think alarm bells should be raised in the fire and rescue service about that matter. We need a proper, thorough-going debate around that, and an inspectorate is a very valid part of that process that we would want to see come out of that.[87]

The FBU carried out its own research into firefighter fatalities and proposed improvements. In 2015, the union published its commissioned report by Professor Andrew Watterson, making a series of recommendations for action. Sadly, these were mostly ignored.[88]

Fire governance

In Cameron's second administration, Mark Francois was DCLG fire minister. Despite lasting barely a year, central government managed to further damage the fire and rescue service. Ministers announced proposals to enable police and crime commissioners (PCCs) to take over fire and rescue authorities. They favoured allowing PCCs to create a single employer for police and fire staff, making it easier for them to share back office functions and streamline management. The FBU made a forceful submission in opposition.[89]

In January 2016, ministerial oversight of fire and rescue transferred to the Home Office from DCLG. Theresa May was home secretary and Mike Penning became fire minister. The Home Office announced it would take forward legislation to enable PCCs to take over fire and rescue authorities.[90] It ignored objections to the PCC model, including the weakness of self-appointed scrutiny panels and the greater risk that PCCs would outsource, sell off or contract out core public services in the name of efficiency.

The home secretary set out the new approach, which included imposing a duty to collaborate on the emergency services and the creation of a fire inspectorate in England, in a speech to the Reform think tank event in London.[91]

Cameron's government continued with austerity cuts. The FBU warned about the impact. In 2015, the FBU sent its *Fire and Rescue Service Matters* bulletin to all MPs. The union explained that over the previous year, more than 1,800 frontline firefighter jobs were cut – the worst single year of job cuts in the service's history. Between 2011 and 2015, nearly one in eight (12%) of the total firefighting force were cut.[92]

The new administration launched its spending review. The FBU warned that 'Government ministers are now planning further cuts of anything between 25 per cent and 40 per cent across government departments. Cuts on this scale would decimate the fire and rescue service as we know it'. The union argued that 'Emergency response times are slowing, emergency response is increasingly under-resourced and public safety is being put at risk'.[93]

Unfortunately, ministers failed to listen. DCLG confirmed cuts of over 20 per cent for central funding allocated to fire and rescue authorities in England over the next five years. The FBU again warned MPs of the consequences of such austerity.[94]

MAY'S GOVERNMENT

In July 2016, David Cameron left office in disgrace after losing the Brexit referendum. Theresa May became prime minister. Philip Hammond was appointed chancellor. May continued with the deregulation agenda. She wrote in the *Financial Times*: 'We will show that capitalism and free markets continue to be the best way to create prosperity, spread opportunity and give people the chance of a better life.'[95] May reinforced this view in a speech shortly afterwards to the CBI annual conference:

> For we believe in free markets. They are the means by which we spread opportunity and lift people out of poverty. We believe in capitalism – the means by which we drive economic growth, putting people into work to provide for their families. And we believe in business – the entrepreneurs and the innovators who employ millions of people up and down this country – the basis for our prosperity. The government I lead will always believe in these things.[96]

In April 2017, May called a snap general election. The Conservative Party again put deregulation at the heart of their general election manifesto: 'Poor and excessive government regulation limits growth for no good reason. So we will continue to regulate more efficiently, saving £9 billion through the Red Tape Challenge and the One-In-Two-Out Rule.'[97]

The general election resulted in a hung parliament, with no party winning an overall majority. Theresa May remained prime minister and formed a new government. This was less than a week before the Grenfell Tower fire.

Building safety

Theresa May appointed Sajid Javid DCLG secretary of state, with responsibility for the building regulations and guidance. Gavin Barwell was the minister responsible for the building safety, until he lost his seat at the 2017 general election.

Under the May government, complaints continued about the building control regime. The All-Party Parliamentary Group (APPG) on the Built Environment published a report, *More Homes, Fewer Complaints*, setting out the problems:

> Concern was raised that in some cases fewer inspections were being undertaken by building control inspectors and approved inspectors (their private counterparts) to establish homes' compliance with Building Regulations because competition in the market was driving fees down and affecting their capability for doing a thorough and full set of inspections.[98]

The report estimated that the NHBC had around 80 per cent of the warranty provision, but less for the building control service. A decade earlier, the NHBC had a virtual monopoly on warranties, but by 2016 it shared the market with Premier Guarantee and LABC Warranty. In addition, there are small and independent approved inspectors marketing warranties that together could account for a small slice. The APPG report stated:

> We are concerned that competition in building control might be fuelling a race to the bottom and we are therefore recommending there should be a defined minimum number of inspections that local authority building control and approved inspectors in

> the private sector and warranty providers should not fall below. We suggest that the minimum level should be considered by DCLG in consultation with the industry.[99]

The new government continued to procrastinate over changes to the Building Regulations. Barwell told MPs, 'We have not set out any formal plans to review the Building Regulations as a whole, but we have publicly committed ourselves to reviewing Part B following the Lakanal House fire.'[100]

Labour MP Rushanara Ali secured a debate in the House of Commons about the regulation of social landlords and how they manage their properties. Barwell insisted that 'the government are committed to deregulating the sector'.[101]

Barwell captured the government's complacency on building safety just weeks before the Grenfell Tower fire. He told MPs:

> Responsibility for compliance with the building regulations rests with those building new homes. All new homes are subject to supervision by a building control body, which can be a local authority or approved inspector. Building control bodies must take all reasonable steps to ascertain if the building work complies with the relevant requirements of the building regulations and not give a compliance certificate until satisfied that the requirements have been met.[102]

Fire 'reform'

Theresa May appointed Amber Rudd home secretary, with responsibility for the fire and rescue service. Brandon Lewis was minister of state for policing and the fire service. Fire and rescue policy continued along the lines of the previous administration. Lewis spoke at the 2016 CFOA conference, advocating the government's fire reform proposals and lauded chief fire officers' plans to transform their organisation into the National Fire Chiefs Council (NFCC):

> I want this reform programme to be in your hands, owned by the service, for the service … In policing we supported the creation of the National Police Chiefs Council. As you have heard, this single body brings together all the operationally independent

> and locally accountable chief constables and their chief officer teams to coordinate national operational policing and work closely with the College of Policing to develop national standards. I am heartened by the steps being taken by CFOA to effectively replicate this model and I look forward to supporting and working with the new body from next April.[103]

Lewis told the Fire Protection Association Sector Summit that his role was to deliver 'the radical and ambitious package of reforms the prime minister, when former home secretary, announced earlier this year'. He also joked about his previous roles, assuring the audience with some irony, 'I have no plans to privatise the fire service'.[104]

The Policing and Crime Act received Royal Assent in January 2017. As the bill finished its final stages through parliament, Lewis made clear the wider aims of his collaboration agenda. He said:

> My hon. Friend makes a good point and highlights the considerable efficiency savings that could be found through collaboration and which could allow extra money to go back into the frontline for both police and fire. On the timeframe, it will be down to the speed with which the police and crime commissioner can present a business case. If there is local agreement, I would hope to see the first police, fire and crime commissioners coming forward a matter of months after Royal Assent.[105]

Firefighter safety

In 2016, the inquest took place into the death of firefighter Stephen Hunt, who was killed in a fire at Paul's Hair World in Manchester. The FBU carried out a systematic investigation into the fatality and submitted a report, making 13 recommendations. The coroner produced a report to the home secretary and the chief fire and rescue adviser, *Regulation 28: report to prevent future deaths*. This report raised ten areas of concern to mitigate the risk of any future deaths.

Senior FBU officials met with the chief fire and rescue adviser, Peter Holland, to discuss the coroner's report. Holland indicated that the majority of the coroner's concerns would be addressed through guidance under the remit of the National Occupational Guidance (NOG) group.

In October 2016, Wrack wrote a further letter to Rudd reiterating FBU concerns and disappointment with the guidance-only approach and highlighted where it was inadequate (for example, on incident command and about fire risk assessors). Wrack wrote:

> Alongside the necessity for guidance to be robust and mandatory, it is essential that the following additional factors are introduced. These factors are specifically not included in the terms of reference of NOG:
>
> - Training packages designed to ensure the application of tactical guidance
> - Monitoring the implementation of national guidance and its application into fire and rescue services' operational policies
> - Monitoring the implementation of training packages
> - Monitoring the quality of training delivery programmes and methods
> - Monitoring the quality of assessment programmes and procedures
> - Robust independent inspection of the service's risk assessment, resources and standards of services delivery; essentially the IRMP
> - Provision of feedback of inspection outcomes and required improvements
> - A review mechanism to oversee the implementation of improvement requirements
> - An enforcement protocol in the event of unsatisfactory improvement.[106]

In November 2016, the FBU organised a parliamentary lobby, entitled, *Make Firefighter Safety a Priority*. Three hundred FBU representatives visited Westminster to campaign for greater professional standards in the fire and rescue service, to better protect firefighters and the public. The FBU demanded a professional standards forum to oversee improvements in firefighter safety and other operational matters, with the FBU centrally involved.[107]

Fire deregulation

Ministers also continued with their deregulation agenda on fire safety. Asked what the government was doing to promote sprinkler systems, Lewis replied:

> Building regulations already cover the use of sprinklers where they are necessary to protect people's lives such as in high rise flats, shopping malls and large retail warehouses open to the public ... While we recognise that sprinklers are effective, in many cases, they are not the only, or the most cost-effective, option for fire protection. The part sprinklers play in any fire safety strategy should be determined by the findings of the fire risk assessment for the building or premises.[108]

Labour's Carolyn Harris asked what discussions the home secretary had had with DCLG to revise building regulations fire safety guidance. Lewis replied: 'Home Office officials have discussed with the Department for Communities and Local Government plans for the future development of the fire safety aspects of building regulations. The Department for Communities and Local Government will make a statement in due course.'[109]

The FBU warned about the slow creep towards privatisation, deregulation and contracting out of the UK fire and rescue service. In *Firefighter* magazine, investigative journalist David Wibberley traced the long road towards privatisation.

The Fire and Rescue Services Act 2004 allowed fire and rescue authorities to enter agreements to secure assistance to discharge their functions. Wibberley pointed to the example of Surrey Fire and Rescue Service, which had outsourced its water rescue capability. In 2012, Specialist Group International (SGI) signed a 12-month pilot contract with Surrey County Council to provide a diving service, rope, confined space and swift-water rescue capability for the fire service. As part of this contract, SGI also provided fire cover at times of industrial action.

Cambridgeshire Fire and Rescue Authority used private contractor Serco to provide cover for its chronic shortages of firefighters. Wibberley highlighted another transfer of assets that could have gone badly wrong for several brigades. This involved Cosalt Plc, a non-trading holding company supplying workwear to the emergency services. Several UK fire services had contracts with the company. In the week Cosalt was due to take over management of North Yorkshire Fire and Rescue Service's contract for PPE, the company went into administration. Only a last-minute deal saved the outsourcing of these assets.[110]

Austerity

In 2010, the FBU had predicted the consequences of cuts for firefighter jobs. It turned out to be an accurate estimate. In 2016, the FBU sent MPs a briefing with the latest job figures. Over 9,600 frontline firefighter jobs had been cut – nearly one in six of the total firefighting force.[111]

In 2017, DCLG confirmed its local government settlement, which cut the central grant (the Settlement Funding Assessment) to fire authorities by a further 20 per cent over four years. The FBU sent MPs a bulletin, warning that austerity continued.[112]

The FBU kept on agitating about job cuts. By the time of the Grenfell Tower fire, more than 10,000 frontline firefighter jobs had been cut from fire and rescue services across the UK.[113]

5

Building safety downgraded

The deregulation of building safety, including for residents of high rise residential buildings, began with the Thatcher government. The previous chapters set out successive Westminster government's deregulation, and how this impacted on building safety.

The diminution of building regulations and the introduction of weak, 'approved' guidance, private 'approved inspectors' in building control, together with the privatisation of the Building Research Establishment (BRE) all contributed to the systemic failure of the building safety regime in the decades before the Grenfell Tower fire.

This chapter explains the implications of deregulation for building safety. It examines specific high rise residential building fires. The chapter also looks at the risks of flammable cladding and when central government knew of those risks. It highlights the repeated warnings given by fire professionals, including the FBU, to politicians and senior civil servants. These warnings were ignored by successive administrations, with terrible consequences for Grenfell Tower and other high rise residents.[1]

HIGH RISE FIRE RISKS UNDER THATCHERISM (1979–97)

During the 1980s, efforts were made to improve conditions in social housing. The solution offered by the construction industry was 'overcladding', which meant adding thermal insulation and additional external cladding systems to the exterior of existing high rise residential buildings. In 1986, BRE published a report on overcladding external walls of large panel system dwellings. The report stated:

> The probability of fire in the overcladding or affecting the overcladding is low ... The risks depend mainly on combustibility of materials used in insulation or overcladding, and hence spread of fire in the overcladding itself. There is an obvious risk of spread on the outer surface ... but a small risk also exists for fire propagation within any cavity containing combustible insulation, for example with polyisocyanurate foam or polystyrene ... There will be some risk in fire of parts of the overcladding becoming detached and falling to the ground ... There is little risk of fire which is affecting overcladding entering the building through window openings. Provision of cavity barriers is nevertheless recommended ...[2]

The risk was clearly deemed significant, because the Westminster government issued some specific advice on cladding. In 1986, the Department of the Environment warned about fire spread with overcladding on multi-storey buildings:

> A risk of increased vertical fire spread has been identified during the laboratory testing of overcladding systems incorporating combustible insulants ... Where the cladding is sheet aluminium, laboratory tests have shown that a fire within the cavity can melt the aluminium and burn through to the surface several storeys above the fire. These emergent flames could re-enter the block via windows. Fires of such severity are rare. Multi-storey blocks have been clad for 10 years with systems which have a potential for fire spread within cavities but no fires leading to excessive vertical spread have been reported. However, it is advised that both existing and proposed overcladding systems should be examined to determine if modifications are required as a precaution against fire spread.[3]

BRE performed large scale fire tests as part of their assessment of potential fire hazards from the use of combustible materials within rainscreen systems. A BRE report published in 1988 warned that 'proposed systems incorporating combustible insulants with sheeted overcladding should be designed to incorporate fire barriers in the ventilated cavity every two storeys'.[4]

Knowsley Heights, Merseyside (1991)

In 1988, the Department of the Environment made funding from its Estates Action Programme (EAP) available for local councils to implement overcladding schemes on their stock of residential tower blocks. One of the pilot projects for this scheme was Knowsley Heights in Merseyside. Knowsley Heights was an eleven-storey block, containing 64 flats. The overcladding of the block was completed in 1989 and was initially considered a success.

On 5 April 1991, fire destroyed all the cladding on one vertical face at Knowsley Heights. All 130 tenants were evacuated. Although nobody was killed, flames were reported as 'coming from every landing window between the ground floor and the roof'. Fire crews told the *Liverpool Echo*, 'it was the most frightening thing any of us had ever seen as firefighters'.[5]

The BRE investigation found that a deliberate rubbish fire spread to the ventilated cavity of the overcladding system and propagated upwards. Fire penetrated the uPVC window frames at each floor on the façade. The cladding panels on all floors melted, fell away or were taken down later for safety. The Capex rainscreen cladding consisted of mineral fibre insulation with aluminium rails supporting panels of a Class 0 surface spread of flame rating. There were no cavity barriers. The BRE summary stated:

> Regulations are mainly concerned with the problem of internal fires spreading out of a building and not to the rare event of an external fire penetrating the building, as in this case. It was most fortunate that there was no serious injuries or life loss …
>
> Departmental guidance on cavity barriers at the time of the fire was called into question following this fire as the fire spread up the whole vertical height of the building … Where Class 0 is called for, BRE suggests that it should be Class 0 on both sides of the cladding exposed to air …
>
> There is no reason to suggest a life risk associated with cladding unless there are cavities large enough to allow vertical fire spread. There are implications for the protection of window reveals especially where refurbishment has involved the use of cellulosic and polymeric materials in close proximity.[6]

Two months after the fire, *Private Eye* magazine observed 'the Building Research Establishment is not expected to make a great fuss of its report into the fire at Knowsley Heights, a showpiece council tower block in Merseyside'. They added that 'most firemen who study these things believe that it is only a matter of time before there is a major national fire disaster in Britain's prematurely ageing tower blocks.'[7]

For the public inquiry, Luke Bisby wrote a withering assessment of the BRE investigation:

> The fact that the rainscreen cladding at Knowsley Heights was combustible (and possibly also not Class 0 on its inside face), appears never to have been openly stated or discussed in any documentation that I have reviewed in my role as expert witness to the Inquiry ... On the basis of the above summary it is apparent to me that the BRE investigation into Knowsley Heights failed to fully address the degree to which the presence of a combustible rainscreen may have contributed to the spread and magnitude of the fire. Even with the considerable benefit of hindsight, I struggle to understand how this factor could have been overlooked during these investigations.[8]

By 1991, BRE was already run like a business, while still subject to government deregulation policy. Government complicity can be gleaned from internal communications, which have since been made publicly available in the National Archives.[9]

On the same day as the fire, Alison Curtis of the government's Housing Management Estates Action (HMEA) division drafted a handwritten note to BRE's Penny Morgan, who would carry out the on-site inspection into the fire. Curtis claimed that the Knowsley fire was 'insignificant', the block had 'performed well' and that 'all materials used in the over cladding and insulation are non-combustible'.[10]

Another handwritten note found in the archives, undated and signed only by 'Lyn' read: 'We have received via HMEA a request from M St Press Office to play down the issue of the fire. Our briefing for S of S will be purely factual and as far as we are aware Knowsley will not be making an issue of the fire.' The 'S of S' (secretary of state) at the time was Michael Heseltine, the original architect of deregulation of building safety a decade earlier. The 'M Street Press Office' refers to government offices at Marsham Street. 'Knowsley' here refers to the council, the landlord of the block.[11]

In 1994, BRE carried out large scale external fire spread tests on various cladding systems. The project focused on the properties of the rainscreen products used, and on the type and placement of cavity barriers. Raymond Connolly from BRE concluded that 'it is clear that the [British Standard] BS 476 Parts 6 and 7 tests do not accurately reflect the fire hazards that may be associated with cladding systems'.[12]

In 1997, Labour MP Gwyneth Dunwoody asked the Secretary of State for the Environment 'what research has been carried out, and by which organisations, into building and other fire safety issues raised by the fire at Knowsley Heights in Liverpool in April 1991'. Environment minister Robert Jones replied:

> The Building Research Establishment was commissioned by the department to investigate the fire at Knowsley Heights. This subsequently led to a programme of research by BRE into the spread of fire in relation to cladding systems, particularly those of the 'rainscreen' type. The project included appraisal of some of the hygrothermal properties of cladding systems.[13]

However, little seems to have been done to tackle those risks. Bisby opined: 'I consider the Knowsley Heights fire, its investigation, and Connolly's subsequent research to represent significant missed opportunities to explicitly address the potential hazards associated with combustible Class 0 rainscreen products.'[14]

A key reason why central government failed to pursue the concerns around rainscreen cladding was the privatisation of BRE, pushed through in the last days of the Major administration. The narrative of BRE's privatisation is set out in chapter 2. However it is worth highlighting the role played by industry lobbyists in facilitating this privatisation.

The Construction Industry Council (CIC) was probably the most influential. Founded in 1988 as the Building Industry Council, by the mid-1990s it had fortnightly meetings with ministers. As Bisby put it, 'the CIC became a key part of the mechanism for realising the vision of creating a private building control industry'.[15]

In 1996, environment minister John Gummer nominated the CIC as a designated body for approved inspectors. The Construction Industry Council Approved Inspectors Register (CICAIR) became the body charged with licensing privatised building control. Although the CIC wanted a National Centre for Construction to take over BRE, Gummer eventually opted to sell it to BRE's own management team. Bisby's verdict is significant:

> Thus, in the period from 1986 until 1996, the vision that Heseltine had initially set out in 1979 was largely realised. The construction industry had been granted the flexibility that it had been seeking, essentially since the 1930s, and the creation of private building control meant that designers and contractors were no longer (necessarily) limited by constraints applied by Local Authority Building Control. The 'race to the bottom' had begun.[16]

FBU warnings

The FBU opposed the Westminster government's deregulation agenda, which undermined building safety by watering down building regulations, part-privatising building control, producing ambiguous guidance and privatising BRE (see Chapter 2).

In 1995, the FBU published, *A Fighting Chance*, raising specific concerns with ministers about the Building Regulations and guidance. The union argued that 'the principles of Part B of the Building Regulations needs to be revisited'. More specifically, the FBU stated:

> We are also concerned about the use of combustible linings being taken across division walls and the use of Class 0 linings which only give Class 0 on the presented side instead of using completely non-combustible linings ... It has been suggested to us that some 90 per cent of buildings are inadequately compartmentalised by the use of ineffective fire stopping materials. If this statistic is true then it is a very worrying one for our members and the fire service generally.[17]

FBU members saw first-hand the risks at high rise residential buildings. In 1992, crews were dispatched to an incident at Charlecote Tower, West Midlands. Firefighters Iain McPhee and Chris Ryder were instructed to don breathing apparatus and tackle the fire in a flat located on the ninth floor. A flashover engulfed the firefighters, requiring their rescue by other crew members. Tragically, Iain McPhee died. Firefighter David Burns was awarded the George Medal and firefighter David Scott awarded the Queens Gallantry Medal for their roles in the rescue. The cause of the fire was arson, carried out by the 19-year-old female resident of the flat, by setting fire to the bedroom.[18]

HIGH RISE RISKS UNDER NEW LABOUR (1997–2010)

The New Labour administration did not reverse deregulation. Instead, they extended it, much to the disquiet of some fire professionals. The FBU made several interventions on building safety in those years. In 1997, the union made a submission to the DETR consultation on Approved Document B.[19] In 1999, the FBU's executive council warned members of growing risks:

> We are also concerned that many legislative fire safety requirements, particularly those contained in the Building Regulations and building standards, have a direct effect upon the safety of firefighters, and we have lobbied government for improvements in these areas for many years. These matters particularly, need to be viewed strategically and in light of the threat that some new building materials and construction techniques can pose to firefighters.[20]

Garnock Court, Scotland 1999

On 11 June 1999, a fire at Garnock Court, a 14-storey block of flats in Irving, North Ayrshire led to the death of one man and five injured. The fire started in the living-room of a flat on the fifth floor and spread to the outside of the tower, as a result of the glass reinforced polymer (GRP) cladding.

The Garnock Court fire occurred within the constituency of Labour MP Brian Donohoe, who was also a member of the

Environment, Transport and Regional Affairs Committee at Westminster. The select committee agreed to launch a short inquiry. The FBU submitted a memorandum and the FBU fire safety adviser Glyn Evans gave oral testimony. The FBU outlined the risks from cladding:

> The primary risk therefore of a cladding system is that of providing a vehicle for assisting uncontrolled fire spread up the outer face of the building, with the strong possibility of the fire re-entering the building at higher levels via windows or other unprotected areas in the face of the building. This in turn poses a threat to the life safety of the residents above the fire floor.
>
> A secondary problem of fire spread through external cladding may be caused by the method of fixing the panels to the exterior facade of the building. If lightweight fixings (aluminium or metal alloys, etc) or resin bonded systems are used to attach the panels, [t]here is a risk of the panels becoming detached when exposed to fire and falling from the face of the building posing the associated missile risk to firefighters and members of the public in the vicinity of the building …
>
> If the flame front gets past them then the probability is that it will re-enter the building through window openings or balconies higher up the building and consume the contents of those rooms thus becoming self perpetuating. This fire scenario is known as 'roll up' because the fire rolls up the building jumping from floor to floor through window and balcony openings and can occur whether or not cladding is present.[21]

The FBU also criticised the test for limited combustibility under Approved Document B:

> We have been particularly concerned for some time with the principle of small scale fire testing of large building components such as composite cladding, or insulated sandwich panel systems. We believe strongly that such testing and its findings should be validated by large scale testing of the complete system under realistic fire conditions. However, it appears that the real barrier to large scale testing is the question of cost rather than

> that of scientific prudence ... Whatever happens in the future, we believe that the existing small scale test method is unsatisfactory and that a new test for both internal and external cladding systems and sandwich panels should be developed.[22]

The FBU concluded starkly that 'all cladding used on multi-storey buildings over 25 metres in height and the fixing systems should be completely non-combustible, or achieve a fire resisting standard equivalent to the external walls.'

The FBU proposed tackling the risks posed in existing buildings:

> It would seem logical to carry out inspections of all high rise residential premises fitted with external cladding systems to ensure that they conform to the current Building Regulations or Standards. Where they do not then they should be either upgraded, or replaced, to that standard as a matter of urgency.[23]

During oral testimony, Glyn Evans was asked what local authorities should do about the risks. Evans replied: 'We certainly feel it would be worth local authorities conducting an inspection of their existing systems to find out just what they have got pinned on the walls of their buildings.'[24]

In 2000, the select committee published its report. It came to a feeble conclusion about the risks from cladding: 'The evidence we have received during this inquiry does not suggest that the majority of the external cladding systems currently in use in the UK poses a serious threat to life or property in the event of fire.' The committee did make some serious recommendations:

> We believe that all external cladding systems should be required either to be entirely non-combustible, or to be proven through full-scale testing not to pose an unacceptable level of risk in terms of fire spread ... We recommend that DETR and the Housing Corporation instruct local authorities and Registered Social Landlords to undertake a review of their existing building stock with a view to ascertaining how many multi-storey buildings are currently using external cladding systems; and how many cladding systems are in use which, whilst complying with

> the regulations in force at the time when they were installed, do not comply with current regulations.[25]

Ministers responded by minimising the risk from flammable cladding and resisted many of the select committee's proposals. Ministers claimed: 'Since January 1993 all new cladding and over-cladding should have included fire barriers and therefore pose a minimal risk. External cladding before that date may or may not constitute a risk depending on the design of the cladding, the materials used and the subsequent maintenance.'[26]

The government argued that 'a visual inspection of a tower block would not suffice to assess whether there is a problem; that would require more investigative techniques undertaken by a structural or fire engineer, as envisaged in the select committee's recommendation'. However ministers concede that 'a stock condition survey could identify the age of the building and the apparent age of cladding work. Analysed alongside information on repair and maintenance activity, this data could be a trigger to instigate more detailed investigative work'.[27]

In 2001, the government was asked about progress in implementing the recommendations of the select committee's report. Lord Falconer of Thoroton replied that the government was reviewing the guidance document, BR 135 and had consulted on a British standard.[28]

BRE investigations

BRE, now a private company, was commissioned to produce three reports into the Garnock Court fire.[29] The first was prepared for North Ayrshire Council by Penny Morgan, Brian Martin and Tony Morris. The second for North Ayrshire Council, was authored by Morgan. A further report by Morgan was for the Department of the Environment, Transport and the Regions (DETR). As a privatised firm, BRE kept these reports confidential. They were only made public by the public inquiry.[30]

Bisby carried out a comparison of the BRE reports. He found 'some potentially significant differences' between them. In its first report, BRE claimed that 'The GRP [cladding] used in the refurbishment in 1991 should have been Class 0 as defined in the

Building Regulations, Approved Document B'. BRE found that the GRP may not have met the Class 0 specification. In their report to North Ayrshire Council, BRE confirmed that 'the GRP samples that we collected from the Irvine site are not Class 0 and it is doubtful if they ever were'. However BRE's report to DETR made no mention of Class 0. Bisby argued that the removal of mentions of Class 0 from the reports to DETR 'appears to have been performed intentionally'.[31]

BRE carried out further cladding research for central government. In 2000, BRE submitted its literature review on the fire performance of external cladding systems to DETR. Bisby pointed out that it indicates an awareness that aluminium composite material polyethylene (ACM PE) products were already in use in the UK.[32]

BRE sent DETR another confidential report, outlining the results of its cladding survey and proposing options for large scale experimental studies. The report confirmed that 'the level of knowledge within the local authorities with regard to both the number and types of cladding systems installed is extremely limited'. Bisby argued that the report indicated that 'regulatory oversight of residential overcladding projects appeared, at that time, to have been weak across the industry'.[33]

BRE was contracted to carry out 14 large scale tests over the following months. Bisby was critical of the test design, but thought that the aluminium sheet tested was probably ACM PE. He argued that 'the testing outcomes from this work represent perhaps the most important of the numerous missed opportunities' within his remit for the public inquiry. None of the rainscreen systems passed their tests and the aluminium product was 'obviously unsuitable for external cladding applications'.[34]

The Westminster government did not take the opportunity to revise Approved Document B, nor did it discontinue Class 0 as a means of classifying cladding materials (see Chapters 3 and 4). After Approved Document B was revised in 2006, the FBU wrote to CLG supporting longer time limits for prosecution of breaches of the building regulations, demanding that proposals were implemented as soon as possible.[35]

Harrow Court: another missed opportunity

In the early hours of 2 February 2005, a fire occurred in Flat 85 Harrow Court, on floor 14 of a 17 storey residential tower block in Stevenage, Hertfordshire. Firefighters Jeff Wornham and Michael Miller lost their lives after entering the flat to rescue a resident, who also died. Several other residents and firefighters were injured.

The FBU launched a serious accident investigation. Delegates at the union's conference in May called on central government 'to fit domestic sprinkler systems into high rise domestic properties'. Speakers highlighted 'ineffective smoke lobbies, protective doors that don't fit or close properly … and [defective] wet and dry risers due to vandalism or poor maintenance and testing'.[36]

In 2007, the FBU published the Harrow Court serious accident investigation report. The union recommended regular firefighter training on high rise procedures, arrangements for bespoke equipment, regular inspections of all high rise buildings and sufficient resources to ensure that the weight and speed of response delivered sufficient firefighters and operational equipment on the initial attendance to high rise incidents. The FBU also made crucial recommendations to DCLG, including the revision of Approved Document B and high rise firefighting guidance.

The FBU recommended that the council survey all flats in the block 'to ensure that the integrity of the fire resisting entrance/internal hall has not been compromised, that all the internal self-closing fire resisting doors are in place and work correctly'. More significantly, the FBU demanded that the local council and fire and rescue service 're-evaluate its entire fire safety evacuation strategy for blocks of high rise apartments and in particular the apparent contradiction between the "Stay Put" and "evacuation" strategies …'[37]

The FBU directed a number of recommendations at Hertfordshire Fire and Rescue Service (HFRS). It demanded the brigade 'immediately revise its high rise incidents procedures', 'reintroduce the practice of regular inspections of all high rise buildings', 'ensure that the passive and active fire safety measures … are present and effectively maintained' and that 'firefighters receive regular training'. The FBU emphasised emergency preparedness within integrated risk management plans (IRMPs):

> The HFRS IRMP should be revised to ensure that the services intervention capability is sufficiently robust enough to ensure that the weight and speed of response, delivers sufficient fire-fighters and operational equipment on the initial attendance to enable their high rise procedures to be implemented in full from the very start of every incident.[38]

The FBU also made crucial recommendations to central government:

> 16. The issue of creating a national (England and Wales) fire and rescue service standard operating procedure for firefighting in high rise residential buildings which aligns with the guidance for the fire safety design strategies in such buildings that is contained in Approved Document Part B and other British Standards needs to be addressed at a national level. This work needs to be carried out urgently …
>
> 17. We believe that in light of the incident at Harrow Court in Stevenage that paragraph 18.12 of Section B5 – Access to Buildings for Fire-fighting Personnel should be withdrawn and in all new high rise apartment buildings in excess of 18m in height the staircase enclosures should be designed and constructed as firefighting shafts and each firefighting shaft should incorporate a firefighting lift and a rising main facility within the firefighting lobby between the staircase and the accommodation …
>
> 46. DCLG should immediately revise the 'High Rise Incidents' Generic Risk Assessment GRA 3.2 taking into account the final outcomes from this particular investigation, and that of the Petershill Court, Glasgow fire which resulted in Strathclyde FRS receiving an improvement notice dated 29th March 2003 …[39]

Coroner Edward Thomas held an inquest into the deaths and recorded a narrative verdict on the firefighters' deaths. His Rule 43 letter to DCLG attached the recommendations from the FBU's and HFRS's reports.[40]

In 2009, the Health and Safety Executive (HSE) carried out an inspection of Hertfordshire Fire and Rescue Service. Although HSE did not pursue any prosecutions, it subsequently served two improvement notices, criticising the brigade over breathing apparatus training, dry suits and cleaning personal protective equipment. Matt Wrack said: 'Although these improvement notices are served on Hertfordshire, they have national implications. Other fire brigades across the UK should be making sure they can satisfy the expectations of the Health and Safety Executive.'[41]

In the last year of the Labour administration, there were two serious fires in high rise residential buildings, with fatalities and injuries.

The Lakanal House fire on 3 July 2009 resulted in the deaths of six people, with 15 residents and a firefighter injured. Firefighters rescued 40 residents. More than 90 families had to vacate their homes as a result of the fire.[42] The FBU called for a public inquiry into the fire. The union also had to challenge disgraceful allegations in *The Sun* that firefighters had walked away from the scene.[43]

Ministers commissioned a number of reports into the fire. Ken Knight, the chief fire and rescue adviser, wrote a rapid report, published within a month of the fire. FBU fire safety adviser Dave Sibert assisted Knight with his investigation.[44] BRE was also commissioned to carry out an investigation for the Metropolitan Police.[45]

On 6 April 2010, firefighters were called to a large high rise fire on the ninth floor of Shirley Towers in Hampshire. Although all residents living in the block were successfully rescued or evacuated, firefighters Alan Bannon and James Shears were overcome by extreme temperatures and died. The FBU assisted the brigade with a serious accident investigation and called for lessons to be learned, to prevent a repetition.[46]

WESTMINSTER FAILS TO TACKLE HIGH RISE RISKS AFTER 2010

Despite high-profile and widely reported fatal fires, Cameron's coalition government carried on with business as usual. In a political environment stifled by deregulation, no significant changes to the Building Regulations, Approved Document B or other measures were implemented, despite clear failings.

The Lakanal House and Shirley Towers fires should have triggered a reaction from central government. DCLG was also aware of other significant high rise residential fires. A 2011 BRE report for DCLG on investigation of real fires, prepared for Brian Martin, carried detailed reports of four flat fires in London over the previous year, where external cladding had been involved.

On 12 July 2010, a fire occurred at the Madingley Block, a 15-storey building in Kingston-upon-Thames, London. The fire was started deliberately on the balcony of a flat on floor 12. No injuries were reported. BRE stated:

> The combustible components of the cladding on the exterior walls of the building may have provided a route for the fire to spread up the exterior of the building. Similarly, the combustible cladding around the roof of the building may have assisted fire spread from the uppermost floor onto the roof.[47]

On 31 December 2010, a fire took hold in St Clair House, London, a four-storey purpose built block of flats. One woman was hospitalised for smoke inhalation and burns. Another person was treated by London Ambulance Service. Flames from tea-lights had ignited the external cladding to the block. BRE recounted:

> The ignitability of the cladding system is of some concern, although the height and separation of the building means that there are no recommendations in Approved Document B (ADB) regarding the fire performance of the external surface of the wall. (i.e. The building was not tall enough, nor was it close enough to neighbouring buildings, for ADB to recommend any particular level of performance in relation to fire.)[48]

On 22 March 2011, a flat fire occurred at Indescon Court, London, a modern purpose built block of flats of 8 and 16 storeys. BRE reported that 'external surfaces of the building are covered in a variety of cladding systems which appear to have been installed to enhance thermal performance as well as appearance'. The London Fire Brigade (LFB) found that the fire started when a plastic cup was misused as an ashtray. BRE reported:

> The fire spread directly to involve the phenolic insulation in the cladding system on the end walls of the balcony, as well as the insulation behind the composite panels on the rear walls of the balcony. From these, the fire then spread to the expanded polystyrene insulation in the cladding of the ceiling above.[49]

On 15 May 2011, a fire broke out at a 21-storey block of flats in Camden, London. Seven people suffered smoke inhalation injuries and two hospitalised. BRE's investigation found:

> The external envelope of the building had, during one of the refurbishments, been covered using an external cladding system. More information regarding this cladding system is awaited from the local authority ... Smoke is also understood to have entered flats on upper floors of the building by passing through the external cladding system and entering the flats through gaps between the external cladding system, the window frames and the structure of the building.[50]

The following year, a similar report by BRE for Brian Martin at DCLG reported on other fires at blocks of flats. It also noted that 'there have been two overseas fires involving the rapid fire spread up cladding systems'.[51] Although these reports were private and confidential, so that most fire professionals and the public would not have seen them at the time, it is clear that senior civil servants and BRE researchers were aware of cladding risks in high rise residential buildings in the immediate years before the Grenfell Tower fire.

Worse, DCLG changed the terms of the contract with BRE in 2012, which BRE accepted, that reports would 'not contain any policy recommendations' nor propose 'revision to an Approved Document or supporting guidance'. This was further evidence of the depth of deregulation during the crucial years before the Grenfell Tower fire.[52]

FBU warns DCLG

The FBU was not privy to these BRE reports until they were published by the public inquiry. However the union did take up matters of high rise building safety with ministers at the time.

In 2011, FBU assistant general secretary Andy Dark wrote to Brian Martin at DCLG about standards in building regulation compliance. The immediate trigger for the letter were reports to the union from members about the Pacific Wharf development in London, where fire separation, compartmentation and fire protection were found to be badly lacking. Dark wrote:

> The FBU is concerned for the safety of anyone in the event of fire, but in this particular case, it is clear that should a fire have broken out in Pacific Wharf, not only residents but firefighters could easily have been injured or killed as they attempted to rescue occupants and extinguish fire.

The FBU endeavoured to gather more evidence of similar failings elsewhere. David Sibert, the FBU's fire safety advisor, surveyed local fire safety enforcement officers for examples they felt was below an appropriate standard. FBU members involved in fire safety enforcement underlined that fire safety standards were not enforced. They highlighted the decline in local authority building control due to private approved inspectors.

The FBU letter attached a number of examples. One concerned a development consisting of first floor commercial premises, with domestic flats from second to seventh floors. Fire officers reported excess travel distance from top floor flats, with engineered solutions such as pressurisation, smoke extraction and a dry riser implemented without consultation with the local fire and rescue service. There was no firefighting lift and no firefighting shaft. A building control consultation had arrived seven days prior to occupancy of several flats. The FBU offered to meet with ministers and senior civil servants, but the offer was ignored.[53]

The FBU worked with allies in the fire sector and the wider labour movement on fire safety matters. In 2010, Dave Sibert was asked for an expert view on cladding by Unison Northern Ireland.

He advised FBU officials to 'leave no stone unturned' to ensure the regulations were 'complied with in letter and spirit', and the highest standards of good practice were observed, 'even when these go beyond the regulatory minimum'.[54]

While representing the FBU, Sibert was also a leading member of the Fire Sector Federation, a not-for-profit, non-government organisation, established in 2012, which brought together representatives from a range of stakeholders which make up the UK fire sector.[55]

Sibert played a prominent role in the Fire Sector Federation in the years before the Grenfell Tower fire, including chair of its sub-committee on fire risk assessors (see chapter 6). The FBU was part of a network of organisations within the fire sector to warn ministers and the public about fire safety risks and how they must be remedied.

LGA high rise guidance

Another example of complacency by ministers and their advisers was the guidance titled *Fire Safety in Purpose Built Blocks of Flats*. It was drafted by CS Todd & Associates Ltd for the Local Government Association (LGA). The final content received input from representative groups from the housing sector, as well as DCLG and the Chief Fire Officers' Association (CFOA). The FBU was not responsible for this publication.[56]

Eric Pickles told the public inquiry that the LGA guidance was commissioned as a result of Ken Knight's report into the Lakanal House fire. Pickles claimed that DCLG contributed to the cost of the guidance and that he 'read it in outline at publication due to my interest in this area'.[57]

There is no doubt that this guide was officially endorsed by central government. In 2013, Colin Todd wrote to ministers and the Fire Sector Federation regarding the status of the guidance. Dave Sibert for the Federation perceived it as taking precedence over previous government guidance on fire safety risk assessment in sleeping accommodation. Sibert pointed to a parliamentary question, where fire minister Brandon Lewis endorsed the guide, specifically mentioning stay put. Lewis stated:

> There is a high level of confidence in the existing guidance. My Department therefore continues to make it available on the fire safety pages of the Government's website, to help the owners of purpose built blocks of flats to understand and discharge their fire safety responsibilities under both the Housing Act 2004 and the Regulatory Reform (Fire Safety) Order 2005.[58]

Despite some useful advice, the LGA guidance has been widely criticised since the Grenfell Tower fire for its rather complacent comments about the risks facing high rise residents. It stated:

> People living in flats experience more fires than people living in houses. However, a fire in a flat is no more dangerous than a fire in a house. High-rise does not mean high-risk! … Very few people die as a result of a fire in a neighbour's flat or the common parts. Nearly all fire deaths occur in the flat in which fire starts.[59]

The guidance did not take into account the very severe risk posed by multiple breaches of compartmentation. It did not give any advice on the circumstances in which it might be appropriate to move from 'stay put' to 'get out'. Instead it restated the 'stay put' policy:

> Some enforcing authorities and fire risk assessors have been adopting a precautionary approach whereby, unless it can be proven that the standard of construction is adequate for 'stay put', the assumption should be that it is not. As a consequence, simultaneous evacuation has sometimes been adopted, and fire alarm systems fitted retrospectively, in blocks of flats designed to support a 'stay put' strategy.
>
> This is considered unduly pessimistic. Indeed, such an approach is not justified by experience or statistical evidence from fires in blocks of flats … It is also differs from the principles of fire risk assessment … Accordingly, proposals of fire risk assessors, and requirements of enforcing authorities, based on a precautionary approach (e.g. abandonment of a 'stay put' policy simply because of difficulties in verifying compartmentation),

> should be questioned. Before committing resources, it might be appropriate to seek a second opinion.[60]

The LGA guide did recognise that many blocks would contain residents with a diverse range of physical and mental capabilities. However paragraph 79.11 stated that it was not realistic to expect responsible persons to hold information relating to residents with mobility or other conditions affecting their ability to escape, made available in a premises information box. After the fire, these passages were redacted by the Home Office and criticised by the public inquiry.[61]

Inquest into the Shirley Towers fire

After two firefighters died while tackling a fire at Shirley Towers, Hampshire, the HSE investigated the incident, but did not impose any notices or pursue any prosecutions. Its only national recommendation was to 'consider the need for national guidance on the content and frequency of familiarisation.'[62]

The FBU carried out a serious accident investigation, which identified problems with control, familiarisation, water use, thermal imaging cameras, risk assessment, incident command, cabling, radio sets and warning alarms. The FBU and Hampshire Fire and Rescue Service worked together to agree 10 key recommendations to raise with the fire minister.[63]

In 2012, coroner Ken Wiseman recorded a verdict of death by misadventure for both fatalities. Wrack said:

> We owe a duty to all firefighters to learn those lessons, no matter how painful that process may be. During this inquest it has been established that previous recommendations stemming from the deaths of two firefighters and a member of the public in a tower block in Stevenage, Hertfordshire had not been properly implemented. This tragedy happened in Hampshire, but a similar tragedy could happen again in any number of fire services. We are deeply committed to doing all we can to prevent other families facing the loss of loved ones.[64]

The coroner made nine recommendations in his Rule 43 letter to Ken Knight, the chief fire and rescue advisor for England, including on BA procedures and plastic trunking, cable clips and ties. The most relevant were:

> It is recommended that a review of training given to control staff is undertaken by all FRSs in the UK in light of the guidance given in recent GRAs including GRA 3.2 of September 2008. All FRS should further consider the implementation of measures to ensure that control staff are properly supervised when taking calls and are trained to capture and relay relevant information likely to assist operational firefighters.
>
> It is recommended that there should be an obligation to: a) provide signage to indicate floor levels both in stairwells and lift lobbies in high rise premises, to assist the emergency services; b) ensure that signage indicating flat numbers and emergency exits in high rise premises are placed at a low level to increase visibility in smoke conditions. This could potentially be achieved by amending Article 38 of the Regulatory Reform (Fire Safety) Order 2005, which relates to maintenance of measures provided for the protection of fire-fighters. Alternatively new legislation may be required.[65]

Inquest into the Lakanal House fire

In 2013, coroner Frances Kirkham held inquests into the Lakanal House deaths. The FBU demanded lessons must be learned. Andy Dark said:

> The fire shows the need for maintenance and continuous improvement in the fire protection systems of buildings. The fire also shows the importance of introducing a high-quality risk assessment process for such buildings, coupled with rigorous and frequent inspection of high-rise buildings by the fire and rescue service.

The FBU was highly critical of LFB, especially its practice of selling one-day training courses to fire risk assessors checking high rise buildings. Peckham fire station, the closest to Lakanal House, was set to lose a fire engine if mayor of London Boris Johnson imposed his cuts. The mayor's proposals would see the borough of Southwark lose one third of its appliances and one quarter of its fire stations.[66]

On 28 March 2013, the coroner sent Eric Pickles a Rule 43 letter, making recommendations.[67] Pickles' reply revealed alarming levels of complacency within central government only a few years before the Grenfell disaster. The coroner recommended that DCLG should 'publish consolidated national guidance in relation to the "stay put" principle and its interaction with the "get out and stay out" policy, including how such guidance is disseminated to residents'.

Pickles claimed that detailed national guidance was already available in the LGA's *Fire Safety in Purpose Built Blocks of Flats*. He supported a review of that guidance in light of the coroner's recommendations, claiming his officials were already engaged with the LGA. No further action was taken. Pickles and the Westminster government squandered this opportunity to improve guidance on when and how to move from 'stay put' to 'evacuate'.

The coroner also recommended central government 'require high rise residential building owners to provide relevant information on or near the premises, such as premises information boxes or plates'. Pickles' response was that 'a regulatory requirement is unnecessary and disproportionate'. The recommendation was therefore not implemented.

The coroner further recommended that central government provide clear guidance on the definition of 'common parts' of buildings containing multiple domestic premises. The 'common parts' were not defined by the Regulatory Reform (Fire Safety) Order 2005. In blocks of flats, the Fire Safety Order applied to lobbies, stairways and plant rooms, while external walls of the block were outside the scope of the Order.

The coroner sought clear guidance on who should inspect the common parts for breach of compartmentation. It was for the Westminster government to provide the clarification. However ministers failed to do so.

The coroner also recommended that central government 'encourages providers of housing in high rise residential buildings containing multiple domestic premises to consider the retro fitting of sprinkler systems'. Although ministers made laudatory comments in support of sprinklers, this was invariably followed by the caveat about being a matter for owners and avoiding the 'burden of red tape'. Central government did not implement this recommendation.

The coroner recommended a review of Generic Risk Assessment 3.2 on high rise firefighting. This was already under way. The revised guidance is discussed in Chapter 6.

The coroner's final recommendation pressed for a review of Approved Document B, 'with particular regard to the spread of fire over the external envelope of the building' and guidance 'to those involved in maintenance or refurbishment of older housing stock.' Pickles' reply was tardy:

> Finally, in relation to Building Regulations, I have noted your concerns about the difficulties that some of those involved in the Inquests had with the interpretation of Approved Document B. I can assure you that my department is committed to a programme of simplification. However, the design of fire protection in buildings is a complex subject and should remain, to some extent, in the realm of professionals. We have commissioned research which will feed into a future review of this part of the Building Regulations. We expect this work to form the basis of a formal review leading to the publication of a new edition of the Approved Document in 2016–17. The revision would be drafted in accordance with a new 'style guide' for Approved Documents, aimed at ensuring the guidance is capable of being more easily understood, and that the need to cross-reference is reduced.[68]

This was never implemented before the Grenfell Tower fire, despite repeated promises by ministers.

Final opportunities missed

In the aftermath of the Lakanal House inquest, numerous warnings from real fires and from fire safety experts, coroners and other professionals, ministers kept on equivocating about changes to regulations and guidance that might have made high rise residential buildings safer.

The public inquiry has published a range of internal communications to and from DCLG, which indicate that the risks were raised repeatedly with senior civil servants and with ministers.

On 25 November 2013, BRE's Tony Baker emailed Brian Martin at DCLG with a question about the applicability of Approved Document B to the use of combustible rainscreen products. Martin flippantly replied that 'there's no such thing as a Class B material'.[69]

On 2 July 2014, the Centre for Window and Cladding Technology (CWCT) convened a meeting to discuss fire risk and facades. It took place at Arup's London offices. Bisby reported a partial list of attendees, included himself, David Metcalfe (CWCT), Sarah Colwell (BRE), Dave Cookson (Kingspan), Alan Keiller (CWCT), Gavin Kerr (Arup facades), Barbara Lane (Arup), Brian Martin (DCLG), Ivor Meredith (Kingspan), Chris Mort (Siderise) and Stuart Taylor (Wintech).

Bisby subsequently reflected on the significance of the meeting. He wrote: 'In July 2014, clearly articulated to all present at the meeting both the potential concerns associated specifically with combustible ACM cladding products and the confusion within the industry as regards the application of Clause 12.7 specifically to ACM cladding products.'[70]

In 2014, David Amess, chair of the All-Party Parliamentary Fire Safety and Rescue Group (APPG), wrote to Stephen Williams, DCLG undersecretary of state, requesting the amendment of Approved Document B with regard to the external walls of buildings above 18 metres. Williams replied: 'I have neither seen nor heard anything that would suggest consideration of these specific potential changes is urgent and I am not willing to disrupt the work of this department by asking that these matters be brought forward.'[71]

Bisby also pointed to three further BRE reports concerned with external fire spread. His verdict was cutting: 'The resulting report and papers are in places incomprehensible, and they appear to lack in any real insights or practical significance.'[72]

Whatever knowledge might have been gleaned by BRE investigations in to real fires and through testing, ministers failed to address the risks. In 2015, Williams told MPs:

> Following the Lakanal House fire ... the coroner called on the government to simplify the guidance in Approved Document B of the building regulations. My department's secretary of state committed to a review, which will deliver a revised document in 2016–17; the intention is to simplify the guidance where possible and update and revise the technical content at the same time.[73]

In October 2016, communities minister Gavin Barwell said: 'We have not set out any formal plans to review the building regulations as a whole, but we have publicly committed ourselves to reviewing Part B following the Lakanal House fire.'[74]

In February 2017, fire minister Brandon Lewis responded to a written question in parliament that Home Office officials had discussed with DCLG 'plans for the future development of the fire safety aspects of building regulations'. The DCLG would make a statement 'in due course'.[75] Later that month, Southwark council pleaded guilty to breaking fire regulations in years leading up to the Lakanal House fire.[76]

In the year before the Grenfell Tower fire, ministers had received seven letters from the APPG on relevant building safety and fire matters, as well as communications from the FBU, Business Sprinkler Association, the London Fire Commissioner Dany Cotton and the Fire Sector Federation.[77]

HOW BUILDING SAFETY REGULATION AND GUIDANCE WAS WEAKENED[78]

The Building Act 1984 laid down primary legislation for building regulations in England and Wales. The Building Regulations 1985 created functional requirements, removed technical details and were truncated in length. Instead, approved but voluntary guidance was published, including Approved Document B.[79]

The functional requirements for fire safety were set out in Part B of Schedule 1 to the Building Regulations 1985:

- B1 Means of escape.
- B2 Internal fire spread (surfaces).
- B3 Internal fire spread (structure).
- B4 External fire spread.

The regulations were revised in 1991, 2000 and 2010. The most significant change was to B1. In 1985, compliance remained prescriptive. It meant following the *Mandatory Rules for Means of Escape*. This was removed in 1991. At the same time, B5: Access and facilities for the fire service, was added. In 2000, the current wording of B4 on external fire spread was formulated. The key passage stated:

> B4. (1) The external walls of the building shall adequately resist the spread of fire over the walls and from one building to another, having regard to the height, use and position of the building.

In 1985, ministers published the first version of Approved Document B to support the new Building Regulations. It set out guidance on fire safety matters by which compliance with the functional requirements could be achieved. However it stated on the first page that 'there is no obligation to adopt any particular solution in the documents if you prefer to meet the requirement in some other way'.[80]

The public inquiry's Phase 2 report was right to conclude that 'the language used in the Approved Documents from 1985 onwards introduced ambiguities and a lack of clarity in relation to the definition of Class 0 which had not existed in the Building Regulations of the 1960s and 70s'.[81]

Approved Document B 1985 altered the longstanding requirement in the Building Regulations that external walls should be non-combustible. Instead, all external walls should be constructed of materials of 'limited combustibility', if the building was more than 15 metres in height. BS 476-11 was introduced as a method of testing to that standard. Approved Document B 1985 also redefined the Class 0 classification. It stated:

Class 0 which restricts both the spread of flame across a surface and also the rate at which heat is released from it, imposes a more strict control than Class 1. Class 0 is not a classification identified in a British standard test, and is considered a higher class than Class 1.

A Class 0 material or the surface of a composite product is either:

(a) composed throughout of materials of limited combustibility, or

(b) a Class 1 material which has a fire propagation index (I) of no more than 12, and (i) of not more than 6.[82]

As the public inquiry found, the definition of Class 0 therefore changed in two important ways when Approved Document B was first introduced:

> First, a requirement that materials or surfaces of materials should be of limited combustibility was introduced in place of the requirement that they be composed of non-combustible materials; secondly, the requirement to consider the substrate and the surface of a composite product together was removed. As a result, the definition of Class 0 no longer made it clear that any test of a composite product had to be carried out on the surface in conjunction with its substrate.[83]

The revised Approved Document B 1992 contained a section on the construction of external walls and provided the crucial guidance on external fire spread. Section 12.7 warned:

> The external envelope of a building should not provide a medium for fire spread if it is likely to be a risk to health or safety. The use of combustible materials for cladding framework, or of combustible thermal insulation as an overcladding or in ventilated cavities, may present such a risk in tall buildings, even though the provisions for external surfaces in Diagram 36 may have been satisfied.

Approved Document B 1992 introduced a separate performance standard for insulation for the first time. It stated that 'In a building with a storey at more than 20m above ground level, insulation material used in the external wall construction should be of limited combustibility'. The restriction did not apply to masonry cavity wall construction.[84]

Approved Document B 2000 was further weakened in paragraph 13.7. First, it introduced an alternative to meeting the external wall surface classification in Diagram 40, with reference to *Fire Note 9: Assessing the Fire Performance of External Cladding Systems: A Test Method*, published by BRE in 1999. It contained a large scale test method as an alternative method of assessing the fire performance of an external wall. Second, the requirement of limited combustibility applied only to insulation used in ventilated cavities, not to insulation generally.[85]

Approved Document B 2000 was amended in 2002, when the European classification system of fire performance was added as an alternative to the national system. The guidance contained in Diagram 40 was that any surface over 18 metres from the ground should be national Class 0 or European Class B-s3, d2 or better.

Approved Document B 2006 introduced more important structural and textual changes to the guidance on the construction of external walls. It was split into two volumes; Volume 1 on dwelling houses; Volume 2 on buildings other than dwelling houses. Blocks of flats came under Volume 2. Paragraph 12.5 stated:

> The external envelope of a building should not provide a medium for fire spread if it is likely to be a risk to health or safety. The use of combustible materials in the cladding system and extensive cavities may present such a risk in tall buildings.
>
> External walls should either meet the guidance given in paragraphs 12.6 to 12.9 or meet the performance criteria given in the BRE Report *Fire performance of external thermal insulation for walls of multi storey buildings* (BR 135) for cladding systems using full scale test data from BS 8414-1:2002 or BS 8414-2:2005.

Approved Document B 2006 offered two alternative routes to compliance. The 'linear' route, said all the individual components of the cladding system should meet certain requirements, which were specified in the sections 12.6 to 12.9. The other 'test' route involved subjecting the whole system to a large scale test, defined in BS 8414-1 and BS 8414-2. The criteria for a successful test was given in the BRE publication BR 135.

Section 12.6 specified requirements for the external surfaces of walls. For residential buildings over 18 metres high, the relevant provisions were given in Diagram 40e: the surfaces should have either a national Class 0 rating or a Euro Class B rating. This section was more ambiguous than previous version of Approved Document B in three respects:

- The restriction of the requirement to insulation material in ventilated cavities only was removed.
- A new category of 'filler material' was added.
- An undefined et cetera was added after 'filler material'.

The other 'test' route to compliance in ADB 2006 also significantly weakened the fire safety requirements. First, the change in wording to '*full-scale test data*' seemed to permit the use of desktop studies, because they use 'test data' despite not being tests themselves. Second, the role of the large scale test (BS 8414) was expanded from an alternative to meeting the provisions of Diagram 40 only, to being an alternative to meeting the limited combustibility requirements for insulation also. It became an alternative to the 'linear route' to compliance.[86]

The general warning was similar to previous versions of Approved Document B, but no longer mentioned that the use of combustible materials might present a risk, even though the provisions for external surfaces in Diagram 40 had been satisfied. This important warning had disappeared.[87]

Successive changes to Approved Document B opened up the opportunity for aluminium composite material cladding panels to be installed on high rise buildings such as Grenfell Tower. Despite the formal wording found in the regulations, Approved Document B provided two flawed routes to permit the use of ACM panels: either through bogus 'tests' or by meeting lesser requirements (national Class 0/Euro Class B) rather than non-combustibility.

A number of politicians warned of the consequences of removing statutory stipulations and replacing the law with guidance.

Arguably, the most far-sighted comment was uttered by Labour peer Lord Sydney Irving of Dartford as the changes became law. In 1984, Irving told parliament:

> I hope that when the government come to consider the building regulations and the guidance in the approved documents they will not permit any relaxation in such matters as non-combustibility and remember that on such occasions when building standards have been relaxed or building regulations have not been applied.[88]

There were also warnings from fire professionals outside Westminster. Probably the most prescient was given in 1986 by Bill Malhotra, working for BRE. He wrote:

> Historically over the last three centuries we have moved from strict constructional specifications to functional or semi-functional requirements with performance oriented objectives as and when feasible. Rigid controls are being replaced progressively by a more flexible system which permits alternative solutions to be considered. The burden of responsibility is being shifted from the central or the local authorities to the individual or corporate designer/contractor for the adequacy of his system ... It will be perhaps another two or three decades before the consequence of this approach can be seen.[89]

6
Fire safety fragmented

The decimation of the fire and rescue service took place over forty years before the Grenfell Tower fire. Deregulation took to the form of new legislation, weaker than the statutory underpinning that had gone before. National resilience was undermined as national standards were replaced by whatever could be risked locally. Scrutiny by the inspectorate was replaced by chief fire officers marking their own or their friend's homework. The FBU was systematically excluded from the corridors of power, ignored by ministers and fighting rear guard actions against sustained attacks.

This chapter examines the results of deregulation and austerity in the years just before the Grenfell Tower fire. It looks at the impact on response times and other measures of performance. It shines a light on the role of chief fire officers in buttressing the new regime. In particular, it exposes their failure to produce robust high rise firefighting guidance. Finally, the impact on the London Fire Brigade is drawn out, on the eve of its worst modern tragedy.

HOW 'MODERNISATION' WRECKED THE FIRE SAFETY REGIME

The post-war fire sector was governed by the Fire Services Act 1947. The legislation established a robust regulatory regime, which facilitated a resilient, adaptable and integrated emergency response to the public. This fire safety regime included national standards of fire cover, setting the required number of fire engines and attendance times for different fires.

To ensure these standards were met, minimum staffing levels for fire brigades (known as 'establishments') were instituted. This meant local fire authorities could not reduce fire cover without the permission of ministers.

The 1947 Fire Services Act created the Central Fire Brigades Advisory Council (CFBAC) as the statutory stakeholder body to provide ministers with expert fire advice. The CFBAC was chaired by the fire minister and included representatives from the Home Office, local government, chief fire officers, the FBU, fire inspectors and other fire professionals.

Subsequent regulations also provided for appointments and promotion. In England, the Fire Service College led on training. Fire research and statistics were coordinated by the Joint Fire Research Organisation and the Fire Research Station (later part of BRE).

The 1947 act established a fire inspectorate within the Home Office for England and Wales, with a similar arrangement in Scotland. The HM Chief Inspector of Fire Services produced annual reports based on their inspections. However the old inspectorate ceased in England after the Fire and Rescue Services Act. In 2007, it was formally abolished.[1]

The post-war fire regime provided national resilience alongside local democratic control. It was flexible enough to adapt to changing risks. It incorporated local fire prevention and protection work into firefighters' roles, as well as emergency intervention at non-fire incidents (known as 'special services'), such as road traffic collisions. This was confirmed by the Holroyd report.[2]

The CFBAC was pivotal to making the fire regime resilient. Almost every major improvement in the professionalisation of the fire and rescue service for the fifty years of its existence owed something to the deliberations of the CFBAC. As a statutory body it had real weight at Westminster and throughout the sector. As a representative body it gave a voice to wide sectors of the industry and a table at which all the main interested parties could contribute. Its sub-committees drew in expert researchers and carefully implemented changes. The CFBAC pioneered fire prevention, the introduction of more efficient appliances and personal protective equipment. It oversaw appointments and promotion, firefighters' health and safety, as well as undertaking work on particular incidents so lessons could be learned. It was a sounding board for legislation and a powerful vehicle to get buy-in for improvements.

However the fire sector came under sustained attack from the Thatcher government, starting with the Home Office report, and including criticism from the Audit Commission, National Audit Office and numerous reviews (see Chapter 2). Although these attacks were mostly resisted for two decades, thanks to campaigning by the FBU and other fire professionals, all political parties at Westminster agreed to press on with 'modernisation' at the turn of the century (see Chapter 3).

Fire and Rescue Services Act 2004

In 2000, the New Labour government proposed a White Paper on fire 'reform', based on previous plans for cuts and deregulation. These proposals were crystallised in the Bain report in 2002, and taken up with considerable malice by ministers, notably John Prescott and Nick Raynsford.

In 2003, Raynsford was quite explicit about the deregulatory and cost-cutting nature of so-called reforms. He told parliament that the changes were 'consistent with the principle of cutting back on consent regimes and red tape'.[3] He also made some outlandish claims based on a fire service emergency cover methodology developed by management consultants to justify the proposed carnage:

> The model has been tested twice in computer simulations. The first test run suggested that you could spend twice the current fire service budget without achieving much reduction in risk. The second test run suggested that you could halve expenditure without much increase in current levels of loss of life and property.[4]

The result was a new legal framework governing fire and rescue. This was the Fire and Rescue Services Act 2004 in England and Wales, with similar legislation in Northern Ireland and Scotland, as well as the Regulatory Reform (Fire Safety) Order 2005. The new deregulated framework hacked away the old regime while putting only weak alternatives in their place:

- Scrapped national emergency response standards and norms, leading to increasing fragmentation of standards and slower response times.

- Removed establishment provisions, which facilitated cuts to firefighter numbers and station closures.
- Scrapped the CFBAC, excluding firefighters' voice (the FBU).
- Scrapped the inspectorate in England and Wales, giving chief officers a free hand to avoid valuable oversight and accountability.
- Set a weak National Framework with only limited oversight at Westminster.
- Allowed local IRMPs to become effectively 'resource' management plans for implementing cuts.
- Chief fire officers had a free hand to build their own empires, enrich themselves while damaging resilience.
- Fire safety became self-regulating, trusted to landlords and business owners, with weak enforcement.

THE FIRE AND RESCUE SERVICE DEFENESTRATED

The 'modernisation' reforms abolished national standards of fire cover. Instead, local fire and rescue services are allowed to set their own standards. Almost everywhere this has led to slower response times.

In England, average response times for the first appliance attending primary fires (potentially more serious fires that harm people or cause damage to property) slowed by almost 2.5 minutes, from 6.07 minutes in 1994–95 to 8.38 minutes in 2016–17. Within that category, average response times to dwelling fires slowed from 5.33 minutes to 7.46 minutes over the same period. Response times to other building fires, including workplaces and businesses, also deteriorated substantially.

The FBU believes that cuts were the central reason for the slowdown in response times. Fewer firefighters, fire stations and appliances have led to a worsening of the speed and weight of emergency response. Response times have continued to slow since the Grenfell Tower fire. By 2023, response times for all primary fires were 9.13 minutes and dwelling fires slowed to 8.01 minutes.[5]

The FBU protested vigorously about slower response times in the years before the Grenfell Tower fire. In 2010, the union published a report, *It's About Time*, making the case for national standards of fire cover. The FBU regularly published statistics obtained by MPs from parliamentary questions on response times, while pressuring ministers to publish annual figures. The union used its submissions to spending reviews and a major report, *Sounding the Alarm* (2014), to press the case for uniform standards of emergency response.

Fire and rescue incidents

Ministers frequently fell back on claims that because the number of incidents attended by firefighters had fallen, this meant a lower risk and therefore needed fewer firefighters. This was a very poor argument, especially from the vantage point of risk management. It was also a significant misuse of official statistics.

Officially published data shows that there are still high risks of fires and fire deaths. It also shows that firefighters respond to an ever-growing range of emergencies to assist the public. There was never justification for cutting firefighter numbers.

The total incidents fire and rescue services attend are made up of fires, false alarms and non-fire incidents. Since the turn of the century, there were significant reductions in the number of fires and false alarms attended. (Many fire and rescue services choose not to attend fire alarm actuations, which they would previously have attended). The number of non-fire incidents attended has risen.

At the turn of the century, firefighters responded to more than a million incidents a year. There was a downward trend in total incidents until 2012, when total incidents plateaued at around 700,000 a year. The downward trend in the number of fires attended by fire and rescue services was driven by changes in fire safety, technology and smoking habits, as well as fire regulation, education and prevention work by firefighters. Since 2012, the number of fires attended levelled off at around 200,000 each year.[6]

The risk of death and injury from fire at home, work and the wider community tragically still exists. Around three-quarters of fire deaths occur in dwellings. Fire deaths have fallen from around 600 a year at the turn of the century. Since then, around 400 people die in fires annually across Britain. The Grenfell Tower fire was a reminder of the terrible consequences of complacency over fire safety.[7]

Fires are not the only emergencies attended by firefighters where people die. The number of deaths firefighters deal with every year at non-fire incidents, including road traffic collisions, floods and suicides has doubled over the last decade. With the emergency medical response trials, this leapt to more than 6,000 deaths just before the Grenfell Tower fire.[8]

Annually, more than 40,000 people are rescued by firefighters across the UK. This equates to more than 100 rescues every day. Around 4,000 rescues take place at fires. But there were around ten times more rescues at non-fire incidents.[9]

The FBU published an assessment of these official figures, with an interpretation, in submissions, bulletins and other publications in the years before (and after) the Grenfell Tower fire.

Cuts and firefighter jobs

The FBU argued that austerity would damage the fire and rescue service. This was born out by official figures and reports. The National Audit Office report, *Financial Sustainability of Fire and Rescue Services*, found that between 2011 and 2015, over 30 per cent of central funding was cut from fire and rescue services in England. Local government settlement figures that period showed that central funding cuts for fire and rescue services in England were planned for 20 per cent over the 2016–20 period.[10]

The impact of these cuts was clear from the reduction in the number of firefighters. Between 2002 and the Grenfell Tower fire, some 10,000 firefighter jobs were cut across England – one in five (20%) of the total number of jobs. The bulk of those job losses were wholetime (full-time) firefighters, with more than 8,000 jobs lost. More than 500 retained (part-time, on call) firefighter jobs were lost, while almost 300 control jobs were cut.[11]

Between 2010 and 2017, 49 fire stations (about 3%) and 11 fire controls closed in England.[12]

Scrapping the statutory advisory body

When the Westminster government scrapped the CFBAC, it established a pale substitute, the non-statutory Practitioners Forum. Minsters entrusted the Chief Fire Officers Association (CFOA) with providing the secretariat for the Practitioners Forum. In hindsight it is difficult to recall any achievements that can be attributed to the forum. It staggered on for a few years, before it was scrapped by the coalition government after 2010. There was no central stakeholder body to learn the lessons from tragedies such as the Lakanal House fire, from flooding, or countless other major incidents.

These same chief officers were asleep at the wheel during the entire experience of IRMPs, implementing flawed resource plans and then justifying each other's decisions through 'peer review'. Rebranded as the National Fire Chiefs Council (NFCC) just months before the Grenfell Tower fire, they continued the 'modernisation' agenda imposed by successive Conservative governments.

The FBU argued for a new statutory advisory body after the CFBAC was scrapped. Almost every FBU submission to Westminster from 2004 until the Grenfell Tower included the demand for a UK-wide stakeholder body, where ministers would get professional advice from a range of key representatives from within the fire and rescue service (see chapters 3 and 4). The FBU also made the demand for a statutory advisory body its central recommendation to the public inquiry after the Grenfell Tower fire (see chapter 9).

The absence of an inspectorate

In October 2007, Ken Knight was appointed chief fire and rescue adviser. He held the post until December 2012. After January 2013, Peter Holland was chief fire and rescue adviser until it was scrapped after the Grenfell Tower fire and replaced with the new inspectorate.[13] The Audit Commission carried out some financial oversight, until it was abolished in 2010. Otherwise, chief fire officers had a peer review system where they were supposed to check each other's practices.

Perhaps the most damning indictment of this system of oversight was given by home secretary Theresa May on 24 May 2016, in a speech to the Reform think tank. She criticised these arrangements and announced the creation of a fire inspectorate in England:

> Local fire and rescue services are examined by a system of peer challenge – which provides no assurance whatsoever to the

> public... in practice it means that chief fire officers handpick their own reviewer, set their own terms of reference, and decide whether or not to publish the results. It is not so much marking your own homework as setting your own exam paper and resolving that you've passed – and it has to change.[14]

HMICFRS was announced as the new fire inspectorate just weeks after the Grenfell Tower fire.[15] During the years after the previous inspectorate of fire services was scrapped in England, the FBU was the only national voice advocating such a body. The FBU supported the re-establishment of the inspectorate in England and our officials engaged constructively with HMICFRS, when it was appointed in 2017.

Unfortunately, HMICFRS failed to hold chief fire officers and their principal managers to account. Instead of inspecting on behalf of the public, HMICFRS pursued a political agenda against the FBU, concentrating on 'reforms' to attack the workforce rather than on measures to improve emergency response (see chapter 9).

The failure of ministerial oversight

The Fire and Rescue Services Act 2004 requires the Westminster government to produce its strategic priorities for fire and rescue authorities, known as the Fire and Rescue National Framework for England. Local fire and rescue authorities must have regard to the framework in carrying out their functions.

The National Framework in force at the time of the Grenfell Tower fire was first published in July 2012. The priorities were for fire and rescue authorities to:

- Identify and assess the full range of foreseeable fire and rescue related risks their areas face, make provision for prevention and protection activities and respond to incidents appropriately.
- Work in partnership with their communities and a wide range of partners locally and nationally to deliver their service.
- Be accountable to communities for the service they provide.[16]

However, ministers put deregulation at the heart of the National Framework for England. Fire minister Bob Neill:

> One of the key principles of which is to acknowledge the proficiency and experience of fire and rescue authorities; and to allow them the freedom and flexibility to deliver the services for which they are respected and renowned without being hampered by Whitehall bureaucracy and red tape.[17]

The problem was compounded by the lack of Westminster oversight. Under Section 25 of the Fire and Rescue Services Act, ministers are meant to provide the Westminster parliament with a biennial report on how well fire and rescue authorities are meeting their statutory responsibilities. Ministers submitted tawdry 'Section 25' reports on fire and rescue authorities' progress with the Fire and Rescue National Framework for England, consisting of scarcely a few pages, mostly boosterism rather than careful evaluation.[18]

The failure of integrated risk management plans

Integrated risk management plans (IRMPs) were a central plank of the Westminster government's 'modernisation' programme. The process began in 2003, when HM Chief Inspector of Fire Services, Sir Graham Meldrum, published a circular on *Fire Authority Integrated Risk Management Planning.*[19]

IRMPs allowed individual fire authorities to make their own local plans based on resources available, not risk – and then reduce the service to the public under the guise of targeting resources, collaboration or other diversions. IRMPs varied widely in content, size, style and even name. Guidance to help services produce these plans was inadequate. This meant 45 different IRMPs covering UK fire and rescue services differ considerably.

The first tranche of HMICFRS inspections in England, carried out shortly after the Grenfell Tower fire, found unacceptable variation across different fire authorities in England. Inspectors stated:

> More than a decade of localism has seen them now operate very differently in many respects. This includes in how things are

> defined, such as response standards and high-risk premises, and how things are done, including how often high-risk premises should be audited, how risk should be mitigated, and how response standards are calculated.

The result was that 'people living in very similar communities up and down the country can receive quite different levels of service from their fire and rescue services'. HMICFRS argued that '45 different ways of defining and doing things is not helpful in some situations. There should be more consistency, for example, in how fire and rescue services define risk and calculate and communicate response standards to the public'.[20]

At the time of the Grenfell Tower fire, national resilience had been diminished. The whole was significantly less than the sum of the impoverished parts.

Role of chief fire officers

Ministers were poorly advised by the chief fire officers' organisation CFOA (renamed NFCC), which claimed to be the professional voice of the fire service. CFOA's embrace of deregulation and the 'modernisation' changes it implemented have seriously affected the management of fire risks in high rise residential buildings.

In the early 1980s, CFOA maligned the CFBAC as 'an amalgam of vested interest'. It argued that firefighters should be exempt from the health and safety at work legislation. CFOA claimed that the cost of fire precautions enforcement was out of all proportion to the cost of compliance. It supported the drive for greater deregulation. In 1981 Home Office minister Lord Belstead claimed that progress towards a self-regulatory system of control was 'thanks in no small measure to the positive and helpful contribution of CACFOA'.[21] (CACFOA, the Chief and Assistant Chief Officers' Association, was the precursor to CFOA).

CFOA supported the New Labour government's 'modernisation' agenda. It supported the abolition of the CFBAC and the substitution of the Practitioners' Forum, for which it provided both the chair and the secretariat. CFOA supported the replacement of the Fire Precautions Act by the Fire Safety Order, which scrapped certification and imposed a weak enforcement regime. CFOA failed to oversee the implementation of recommendations from inquests, including on training, are put into practice across the fire and rescue service.[22]

During the Cameron government's deregulatory drive against red tape, CFOA developed the concept of 'safe enough'. This was explicitly motivated by the wider policy agenda to reduce 'unnecessary burdens' and 'promote economic growth'. It involves a new audit methodology that moved away from compliance with articles of the Fire Safety Order. The approach leaves some individual aspects of fire safety law not complied with, under the guise that risks to people are mitigated and controlled.[23]

The transformation of CFOA into the NFCC occurred with the Conservative government's blessing – and with considerable funding (see Chapter 9). The new name did not remove the flaws the chief fire officers' body persistently demonstrated over many years. The role of chief fire officers was not interrogated by the public inquiry, despite the FBU's efforts to raise the issue.

FIRE SAFETY DIMINISHED

The Regulatory Reform (Fire Safety) Order 2005 was supposed to consolidate fire safety legislation and raise standards of fire protection and prevention. However the deregulatory approach weakened the fire safety regime and its enforcement.

The FBU warned ministers of the risks once fire authorities lost the capacity to issue fire certificates, with the new system relying on the 'responsible person' – the landlord or business owner – to carry out risk assessments thoroughly and to implement any prevention and control measures. The weakening of enforcement, especially after austerity cuts drastically reduced firefighter job numbers, meant less scrutiny by fire and rescue services.

In 2009, DCLG published its first evaluation of the Fire Safety Order. Although the report mostly presented the legislation as a success, it still highlighted concerns about the responsible persons, risk assessment, the competence of fire risk assessors and enforcement. It stated:

> A further concern mentioned by FRAs, in the context of the legal implications of the FSO, was the potential for disagreement over who is the 'responsible person' in some premises – specifically in large multi-site businesses ... The variable quality of the risk assessments that would be carried out by non-specialists under the FSO was raised as a concern among some respondents particularly about the level of detail that had been considered when undertaking the risk assessments ...
>
> There was a concern expressed by some of those interviewed from each of the interested parties (whether enforcers, businesses or the fire safety industry) over the variability in the level of competence evident in the work of independent fire risk assessors or fire safety consultants. This led to some demands for a system of accreditation to be put in place, to quality-assure the work of such organisations or individuals. Few of the 'responsible persons' interviewed were aware of any independently operated accreditation schemes for fire risk assessors.[24]

In 2009, fire professionals formed the Fire Risk Assessment Competency Council, in response to the problems with fire risk assessors. The FBU was represented by Dave Sibert. Most participants advocated a mandatory competency accreditation for fire risk assessors, but were opposed by civil servants. In 2011, the Competency Council published a guide, *Competency Criteria for Fire Risk Assessors*, but it was only voluntary, due to the deregulatory philosophy of ministers. Two years later, it published a *Guide to Choosing a Competent Fire Risk Assessor*.[25]

In 2013, the Fire Sector Federation, another fire professionals' organisation that included the FBU, developed a passport scheme should be established for fire risk assessors. A copy of the proposal was sent to Ken Knight and DCLG officials, including Louise Upton and Brian Martin. Martin argued the Fire Sector Federation was in danger of trying to do more than was necessary or desirable, while Upton described the proposed scheme as 'control freakery'. Knight concurred that the Federation was going beyond what was required.[26]

At a meeting on 17 July 2013, Brandon Lewis was reluctant to pursue the idea of a national fire safety regulator, because he was not attracted to the idea of introducing additional regulation. (In the same memo, he was more interested in the scope of a review of firefighters' terms and conditions, 'potentially in the style of Winsor', demanding a list of possible candidates be drawn up.)[27]

In 2013, the Department for Business, Innovation and Skills (BIS) reviewed enforcement of the Regulatory Reform (Fire Safety) Order 2005. It confirmed significant failings with respect to risk assessments and risk assessors:

> Many small businesses are using commercial providers to carry out their risk assessments – with little assurance available on the quality of their service ... However, it is clear that many businesses use commercial third parties to carry out the risk assessment. Until recently no certification or accreditation existed in relation to these services and none are currently required in the market, meaning that in effect anyone can offer their services. Some businesses reported overselling by assessors that were also equipment suppliers, and a number of fire professionals questioned the quality of some commercial providers. In practice a third party assessment offers no guarantees to a business, and sometimes they will find that a fire protection officer will ask for additional measures beyond those identified in the 'bought in' fire risk assessment.[28]

In 2014, the Fire Sector Federation formed a Fire Risk Management Competency Council, chaired by Sibert, which continued to campaign for standards on fire risk assessors. The public inquiry praised the FBU for challenging home secretary Amber Rudd about the lack of progress on regulating fire risk assessors.[29]

Fire safety enforcement weakened

Official figures published by the DCLG and the Home Office show that in the decade before the Grenfell Tower, under the Fire Safety Order, enforcement was dramatically reduced by fire and rescue services.

Between 2010 and 2017, the number of inspections carried out in England fell drastically under the Fire Safety Order. The number of inspections (audits) fell by a third, from more than 84,000 to less than 54,000 a year. The total hours spent on inspections fell by 40 per cent, from more than 409,000 hours to less than 244,000 hours. The number of enforcement notices more than halved.

Over the same period, fire safety enforcement for purpose-built flats for four storeys or more also declined. The number of inspections of purpose-built flats fell by almost a quarter, from more than 4,000 to around 3,000 a year. The hours spent on inspections of these premises fell by 20 per cent, from more than 18,000 hours to less than 15,000 hours. The number of enforcement notices almost halved.[30]

FBU research revealed that fire and rescue services cut the number of fire safety inspectors in the years before the Grenfell Tower fire. Between 1997 and 2017, the number of fire safety inspectors in England and Wales fell by 40 per cent, from 1,724 to 1,041 inspectors. Between 2010 and 2017, the number of fire safety inspectors fell by 28 per cent.[31]

THE FAILURE OF HIGH RISE FIREFIGHTING POLICY

The failure of ministers, their advisers and chief fire officers to prepare the fire and rescue service for the risks of the Grenfell Tower fire were epitomised by its role in producing the guidance on high rise firefighting, known as GRA 3.2.

In 1998, the HM Fire Service Inspectorate produced *A Guide to Operational Risk Assessment*. Volume three contained a short section, *Generic Risk Assessment 3.2 Fighting Fire – High Rise Buildings*. It defined high rise buildings as those with eight floors or above, or 'one which contains floors at such a height that external rescue and firefighting are not feasible. This height would normally depend on the limits of standard fire brigade equipment available to execute these actions.' This guidance made no mention of stay put or evacuation strategies.[32]

In 2008, DCLG published a revised version of its *Generic Risk Assessment 3.2 High Rise Firefighting* guidance. Parmjit Dhanda reported to MPs:

> Within the last 12 months three reports have been finalised which are in process of being published on the department

> website. These reports cover two further studies on the physiological impact on firefighters of operational activities and a review of the incident ground communication provision of fire and rescue services. Draft reports have been received on the modelling of fires in under-ventilated compartments and it is intended that these reports be consolidated and published on the department website once finalised. A further internal report has been prepared into an assessment of alternative methods of advancing hose from a bridgehead during high-rise firefighting. This report has been used to inform preparation of a revision to the generic risk assessment for high-rise firefighting.[33]

A further revision was made after the Lakanal House fire. The public inquiry commissioned former LFB assistant commissioner Peter Cowup to write a report on the revision of the GRA 3.2 guidance. (Although Cowup's account is diminished by some disparaging asides about the FBU, it revealed multiple failures by the principal managers). The GRA 3.2 document published in 2008 was referred as version 2; the document published in 2014 referred to as version 3. Both documents were published by DCLG.[34]

The GRA series was reviewed between 2010 and 2014, as part of a broader Operational Guidance programme. It was commissioned by DCLG and the chief fire and rescue adviser as the 'owners' of this guidance. Responsibility for programme management and delivery was contracted to Surrey Fire and Rescue Service. Governance for the review process was provided by a project board and all CFOA regions, the devolved administrations and other stakeholders were represented on a larger review committee. On high rise firefighting, Cowup stated:

> GRA 3.2 was allocated to LFB by the programme manager in March 2011 and the decision for LFB to lead on the review of GRA 3.2 was initially opposed by FBU London regional officials, based on their perception that the Brigade's involvement in the Lakanal House fire created a potential conflict of interest when completing this work. This contention was addressed, locally by LFB management and with national FBU officials by the GRA programme manager and agreement was subsequently reached

with the FBU nationally that it would be acceptable for LFB to conduct this review.[35]

In 2011, LFB produced a new draft GRA 3.2 guidance document. It was subjected to consultation over the following year, including with the FBU. According to Cowup's account, the FBU sought to strengthen the status of the guidance and ensure high level health and safety imperatives were built into it. Cowup reports that the review team accepted the FBU's proposal to change 'should' to 'must', only for DCLG advisers to change it back to 'should'.

By 2013, a revised draft was finished – that is, before the Lakanal House coroner's Rule 43 letter. The coroner recommended 'consideration be given to review of Generic Risk Assessment 3.2 on 'High Rise Firefighting' to provide consolidated national guidance'. The draft guidance was further revised by senior civil servants and their advisors during 2013, until publication.

Problems with GRA 3.2 high rise guidance

In 2014, DCLG published a revised version of GRA 3.2 on fighting fires in high rise buildings. It accurately described high rise firefighting as 'a high risk activity' and 'an extremely hazardous environment for firefighters'. It rightly stated that 'additional time and resources may be required to implement safe systems of work for operations at elevated levels' – but this was only a year after it had backed Ken Knight's review, which advocated further cuts to fire service budgets, impacting on resources available on the fire ground.

However, the revised guidance did not give advice on the real difficulty posed by fire spread beyond the compartment of origin, the need for multiple rescues, the details of an evacuation plan or the policies and training necessary for incident commanders to effect such plans. It did not address when an incident commander should move to partial or full evacuation. It merely stated what contingency plans should cover without providing the 'guidance' recommended by the coroner on what those plans should be.

In order to provide that guidance it would have been necessary for the secretary of state to commit resources and expertise to considering the problem, testing possible solutions and providing guidance based on empirical evidence. Done properly, this would have required a serious national effort with a major commitment of central funding. In the absence of such efforts, the guidance in GRA 3.2 fell short of assisting fire and rescues to devise practical contingency plans for evacuating high rise residential buildings in the event of a significant breach of compartmentation or other rapid fire spread.

In particular, the advice to incident commanders to 'follow the evacuation plan devised as part of the premises fire risk assessment' was vacuous, when the only plan likely to be operative was 'stay put'. Instead the GRA 3.2 guidance simply suggested referring to Approved Document B paragraph 4.27 for further information.[36]

But the Approved Document B guidance provided little to assist fire officers in preventing breaches in compartmentation, which would require a very large scale inspection and enforcement programme, or for preparing firefighters for situations where they needed to evacuate very large numbers of people from high rise residential buildings. The reference to ADB 2006 edition was to Section 4, was entitled 'Design for vertical escape – buildings other than flats'. In the 2000 and 1991 editions of Approved Document B, this section was entitled 'Design for vertical escape – buildings other than dwellings'. The guidance was dated and applied to offices, not homes, but no subsequent work on evacuation was indicated. The advice on simultaneous and phased evacuation assumed buildings had been designed for such an eventuality. The document may assist firefighters plan for high rise workplaces, which have central alarm and communication systems, regular fire drills, wide stairways and other measures in place, with most hazardous incidents during daytime. However this section did not address all the specific risks firefighters faced when evacuating high rise residential buildings, particularly at night, when there is only one stairway, no central warning system or central means of communication, as they were at Grenfell Tower.

The Lakanal House coroner had wanted DCLG to deal with these issues, but ministers woefully failed to do so. The lack of central, national guidance was a material cause of the failure of fire and rescue services, (even the UK's largest, the LFB) to develop an alternative evacuation plan in these circumstances and then to provide training and resources for incident commanders and other firefighters to implement on the fire ground.

PORIS

In 2012, DCLG published guidance on the Provision of Operational Risk Information System (PORIS), a model to assist fire authorities with meeting their statutory duties. PORIS is a three-dimensional risk assessment model that can be used to quantify risk and prioritise high risk premises.

The FBU's fire safety advisor Dave Sibert evaluated the model during and after it was published. Sibert pointed to flaws with the risk matrix in PORIS, which valued a firefighter's life as equivalent to, for instance, a listed building. PORIS also required enhanced familiarisation visits, known from the legislation as 7(2)(d) visits, to gather risk information. The model also required enhanced fire safety inspections to gather data. Both had significant training and resource implications.

The FBU argued that it was folly to introduce the new PORIS regime at a time when fire and rescue services were facing cuts and austerity, including in their fire safety departments. Deregulation meant there was no requirement for individual fire and rescue authorities to adopt the PORIS guidance at all. The PORIS model 'adopted an over simplistic approach to risk management and failed to consider the consequences'.[37]

PORIS was another example of the failures of the chief fire and rescue adviser and the CFOA, who produced inadequate guidance while proposing cuts to the firefighters, the workforce necessary for improvements to work in our communities.

LFB AT THE SHARP END OF DEREGULATION

The London Fire Brigade (LFB) was responsible for the emergency response to the Grenfell Tower fire. But the LFB had already been through the mangle for decades and was under duress immediately before the Grenfell Tower fire.

When Grenfell Tower was built, LFB was overseen by the Greater London Council (GLC). After the Thatcher government abolished the GLC in 1986, the London Fire and Civil Defence Authority (LFCDA) became the fire authority. In 2000, under the new London mayor, the London Fire and Emergency Planning Authority (LFEPA) was formed, composed of Greater London Assembly members (AMs) to oversee LFB.

Ken Livingstone was the mayor (2000–08), followed by Boris Johnson (2008–16) and then Sadiq Khan (2016–present). Labour AM Val Shawcross chaired LFEPA between 2000 and 2008. Conservative assembly members chaired LFEPA after that: first Brian Coleman (2008–12), then James Cleverly (May 2012–May 2015). Gareth Bacon chaired LFEPA from then until the Grenfell Tower fire.

Brian Robinson was chief fire officer in London (1991–2003), followed by Ken Knight until 2007 and Ron Dobson from 1 October 2007 until 31 December 2016. Dany Cotton, the capital's first woman chief fire officer, took over the role as London Fire Commissioner from 1 January 2017 in a provisional capacity.[38]

The decade before the Grenfell Tower fire was characterised by bitter industrial relations within LFB, with the fault laying squarely with the mayor, fire authority chair and the chief fire officer. In 2010, Coleman and Dobson issued Section 188 'fire and rehire' contracts to London firefighters, in an attempt to force them to change shift times without consultation. The threat to sack the entire workforce, with re-employment on worse terms and conditions, was met with disgust by firefighters.

The bitterness was captured by Coleman's public remarks that London FBU officials were 'thick', 'thugs and bullies' and 'can't string a sentence together'. Coleman declared: 'We have to break the FBU … they've been a block on modernisation right along the line'.[39]

The FBU held a series of mass meetings and demonstrations, culminating with almost half of all London firefighters lobbying LFEPA on 16 September 2010. A ballot for strike action saw a 79 per cent vote in favour with a 79 per cent turnout. Firefighters went on strike on 23 October and 1 November 2010. Further strikes were planned for bonfire night, but LFB principal managers withdrew the fire and rehire threat. The FBU negotiated a settlement through the National Joint Council, which was endorsed by 84 per cent of London FBU members.[40]

Deregulation

In the years before the Grenfell Tower fire, LFB was subjected to the full range of deregulation and austerity. Three significant interventions stood out:

- The appliances and equipment contract which eventually ended with AssetCo.
- The training contract with Babcock.
- The aborted privatisation of the control room.

In 2000, fire minister Mike O'Brien told parliament that the LFEPA had signed a contract with The Leasing Group Fire Services 'for the provision, management and maintenance of the authority's operational and non-operational vehicles and fireboats and some operational equipment'. The deal did not include fire stations. The Home Office supported the project under the Private Finance Initiative (PFI).[41]

The contract changed hands over the next decade and was finally in the hands of AssetCo PLC. According to the company's accounts in 2007, AssetCo's emergency services division 'owns, manages, maintains and ensures the availability of approximately 650 fire and rescue vehicles and over 50,000 items of operational equipment for the London Fire Brigade', as part of the 20-year PFI contract. AssetCo also had a similar contract with Lincolnshire Fire and Rescue Service. It told shareholders that eight other fire authorities were 'in advanced stages of evaluating the move to an external supply for their fire and rescue equipment and related services'.[42]

AssetCo's accounts also revealed that the firm tendered for the national resilience contract for New Dimensions assets and the fireguard contract for business continuity. The following year, the firm published *The AssetCo Fire and Rescue Report 2008*, with welcoming forewords by Ken Knight, CFRA and Steve McGuirk on behalf of CFOA. Its accounts reported that profits before tax had almost doubled to £10.3 million. In July 2009, AssetCo were awarded a 7-year contract for the provision of an 'emergency fire crew capability service' of up to 700 strikebreakers.[43]

The FBU opposed AssetCo's plans and fought a public campaign against the firm. The outsourcing reached crisis point in 2010, when it became clear AssetCo would not hoover up the lucrative contracts it had wished for. First, AssetCo contractors supplied during the London fire and rehire strikes proved hopeless at putting out fires. FBU members came off picket lines to tackle emergencies. At an FBU picket, a contract driver knocked down London FBU executive member Ian Leahair, who suffered painful injuries.[44]

At the same time, AssetCo ran into serious financial difficulties, with its owners seeking to offload the business. The FBU ran a campaign to expose the misuse of LFB assets and insist they should be returned to public ownership. The union worked with investigative journalist David Hencke to publicise AssetCo's financial woes, with the firm passed around various banks. As Wrack put it: 'Privatising emergency services is stupid and dangerous. The long, slow death of AssetCo is a perfect illustration of this.'[45]

Wrack also wrote to fire minister Bob Neill and Ron Dobson to demand answers about the ownership and control of London's fire engines. The FBU continued to harry ministers and LFB principal managers.[46] Sadly, London's fire engines were not brought back in-house, but were sold for £2. Babcock were awarded the fleet management contract for a 21-year period.[47]

The AssetCo saga ended in ignominy just before the Grenfell Tower fire. The Financial Reporting Council investigated the firm's accounts and the auditing of them. In April 2017 Grant Thornton UK LLP and Robert Napper, a retired partner at the firm, were sanctioned after admitting misconduct in relation to the audits of the financial statements of AssetCo plc for 2009–10. A year later, the Financial Reporting Council announced that three former executives of AssetCo plc had been excluded from the accountancy profession after a disciplinary tribunal found they had committed misconduct in relation to the preparation and approval of the company's financial statements.[48]

London training

Deregulation within LFB went further than fleet management and equipment. In 2010, LFEPA commenced procurement for a 25-year contract for the provision of operational firefighting training, and other training of personnel. The full cost of training delivery was estimated at £25 million. Three contractors were shortlisted: a joint AssetCo and Balfour Beatty bid (Capital Training Solutions); Babcock and Serco. AssetCo collapsed, while Serco withdrew.[49]

Matt Wrack warned of the dangers of outsourcing training in the *Guardian*:

> Such training includes the initial 80-day programme for new recruits, as well as the regular and refresher training, which covers real fire training and the use of breathing apparatus. Providing the first-class fire service the public has been accustomed to has training at its heart. It is critical to all we do, which is much more than putting out fires. It helps us save lives, homes, businesses and our built and natural environment.[50]

Unfortunately, Babcock were awarded the 25-year training contract, worth £364 million and starting from 1 April 2012, despite continued objections from the FBU. FBU officials raised complaints about the quality of Babcock training before and after the Grenfell Tower fire, as did members of the Greater London Assembly.[51]

Babcock's role was also raised during the public inquiry. Ron Dobson confessed to the public inquiry that following his retirement from LFB, he had worked for Babcock on a consultancy basis since April 2017. He claimed to be 'satisfied that no conflict of interest exists'.[52]

Control

During the same period, LFB was on the verge of becoming the first UK fire and rescue service to outsource its emergency call function and mobilisation. In 2011, LFEPA commenced procurement of a 10-year contract to design, build, provide and maintain control and mobilising ICT services. It included a second option to provide managed services, which meant to outsource the entire control and mobilising service. This not only jeopardised resilience in London: it had implications for the future of the fire service national co-ordinating centre role, which London was expected to take on. Sharon Riley, FBU leading control rep said:

> The privatisation of London's control throws a spanner in the works of national co-ordination and national resilience. Every fire authority in England relies on the national co-ordination function that until 1 April was provided by West Yorkshire and now lies with the London fire service. None of them appear to have been asked their views on the London privatisation and its impact on national co-ordination and resilience. It is a clear example of how a locally made decision can have knock-on effects across the fire service.[53]

In March 2012, under Johnson and Coleman, LFEPA awarded Capita a ten-year contract to take over its control centre – constructed and equipped at public expense – and around 120 existing LFB staff, who would be transferred to the company. However Coleman lost his seat to Labour's Andrew Dismore in the May 2012 elections, changing the balance on the Greater London Assembly.

LFEPA reviewed the decision, finding that 'the Brigade already has two 'risk critical' external, private sector providers, one of which is clearly struggling' and that 'outsourcing fire control would impose new high financial risks on the capital's fire and rescue service'. LFEPA concluded that 'the risks of proceeding with this outsourcing proposal outweigh any likely advantages' and the decision was made to award a contract to Capita for a replacement mobilising solution, rather than a fully managed outsourced service.[54]

Although LFB control was spared the disaster of privatisation, staff still faced multiple threats from principal management in the years before the Grenfell Tower fire, which even the public inquiry recognised as disrupting its activities.

The threat of deregulation continued. As late as 2016, LFB's review of brigade control recommended that responsibility for control room training should be transferred to Babcock. This was opposed internally and control training remained within LFB.[55]

The control room suffered significant staffing problems and underwent restructuring between 2009 and 2017. In 2011–12, there was a temporary halt to recruitment, due to the privatisation threat. But control staff numbers continued to fall until the Grenfell Tower fire.[56]

Between 2013 and 2017, probably the next biggest disruption for control staff was the LFB changed its mobilising system Vision, developed by Capita. The public inquiry captured the impact of Vision on staff after the system came into operation in 2015. The Phase 2 report stated:

> For a number of years after its introduction, Vision continued to be plagued by significant system failures. More than 500 faults were reported to Capita in the first six months. There were also six occasions during the first year when the system failed altogether for periods of between 40 minutes and three hours, requiring the use of contingency measures. AC George described instances when the mobilising system slowed to the point of stopping completely, causing the CROs to resort to a secondary mobilising system that he described as 'basically pen and paper'. That was extremely stressful for staff, who had occasionally left the control room in tears. The scale of the difficulties was such that in the period from 2016 to 2017 the Operational Support Team spent about 60% of its time reporting problems with Vision, revising training packages to reflect changes to the system and training staff on ways to circumvent problems. During the first two years in which Vision was in use, ways were devised to circumvent about 100 problems.[57]

Vision generated an enormous amount of additional work for control staff and impacted on the already fraught situation for training. A longstanding problem, caused by short staffing, was that control staff training was not generally done during working hours but while staff were away from their work stations. Instead, control staff had to undertake training while operational capability was maintained, so they only had 'training on the watch'. Control staff often complained to the FBU and to LFB principal management that training was regularly interrupted by the need to recall staff to respond to incoming calls.[58]

This affected training on fire survival guidance. The public inquiry concluded that 'between 2013 and the Grenfell Tower fire, existing control room staff did not receive the full day of fire survival guidance refresher training that had been planned and approved by the Lakanal House Board and promised to the coroner'. Despite some smaller scale exercises, LFB never organised training to test the number of fire survival calls that the control room could effectively handle.[59]

Austerity cuts

Central funding cuts to fire and rescue service were another blight on the LFB in the years before the Grenfell Tower fire. In 1998, the home secretary agreed to the LFCDA's application to close the Barbican and Shooters Hill fire stations, to change the arrangements for the provision of fire cover on the River Thames and to reduce the LFB's establishment by 80 firefighting posts.[60]

In 2004, LFB's London Safety Plan 2 sought to scrap several fire appliances in central London, close Manchester Square fire station in Marylebone and reduce crewing levels across the capital. The FBU opposed these proposals, but sadly LFB pressed ahead. The FBU had more success with defending pre-determined attendance to fires in high rise buildings, after LFB principal managers proposed sending only two fire engines. The union declared a dispute and fought for two years until LFB relented.[61]

The situation worsened after Boris Johnson became mayor of London, although cuts were delayed because of the 2012 Olympics and Paralympics in London. Just before the competition began, Johnson took £30 million from LFEPA's reserves and gave the funds to the Metropolitan Police. Ben Sprung, FBU regional organiser, described the decision as 'playing politics at the expense of the fire service'.[62]

Soon after the 2012 Olympics and Paralympics had finished, Johnson proposed closing 12 fire stations, removing 18 fire engines and slashing around 400 firefighter jobs in the Fifth London Safety Plan (LSP5). LFEPA opposed the mayor's plans, but were overruled.

The FBU fought a high-profile public campaign to defend fire stations, mobilising members and working with campaigners. London FBU regional secretary Paul Embery warned: 'These cuts are dangerous and wrong. They would lead to increased response times for millions of Londoners, which in turn would cost lives.'[63] The union's submission to the LFB consultation warned that the plans would have be particularly damaging for high rise buildings. The FBU submission stated:

> The majority of the 10 stations that are proposed to be closed under this plan have extensive high-rise buildings on their grounds. With indications of major increases over the term of the integrated risk management plan LSP5 of high rise building construction for residential and commercial, it simply isn't conceivable that firefighters' health and safety can be put at risk by extending the duration from the 'time of call' until the eventual arrival at the correct address with thirteen firefighters before firefighting activities can start at the high rise building.[64]

In 2014, ten fire stations were closed, including Belsize, Knightsbridge and Westminster relatively near to Grenfell Tower. Other stations lost a pump. Some 14 appliances were lost across London, including Ealing fire station, which sent firefighters to Grenfell Tower and Peckham, close to Lakanal House. Similarly, two fire rescue units (FRUs), which are specialist heavy rescue vehicles, were lost. As a result of Johnson's cuts, 550 firefighter jobs were lost in one go.

Johnson was not finished wasting resources. In 2014, he bought three water cannons from German police. Home secretary Theresa May banned their use anywhere in England and Wales. Unable to find a buyer, they were subsequently scrapped.[65]

In early 2017, the FBU made a detailed submission to the next London safety plan, drawn up just months before the Grenfell Tower fire. The submission made specific reference to the risks in high rise dwellings and the need to improve response targets for such incidents. It stated:

> The FBU believes that the brigade should introduce a new attendance target for the initial response to a high rise incident. Four appliances are required to safely and effectively begin operations at a high rise incident. As ridership levels can vary between four and six on an appliance, we believe that setting an attendance target for the initial four appliances would provide the necessary numbers as quickly as possible to a high-rise incident. The FBU

proposes a new target of six minutes for the first and second fire engines and eight minutes for the third and fourth ... The FBU welcomes the proposals to introduce attendance times for FRUs and aerials. We want to see a change towards measuring attendance times as a percentile, and for a new high-rise incident attendance target of six, six, eight and eight minutes for the initial four appliances.[66]

LFB firefighters and inspectors

The LFB significantly reduced its firefighting force before the Grenfell Tower fire. Wholetime firefighters were reduced by 22 per cent, control staff by 13 per cent and total staff by 23 per cent in that time (Table 6.1).[67] Staff engaged in inspection and enforcement fell by more than a quarter over the previous decade. The figures indicate a particularly stark fall in operational firefighters carrying out these roles, down by almost a half over the previous decade (Table 6.2).[68]

Table 6.1 LFB staff in post employed by headcount and by role, 2008 to 2017.

Year	*Wholetime*	*Control*	*Support*	*Total staff*
2008	6,047	119	1,068	7,234
2017	4,695	104	785	5,584

Table 6.2 LFB staff (FTE) dedicated to inspecting and auditing fire safety, 2008 to 2017.

Year	*Inspecting officers*	*Operational staff*	*FRS staff*
2008	204	101	103
2017	152	56	96

Before the fire: mistakes of LFB principal management

After the Lakanal House fire, Ron Dobson wrote to social housing providers in London about fire risk assessment, means of escape and evacuation strategy. Dobson also wrote to Ken Knight about cladding test results, but did not move the department to pursue the matter.[69] After the Lakanal House coroner sent LFB a Rule 43 letter, the brigade took some steps to address the criticism.[70]

However, LFB principal management continued with the deregulation and austerity agenda, promulgated by the Westminster government and the mayor of London. LFB principal management made numerous mistakes before the Grenfell Tower fire.

LFB principal management failed to plan for a fire of the type or magnitude as occurred at Grenfell Tower. LFB principal managers failed to develop procedures for such a fire and failed to train and equip incident commanders, operational firefighters and emergency control staff for this eventuality. The public inquiry Phase 1 report made these criticisms. The FBU accepts the criticisms are valid.

LFB principal management failed to plan and prepare for fires involving cladding systems. Although the LFB's fire safety regulation department delivered a presentation title 'Tall Building Facades' to senior staff in late 2016, the LFB did not establish adequate procedures for tackling cladding fires nor did it adequately train firefighters, officers and control staff for such fires.

However the institutional failure lies above the LFB and other individual brigades – at the level of central government. Ministers and their advisors, including CFOA and its successor, the NFCC, failed to research cladding fire risks, including the new materials and international examples or to ensure such research took place. It is central government's responsibility to provide regulations and authoritative guidance to direct local fire and rescue services about managing those risks, along with the necessary resources to implement the guidance.

LFB's policy for fighting fires in high rise buildings at the time of the Grenfell Tower fire, known as PN633, was flawed. Ron Dobson gave a presentation to insurers six months before the Grenfell Tower fire. The presentation was entitled, 'High Rise – Not High Risk' and included slides such as 'How Fire Engineering ensures high rise are safe for people and fire-fighters'.[71] This indicated a culture of complacency among principal managers to underestimate the risks associated with high rise residential buildings.

At the time of the Grenfell fire, LFB's pre-determined attendance for a high rise fire was four appliances under the direction of a watch manager. In the immediate months after the fire, LFB revised this high rise PDA to 'five fire engines, one aerial appliance and the standard officer complement for a five pump fire being mobilised to any high rise fire related incident'. A further interim revision was added: when control received four calls or more to a residential high rise premise, the PDA was upgraded to eight fire engines and one aerial appliance.[72] The FBU believes this is tantamount to an admission by LFB principal management that their PDA at the time of the Grenfell Tower fire was inadequate.

The LFB's high rise policy PN633 had other flaws. LFB's policy failed to incorporate key elements of central government guidance, *Generic Risk Assessment 3.2 – fighting fires in high rise buildings* (2014), known as GRA 3.2. LFB were particularly remiss because their own principal managers took the policy lead revising GRA 3.2 between 2010 and 2014, led by Peter Cowup.[73]

In 2017, LFB's high rise policy PN633 did not explain how firefighters could evacuate a high rise residential building, particularly one where compartmentation had failed. But neither GRA 3.2 nor Approved Document B provided residents and firefighters with clear guidance on evacuation. If LFB was at fault, then so were ministers and chief fire officers for failing to develop such guidance, even after the Lakanal House fire.

Before the Grenfell Tower fire, LFB's policies governing the handling of emergency calls in the control room, emergency call management (PN539) and fire survival guidance calls (PN790), were also flawed. But where these failings reflected national guidance, they were the responsibility of ministers and chief fire officers.

LFB did not train its firefighters properly in how to carry out 7(2)(d) visits. However, 7(2)(d) visits are not the primary mechanism to initially identify the level of risk associated with any premises. The primary purpose of 7(2)d visits is to familiarise crews with the specific characteristics of each building. They are designed to update or confirm any existing risk information.[74] Operational firefighters must carry out 7(2)(d) visits, not others.

The FBU carefully considered the public inquiry's Phase 1 report, which concluded that 'the LFB is an institution at risk of not learning the lessons of the Grenfell Tower fire'.[75] The LFB has produced a number of lessons learned reports and faced substantial scrutiny from Greater London Assembly members, particularly on its Fire, Resilience and Emergency Planning Committee.

The public inquiry's Phase 2 report was similarly critical of LFB principal management before and on the night of the fire. The inquiry highlighted 'systemic failings' in training, incident command, communications and the operation of the control room. It concluded that 'the LFB's failure was attributable to a chronic lack of effective leadership, combined with an undue emphasis on process and a culture of complacency'.[76]

The FBU has long been LFB principal management's harshest critics. FBU officials made many of the criticisms echoed by the inquiry before the Grenfell Tower fire. However, LFB is an institution capable of reform, as long as it consults its workforce through the FBU.

7
Refurbishment botched

The public Grenfell Tower Inquiry (GTI) Phase 2 report posed a key question about the causes of the Grenfell Tower fire and who was to blame for it:

> How was it possible in 21st century London for a reinforced concrete building, itself structurally impervious to fire, to be turned into a death trap that would enable fire to sweep through it in an uncontrollable way in a matter of a few hours despite what were thought to be effective regulations designed to prevent just such an event?[1]

Culpability lies with five important groups of actors: central government, which set the political and legal framework for building and fire safety; the manufacturers of hazardous materials; the private testing and certification bodies; the public bodies, including the council and others; and finally, the private contractors who refurbished Grenfell Tower.

The FBU argued from the beginning of the public inquiry that deregulation, instigated by central government and big business, permeated all the way down through other public and private organisations, to local politicians, firms and individuals.

Deregulation meant the removal, weakening and downgrading of the law governing building safety and fire safety. It meant construction firms could manufacture and sell flammable cladding and insulation, despite the risks. Deregulation meant private testing and certification bodies licensed these products, claiming they were legal when they were not. It meant the refurbishment work on Grenfell Tower was appallingly planned and abysmally carried out, yielding building failures all over the block, inside and out, which contributed to the fire.

This chapter examines the immediate situation before the Grenfell Tower fire, Drawing heavily on the public inquiry's reports and evidence. It examines how an unsatisfactory legal framework, poorly enforced, gave local politicians, housing managers, manufacturers, private construction firms and other contractors the opportunity to make Grenfell Tower unsafe for habitation. Residents of Grenfell Tower warned of the risks to their homes long before the fire.

The public inquiry's Phase 2 report, volumes 2 to 4, exhaustively explained the role each of these actors played in causing the Grenfell Tower fire. The lead counsel to the inquiry, Richard Millett, began and closed hearings by pointing to the 'merry-go-round of buck passing' between key actors involved in the Grenfell Tower fire.[2] Whether their conduct was criminal is now subject to police investigation. The FBU hopes that those found culpable are prosecuted and punished appropriately.

MANUFACTURERS

During the Grenfell Tower refurbishment, flammable materials were added to the block. The rainscreen panels, known as Reynobond 55 PE, were manufactured as plain sheets by Arconic Architectural Products SAS and fabricated into cassettes by CEP Architectural Facades Ltd for Grenfell Tower. Behind aluminium composite material (ACM) panels was a layer of insulation. On the spandrels, this was mostly Celotex RS5000 polyisocyanurate (PIR) polymer foam or Kingspan K15 phenolic polymer foam. On the columns, it was mainly Celotex RS5000 PIR, with a small number of Kingspan K15 insulation boards.[3]

The public inquiry shone a bright light on the cladding and insulation manufacturers. Sam Stein, counsel for one group of residents, described the manufacturers, Arconic, Kingspan and Celotex, as 'crooks and killers', who 'operated without any regard whatsoever for the lives of those living within walls covered in their combustible materials'.[4] Stein said that Kingspan, Celotex and Arconic were allowed to 'wrap buildings housing families in the high-rise and high-tech equivalent of kindling soaked in petrol':

> Arconic, Celotex and Kingspan harboured a disregard bordering on contempt for the rules. They lied, manipulated data, hid results and threatened litigation, all to get their products to market. The evidence from all three companies showed no regard was given to the danger their products posed to the public. Nothing was allowed to stand in the way of market share. If there was a bad test, it was ignored, and the next one rigged until the desired result was achieved. If they found data inconvenient, they simply hid it. If inconvenient questions were asked, they ignored them.[5]

Arconic

At the turn of the century, Arconic began producing sheets of ACM material with a polyethylene core, sold as Reynobond 55 PE. In 2003, Arconic arranged for Reynobond 55 with a fire-resistant core to be tested by Warrington Fire. It was given the Class 0 classification. Reynobond with an unmodified polyethylene core was not tested.[6]

In 2004, the Centre Scientifique et Technique du Bâtiment (CSTB), the French national testing body, tested Reynobond 55 PE at Arconic's request. A test of a riveted specimen achieved European classification B-s2, d0, although Arconic's technical sales support Claude Wehrle admitted that this was due to '"arranging" the system to pass'. A test of a specimen in cassette form was stopped after less than 15 minutes because the heat release rate exceeded 400 kW. The test report recorded that the results could not be used. Arconic kept the cassette test secret.[7]

In 2007, two Arconic managers attended a presentation by Fred-Roderick Pohl in Oslo. Pohl compared the combustibility of 5,000 m^2 of ACM PE to a truck containing 19,000 litres of oil. He explained the greater danger posed by the toxic smoke from burning polyethylene, which could kill in two or three minutes. Pohl posed the question of what would happen if 'one building made out [of] PE core is in [a] fire and will kill 60 to 70 persons, what is the responsibility of the ACM supplier?'[8]

In 2008, Reynobond 55 PE was awarded a BBA certificate. It stated that 'the panels may be regarded as having a Class 0 surface in England and Wales' and that it covered both riveted and cassette forms without qualification. In 2010, an Arconic sales executive wrote to Wehrle and others regarding concerns raised in Spain about ACM PE. Wehrle responded, admitting that Reynobond PE in cassette form did not meet European Class B. This information, he warned, 'we have to keep as "VERY CONFIDENTIAL!!!!"'[9]

In 2011, CSTB tested Reynobond 55 PE in cassette form. The test was stopped early because the heat emitted by the sample was too great. It was classified Class E. A week later, Wehrle reported the result, lamenting that Class B was the minimum requirement for facades in Europe. Clearly aware of the deregulatory context, he opined that, 'For the moment, even if we know that PE material in cassette has a bad behaviour exposed to fire, we can still work with national regulations who are not as restrictive.'[10]

In 2013, CSTB tested Reynobond 55 PE again in both riveted and cassette forms. The riveted specimen achieved only Class C-s2, d0, while the cassette test was stopped early because of 'wide-spread ignition'. CSTB certified it as only Class E. The following year, Wehrle told Arconic's sales staff that all Reynobond 55 PE products had been classified Class E and previous classifications were immediately cancelled.[11]

However Arconic made no attempt to ensure that contractors knew about the performance of the product it supplied for the refurbishment of Grenfell Tower. The public inquiry concluded:

> Arconic itself must take responsibility for the use of Reynobond 55 PE on Grenfell Tower because it knew that the sale of the product had been obtained on the basis of the BBA certificate which it was well aware gave a misleading impression of the way in which the product in cassette form reacted to fire.[12]

Arconic's disgraceful behaviour continued after the Grenfell Tower fire. Arconic did not renounce Reynobond 55 PE ACM panels after the fire. BBA withdrew its certificate in 2019. Arconic's solicitors invoked the French Blocking Statute, which meant its representatives initially refused to appear in person at the inquiry, with only limited testimony after much legal wrangling.

Arconic's closing submissions made a series of outrageous claims. It stated that 'ACM PE panels are not in themselves unsafe nor are they fully combustible unless incorporated into a system in which they face a continuous surface of combustible insulation' and that 'ACM PE was not prohibited by the regulatory regime and was in widespread use before the Grenfell fire'. The same submission criticised firefighters for breaking down doors or wedging them open with firefighting equipment during emergency intervention at the fire.[13]

Kingspan

A small amount of the insulation used on Grenfell Tower, around 5 per cent of the total, was K15 Kooltherm manufactured by Kingspan and marketed for use in rainscreen cladding systems. However the public inquiry found that Kingspan played a key role in creating a false market in insulation for use on buildings over 18 metres in height.

At the turn of the century, Kingspan began to take advantage of the ambiguities in building safety guidance, testing and certification to create 'a new category of insulation products for use on buildings over 18 metres in height, namely, products that were not materials of limited combustibility but were nonetheless suitable for use above that height'. The inquiry highlighted the 'fundamental falsehood at the heart of Kingspan's marketing strategy', because there was no over-18-metre market for combustible insulation products.[14]

In 2005, BRE carried out a test for Kingspan using K15 with a non-combustible cement particle or fibre cement board as the rainscreen. BRE initially appeared to agree that the test had met the criteria in BR 135, but then produced a no 'scope of application' report. Despite BRE's reluctance, Kingspan continued to market K15. Kingspan's promotional flyer headed 'What's lurking behind your façade?' (2006) claimed that K15 had been tested and 'awarded certification to BS 8414-1' and had been 'assessed and approved in accordance with BR 135'. The inquiry argued that both statements were false.[15]

In 2007, K15 was tested, with devastating results. An internal Kingspan report by Ivor Meredith described the result as a 'raging inferno'. The top fire barrier was breached 17 minutes into the test. The system failed the temperature criteria in BR 135 and that the test was terminated early because there had been a danger that the laboratory would be set alight. Meredith said K15 burnt ferociously 'on its own steam' and was 'very different in a fire situation to the previous technology'.[16]

In 2008, Kingspan carried out its second test at BRE. K15 continued to burn for more than 30 minutes after removal of the source of ignition. The public inquiry published emails between Kingspan staff, which revealed that they 'actively designed to conceal and mislead' other staff about the risks. Philip Heath sent an email to his Kingspan colleague Gwyn Davies in which he said, 'I'm spinning so much I'm dizzy'. Meredith asked Heath by email, 'Are we saying that the product supplied which failed their test is the same product that we got to pass the test?'.[17]

Wintech Group Ltd, a facade engineering consultancy, asked questions about the suitability of K15 for use in high rise projects. Despite the recent tests, Heath emailed Meredith: 'Wintech can go fuck themselves, and if they are not careful we'll sue the arse of [*sic*] them.' In another communication, Heath called the situation a 'nightmare' and wrote, 'I'm trying to think of a way out of this one, imagine a fire running up this tower !!!!!!!!!!!!!!!!!'.[18]

Kingspan obtained its first BBA certificate for K15 in 2008, and the following year a certificate from LABC. Heath wrote internally that Kingspan had sent so much fire data to the LABC certificate's author that it had 'probably blocked his server'. He added that the LABC surveyor had been convinced without even having 'to get any real ale down him'.[19] The public inquiry verdict on Kingspan was stark:

> The story of the development and marketing of K15 for use on buildings of over 18 metres in height between 2006 and 2019 is one of deeply entrenched and persistent dishonesty on the part of Kingspan in pursuit of commercial gain coupled with a complete disregard for fire safety …
>
> The effect of Kingspan's dishonest marketing of K15 was to create a spurious market for a polymeric insulation product suitable for use on high-rise buildings generally, which drew in Celotex as a competitor.[20]

Celotex

Celotex RS5000, a polyisocyanurate (PIR) thermosetting foam product, accounted for most of the insulation used in the cladding system at Grenfell Tower. According to the public inquiry, Celotex had a corporate 'culture of maximising profits', as well as a history within the firm of 'data manipulation and dissimulation'.[21]

In 2011, the Celotex FR5000 product was tested and given a Class 0 classification. Celotex marketed FR5000 as having Class 0 fire performance 'throughout'. The Celotex product was intended to compete with Kingspan's K15. In 2013, Jonathan Roper of Celotex prepared a paper entitled 'Above 18m Action Plan', in which he set out the steps required for accreditation of FR5000 for use on buildings over 18 metres in height. Roper had an internal exchange with another Celotex colleague Paul Evans, in which he confessed, 'realistically our product shouldn't be used behind most cladding panels because in the event of a fire it will burn'.[22]

In 2014, Celotex FR5000 was tested twice by BRE. The test was stopped after 26 minutes, when flames overtopped the rig. It was allowed to continue burning for a further period, so Celotex could obtain more data. BRE confirmed that the test failed. No classification report was issued. The second test involved a steel-framed rig, 12 mm magnesium oxide sheathing board, 100 mm Celotex FR5000, Lamatherm fire barriers, 8 mm Marley Eternit cladding over 6 mm magnesium oxide boards over the level 2 thermocouples and 12 mm Marley Eternit cladding over all other areas. The results met the criteria in BR 135. As the inquiry report put it, the test rig was 'so obviously unrepresentative and designed only to meet the performance criteria'.[23]

Celotex launched RS5000 after these tests, in 2014. The inquiry found that the marketing literature for RS5000 contained two messages, 'both of which were false and deliberately misleading'. The first, aimed at the designer or cladding specialist, 'was that RS5000 was suitable for use on any building over 18 metres in height, whereas it was not'. The second was 'the warning aimed at the more conscientious reader that the fire performance and classification for RS5000 related only to the components described as making up the system tested, when in fact the components were misdescribed'.[24]

The inquiry concluded that Celotex RS5000 was not a material of limited combustibility and did not conform to the guidance on the construction of external walls in Approved Document B. The tests on which claims about RS5000 were made took place before it was launched, on a different Celotex product, FR5000. The inquiry argued that 'the test on which Celotex relied ... had been rigged by the inclusion at critical points in the construction of the system under test of fire-resistant magnesium oxide boards'. In any case, BS 8414 and BR 135 did not provide for the testing and classification of individual products, they applied only to a complete system. Celotex 'deliberately tucked that information away in the small print of its marketing literature where it was unlikely to be spotted'.[25]

Almost as soon as it was launched, Celotex RS5000 received its LABC certificate. Within weeks, it was marketed to Harley for use on Grenfell Tower.[26]

PRIVATE TESTING AND CERTIFICATION BODIES

Arconic, Kingspan and Celotex were culpable for their own activities, but they did not act alone. The testing and certifying bodies – BRE, BBA and LABC – were also complicit. At the inquiry, Adrian Williamson, counsel for one group of residents, argued that BRE, BBA and LABC were 'at best asleep at the wheel in engaging with these manufacturers, and at worst positively collusive with them in their sales tactics'. He added that 'they were far too close to their 'clients', and far too reluctant to bite the hand that fed them'.[27] Similarly, Sam Stein drew out the link with deregulation. He argued:

> In essence, the failings of the BBA, BRE and LABC were in part systemic, and in part the result of individual negligence and ineptitude. The watchdogs in place which should have secured the safety of building materials had been privatised many years ago, and instead, their mission had become warped into acting as the lapdogs of the manufacturers. The evidence tells us at this

time there was no independent, no competent certification or testing agency in place whatsoever.[28]

BRE

In Chapters 1 and 2, we explained that BRE had been the government's own testing facility, but was commercialised in the 1980s, before privatisation in 1997. After that, it did contract work for the government, as well as commercial testing for construction manufacturers.

For a decade between 2005 and 2014, BRE staff worked closely with Kingspan. The inquiry was critical of the accounts given by BRE of their relationships with the business. The Phase 2 report stated: 'We did not find Dr Colwell's evidence on these matters very convincing and have been left with the clear impression that she and other employees of BRE were doing much more to assist Kingspan than she was willing to admit.'[29]

BRE was party to tests of K15 in 2005, 2008 and in 2014. Although BRE was subjected to pressure from Kingspan employees, including challenging the results of testing, formal complaints and threats to involve lawyers, BRE did not do enough to highlight the risks of combustible insulation.[30]

The public inquiry was even more critical of BRE's behaviour towards Celotex, especially the testing of Celotex FR5000 in 2014, which was designed to meet the performance criteria in BR 135, rather than the regulations. The inquiry came to damning conclusions about BRE in the years before the Grenfell Tower fire. The Phase 2 report judged:

> In essence, over the years leading up to 2014 BRE had by degrees lost sight of the importance of maintaining a proper distance between itself and clients and of the need for scientific rigour and independence. Its internal controls were not the subject of regular and robust training and there was no independent supervision that ensured that conflicts of interest were properly managed. It had gradually become much closer to its clients and wanted to work with them to find solutions to their problems. Scientific rigour and independence were sacrificed in favour of financial sustainability.[31]

The inquiry did not shy away from the wider political context. It found that 'the effective working of the system was not enhanced by the privatisation of BRE'. BRE's relationship with the DCLG became 'less beneficial after it was required to operate in a commercial environment. The transition from adviser to contractor meant that it did not regard itself as being under a duty to provide robust and independent advice to the government'. It was this status that lay behind much of BRE's work, which was marred by 'unprofessional conduct, inadequate practices, a lack of effective oversight, poor reporting and a lack of scientific rigour'.[32]

BBA

In earlier chapters, we explained how the Agrément Board was originally established by the Westminster government to certify the compliance of products with building legislation. Renamed the British Board of Agrément (BBA) in 1983, it became a not-for-profit commercial organisation. BBA issued certificates of compliance for Arconic's Reynobond 55 PE ACM panels and Kingspan's K15 insulation, both of which were used on Grenfell Tower.

The BBA certificate for Reynobond 55 PE was first issued in 2008 and due for review at three-year intervals. In 2011, BBA staff asked Arconic for relevant materials for the review. Arconic provided a pack of documents, but none concerned the fire performance of Reynobond 55 PE in cassette form and Arconic did not inform the BBA of the results of disastrous cassette test in 2004 carried out by the CSTB. Nevertheless, the BBA certificate remained valid.[33]

The BBA certificate was due for renewal in 2014. Despite six emails and at least two phone calls, BBA received no substantial response from anyone at Arconic during that period. In 2015, BBA's senior management decided to complete the review with the information already obtained. The inquiry described the decision as 'inexplicable'. The BBA had received 'no confirmation of the performance of the Reynobond product from Arconic in the previous seven years and Arconic's failure to provide such information when asked was exceptional and extreme'. The BBA 'could and should have threatened to suspend Arconic's BBA certificate given its lack of response and should have done so if the information it required was not provided'. Yet BBA appeared never to have considered such a step.[34]

Only evidence produced by the public inquiry prompted BBA to act against Arconic. In 2018, a report by the inquiry's expert Barbara Lane revealed the existence of the 2004 test on Reynobond PE in cassette form. BBA suspended the certificate for material non-disclosure in breach of contract. In 2019, BBA withdrew the certificate for Reynobond 55 in all forms.[35]

In 2008, BBA issued a certificate for Kingspan K15. Although Kingspan concealed significant information from the BBA, the inquiry found that the BBA certificate contained 'important statements about the fire performance of K15 that were untrue' and 'used a form of words suggested by Kingspan and drawn from its own marketing literature'. When the BBA certificate was re-issued in 2013, 'Kingspan persuaded the BBA to include a statement that K15 complied with paragraph 12.7 of Approved Document B, which wrongly implied that it was a product of limited combustibility'.[36] The inquiry's Phase 2 was highly critical of BBA's practices. It stated:

> In the case of the BBA the root of the problem lay in the conflict between the need to act as a commercial organisation, and therefore to attract customers in order to generate profits, and the need to maintain a high degree of independence and rigorous investigation in order to satisfy those who might be considering using the products in question that the contents of their certificates could safely be relied on. The BBA failed to manage effectively the conflict between the commercial and (for want of a better word) regulatory aspects of its operations ...[37]

LABC

Local Authority Building Control (LABC) was formed in 2005 to support local authority building control in England and Wales with training, advice and assistance, technical consistency in the interpretation of building regulations and a forum for discussion between its members.[38]

In 2009, LABC issued a certificate for Kingspan K15. It stated that K15 could be considered a material of limited combustibility and that it was suitable for use on buildings over 18 metres in height. Similarly, in 2014 LABC issued a certificate for Celotex RS5000, permitting it 'for use in rainscreen wall construction including above 18m in height'. It claimed it had been successfully tested, met the criteria in BR 135 and complied with Approved Document B. The wording on the certificate was lifted from an email sent by a Celotex employee. The public inquiry accused LABC, like it did BBA, of compromising its independence issuing certificates with 'language that was inappropriate and in some cases misleading'.[39]

NHBC

The public inquiry did not spare the National House Building Council (NHBC) from criticism, and with good reason. Michael Heseltine had announced his building regulation proposals to the NHBC in 1979. The NHBC became the first authorised private approved inspector body in 1985. The NHBC was the largest provider of warranties for newly built properties in the UK, supplying over 80 per cent. Through its subsidiary, NHBC was also the largest private building control body in England and Wales, providing about 60 per cent of the services provided to the residential market by approved inspectors. NHBC did not provide building control or warranty services for the Grenfell Tower refurbishment, but it had a major influence over standards in the housebuilding industry.[40]

The Building Control Alliance (BCA) was formed in 2008 by five member organisations, the Association of Consultant Approved Inspectors (ACAI), LABC, the Royal Institution of Chartered Surveyors (RICS), the Chartered Institute of Building (CIB) and the Chartered Association of Building Engineers (CABE). NHBC was not a member of the BCA, but through the ACAI, senior NHBC staff played a leading role within the BCA. As the inquiry pointed out, 'although the BCA published guidance for the construction industry, it had no statutory standing and was an unregulated, voluntary, professional body'.[41]

By 2010 at the latest, NHBC was aware that combustible insulation was commonly being used in the external walls of buildings over 18 metres in height. BRE published a report entitled *Fire performance of highly insulated residential buildings and modern methods of construction: A literature review*, commissioned by NHBC Foundation, NHBC's research arm. Although NHBC raised questions about Kingspan K15, the inquiry found that 'NHBC's continued endorsement of its use from then on was unjustifiable and amounted to an abdication of its responsibility'. NHBC issued a 'flimsy warning' to its staff, but failed to instruct them to stop accepting K15 for use in the external wall of any building over 18 metres in height immediately. The failure of NHBC to do so reflected 'a desire at the time to placate customers and manufacturers at the expense of safety'.[42]

In 2014, the BCA published, *Use of Combustible Cladding Materials on Residential Buildings*, Technical Guidance Note 18 (TGN 18). It was written by the NHBC's Steve Evans. It proposed a third route, through desktop studies, for compliance with Approved Document B. The inquiry's Phase 2 report found:

> In the circumstances, the inclusion of the third option in TGN 18 was irresponsible. It was not motivated by a desire for rigour in the application of Approved Document B, nor by a desire to improve fire safety standards in high-rise buildings, but by NHBC's desire to assist developers to find a way to justify the use of non-compliant products.[43]

The inquiry was also scathing about NHBC's relations with Kingspan:

> The action of NHBC provides a vivid example of a large body with substantial influence over building control officers nationwide electing to co-operate with manufacturers rather than robustly enforce regulations designed to protect life. The attitude of NHBC ... deserves criticism in the strongest terms.[44]

PUBLIC BODIES

Grenfell Tower was owned by RBKC, but its housing management functions were contracted out to the tenant management organisation (TMO). This arrangement came into force in 1996. It meant 250 staff employed in RBKC's housing services department transferred to the TMO. In 2002, the TMO became an arm's-length management organisation (ALMO). The public inquiry noted this status, but did not interrogate the problems with this form of deregulation.[45]

The status of social housing within these contracted out arrangements certainly deserves further study.[46] It had material significance for the Grenfell Tower fire and the subsequent inquiry, because RBKC legal representatives argued that under the arrangements, they were not the 'responsible person' under the Fire Safety Order. Instead, RBKC claimed that the TMO was the responsible person and therefore any failings or breaches of the law were not down to the council.

The public inquiry certainly felt that RBKC qualified as the responsible person, or at least to the main duties under the Order. RBKC owned Grenfell Tower and paid for its refurbishment. Some of those who carried out work for the TMO, before and during the refurbishment, seem to have believed that RBKC was the responsible person. The FBU's view is that it is perverse for the owner of any building, whether they are a private landlord or public body, to offload legal liabilities meant to hold them to account for safety and other matters onto another subsidiary organisation.[47]

TMO

The TMO's failures pre-dated the refurbishment. In fact, as the public inquiry Phase 2 report, Volume 3 made clear, was already failing to meet its fire safety responsibilities for Grenfell Tower and other homes within the borough. In 2009, Robert Black became the TMO's chief executive. At the time the TMO produced its own fire risk assessments. The London Fire Brigade (LFB) told the TMO these were inadequate and threatened to impose an enforcement notice on the TMO (and RBKC) if matters were not resolved. A 2009 report by consultants Salvus for the TMO drew attention to 19 prospective breaches of the Fire Safety Order. Over the following six months, Salvus carried out fire risk assessments of high risk properties, part of a joint programme for the TMO and RBKC.[48]

Carl Stokes was one of the fire risk assessors contracted by Salvus. Between 1986 and 2009, Stokes had been an operational firefighter, working for Royal Berkshire and Oxfordshire fire and rescue services, including in fire safety departments. Despite training and experience with the Fire Safety Order and a fire risk assessment certificate, Stokes was not registered by any professional body as competent to carry out fire risk assessments. There were no mandatory national standards for fire risk assessors, despite repeated efforts by the FBU and other fire professionals to campaign for them.[49]

In 2010, Stokes began doing fire risk assessments for the TMO in his own right, as a self-employed contractor. The TMO did not tender for the work. The inquiry found that Stokes carried out fire risk assessments of Grenfell Tower in 2010, 2012, 2014 and twice in 2016. In each case, he identified the chief executive of RBKC as the responsible person, although he had no contact with anyone at RBKC.[50] The public inquiry was scathing about the quality of Stokes' risk assessments. It revealed:

> Provided nothing had changed, Mr Stokes's practice was to copy text from one fire risk assessment of Grenfell Tower to the next. He also copied text from fire risk assessments of other buildings. For example … he included some text referring to balconies taken from the assessment of another building, even though there were no balconies at Grenfell Tower. The passage was then repeated … he always included a passage headed 'Pest control' … he reported on the condition of pigeon netting on the balconies, although there were no balconies on Grenfell Tower.[51]

The TMO's failures on fire safety continued in the years before the Grenfell Tower fire. In 2013, consultant Matt Hodgson reviewed the TMO's safety management across the borough. On fire risk assessments, he found nearly a thousand outstanding items of remedial work waiting to be completed. In 2016, Stokes inspected Grenfell Tower before a scheduled LFB audit. He told the TMO that 23 of the 46 recommendations he had made earlier that year, 43 described as 'high priority', were still outstanding.[52]

The TMO's terrible attitude towards fire safety carried over during the refurbishment of Grenfell Tower and its failures. This is captured by Claire Williams, the TMO's project manager for the Grenfell Tower refurbishment, who was the primary point of contact with the main contractor and residents. On 12 November 2014, Williams wrote to contractor Rydon: 'I am just writing to get clarification on the fire retardance of the new cladding – I just had a Lacknall [*sic*] moment.' She was referring to the 2009 fire at Lakanal House.

Williams left the TMO a year after the Grenfell Tower fire. In 2020, she told the public inquiry she had destroyed notes of her work on the project, despite knowing of the public inquiry and police investigation. She excused herself as 'just clearing her desk'.[53]

The public inquiry highlighted several failures on the part of the TMO during the refurbishment. The TMO appointed Studio E architects without any tender or assessment of its competence for such a project. The TMO commissioned Exova fire consultants, but failed to check whether it had finished its fire safety strategy. It failed to challenge the principal contractor Rydon, which did not appoint a fire engineer for the refurbishment. The TMO also failed to produce a health and safety file, as it should have done as principal designer under the Construction, Design and Management Regulations 2015. Finally, the TMO failed to engage with and consult the residents.[54] The public inquiry came to a withering verdict on the TMO's failures at Grenfell Tower. It stated:

> Responsibility for the dangerous condition of Grenfell Tower following the refurbishment project, including the presence of combustible materials in the walls and around windows, rests primarily on those who designed, constructed and approved the work and some of those who manufactured and sold the materials they used. However, the TMO itself must take a share of the blame for the disaster.[55]

RBKC building control

In addition to its responsibilities as the owner of Grenfell Tower, RBKC was the building control body for the Grenfell Tower refurbishment. It was involved with the whole project, beginning in 2012 until it issued the completion certificate in 2016. John Hoban was a senior surveyor in RBKC's building control department between 1986 and March 2017, when he retired. The public inquiry was critical of Hoban's work:

> The two most serious errors made by Mr Hoban were, first, the failure to recognise that the presence of unmodified polyethylene cores rendered the ACM panels highly combustible, and second, the failure to recognise that the insulation, which was visible on the tower during his site visits, was not of limited combustibility.[56]

Nevertheless, the public inquiry accepted that Hoban's ability to carry out his task effectively was 'hampered by an excessive workload and poor management of the department as a whole'. It accepted that the restructuring of RBKC's building control department in 2013 'involved a substantial reduction in numbers'. Hoban complained about heavy workloads after the restructuring. He told the inquiry that the team of 15 surveyors lost six members of staff. Hoban also said he was responsible for overseeing 120–130 projects while doing the Grenfell Tower refurbishment.[57]

The inquiry apportioned some blame to RBKC building control for the state of Grenfell Tower after the refurbishment. The Phase 2 report stated:

> Building control was the last line of defence and had a statutory obligation to check for compliance with the Building Regulations. It had a responsibility to protect the public and it wholly failed to perform that function. It therefore bears considerable responsibility for the dangerous condition of Grenfell Tower immediately on completion of the refurbishment.[58]

LFB and Grenfell Tower

The London Fire Brigade was the final public body with responsibilities for Grenfell Tower. LFB had a long association with Grenfell Tower, notably with firefighters at North Kensington fire station. In 1979, Grenfell Tower was labelled a 'death trap' by a local ward councillor after residents attempted to evacuate during a fire.[59] RBKC's chronology sent to the inquiry recorded fires in 1988, 1997 and 2010. Crews also made annual familiarisation visits to Grenfell Tower.[60]

In 2010, a fire broke out in the lift lobby on what was then floor 6 of Grenfell Tower. The TMO told RBKC and LFB that there had been a leakage of smoke from the extraction system into the lobbies of floors 7, 12, 13, 15, 17, 18, 19 and 20. Some residents believed their lobbies were smoke-logged and that they were trapped in their flats.[61]

LFB fire safety inspecting officers also raised concerns. As explained earlier, a year before this fire, LFB had threatened to issue an enforcement notice because the TMO's risk assessments were inadequate.

In 2014, LFB inspecting officer Matthew Ramsey and others inspected the common parts of the building and found significant deficiencies. The fire risk assessment completed by Stokes did not address the smoke ventilation arrangements, a quarter of the automatically opening vents were not working and the emergency lighting was not maintained. LFB asked for a premises information box to be installed in Grenfell Tower, to assist crews in the event of a fire. Ramsey only issued a deficiency notice, as he anticipated these problems would be fixed during the refurbishment.[62]

In 2015, fire safety inspecting officers told Rebecca Burton, LFB's fire safety team leader for the borough, about concerns with Stokes' fire risk assessments. Over the following year, Burton raised the matter with the TMO on a number of occasions. During that time, the TMO promised to install a secure box in the lobby of Grenfell Tower. However, by the time of the fire, no such box with the relevant fire safety information had been installed on the premises.[63]

In 2016, LFB inspecting officer Michele McHugh inspected Grenfell Tower and found safety deficiencies. Panels covering service ducts on the eighth floor were broken, creating a breach in the void. Several lobby doors to the stairs did not close fully into the frame. Flat doors 44 and 53 were not self-closing. The means of escape were not clear. The evacuation plan was stay put, but 'residents interviewed at audit stated that they had not been informed of this'. Fire Action Notices were not displayed in the common parts.

McHugh issued another deficiency notice, giving six months to rectify them. She explained that this was done instead of an enforcement notice because LFB's enforcement policy, based on

CFOA's fire safety guidance, 'encourages co-operation and engagement with the responsible person'.[64]

The LFB's Operational Risk Database (ORD) for Grenfell Tower estimated 400 people might be in the building at night and therefore at risk. Other aspects of the entry were unsatisfactory. There were no plans of the tower, only a small aerial photo. The number of floors was incorrectly recorded as 20, the tactical plan was blank and emergency contact details were out of date.[65] LFB cannot excuse the gaps and errors in the Grenfell Tower ORD entry. However it would be a mistake to exaggerate these mistakes to decry the whole 7(2)(d) process by firefighters.

LFB was not responsible for inspecting the whole of Grenfell Tower. In particular, it was not responsible for the external walls, including the cladding, nor for the internal alterations to individual flats, including their doors, windows and other changes made during the refurbishment. The FBU has been LFB's most strident critic, but the brigade was not culpable for the Grenfell Tower fire.

CONTRACTORS WHO REFURBISHED GRENFELL TOWER

In 2009, RBKC commissioned consultants to produce options for the transformation of the ward in North Kensington where Grenfell Tower was located. The report proposed the demolition of the block, along with a new school. In 2010, RBKC began work on the Kensington Aldridge Academy and Kensington Leisure Centre, known as the KALC project. Late in 2011, RBKC and TMO officials began to discuss overcladding Grenfell Tower and replacing its windows, to improve one of its worst properties and improve its appearance next to the new facilities. This is how the refurbishment of Grenfell Tower was conceived.[66]

The inquiry's Phase 1 report argued that the refurbishment of Grenfell Tower carried out between 2012 and 2016 was most relevant to the immediate causes of the fire on 14 June 2017. A central part of the main refurbishment was the addition to the tower of ACM rainscreen panels, insulation materials, new windows, new window infill panels, flat doors and other remedial works.

Building works were carried out on every floor and every flat. Internal building works included fitting a new heating system, a new cold water distribution system, the refurbishment of the existing environmental ventilation and smoke control system, with some alterations to the lifts and dry riser system. Nine new flats were created from the ground floor to the third floor.[67]

RBKC funded the works. The TMO was the client for the refurbishment. The RBKC department of building control acted as building control authority. The inquiry's Phase 2 report, chapter 50, described the organisations and individuals involved. The main private contractors were:

- Studio E, the architect for the refurbishment.
- Exova Warringtonfire (Exova), fire engineering services.
- Rydon Maintenance Limited (Rydon), the design and build contractor.
- Harley Facades Ltd (Harley), cladding subcontractor to Rydon.[68]

Studio E

In 2011, Studio E Architects was commissioned by RBKC to design the KALC project. Studio E retained fire engineers Exova as sub-consultant. In 2012, Studio E was appointed by the TMO for the Grenfell Tower refurbishment and provided professional services throughout the project. Studio E did not have any significant experience in refurbishing or overcladding high rise residential buildings. It is unlikely that the firm would have won the commission if it had been put out to tender, because of its lack of relevant experience.[69]

The public inquiry laid out the litany of Studio E's failures. Studio E did not take active responsibility for the choice of the materials added to the external walls, including the ACM cladding and insulation. It did not investigate whether those materials were legal under the building regulations and guidance. Studio E failed to devise a proper cavity barrier strategy for the overcladding system, nor did it take a close interest in Exova's fire safety strategy (and the failure to complete the strategy).[70]

Although, Studio E's services were eventually transferred to Rydon after it became principal contractor for the refurbishment in 2014, Studio E was still responsible for the ongoing work. Studio E was also supposed to co-ordinate with RBKC building control, but failed to do so professionally.[71] The inquiry's verdict on Studio E was highly critical:

> Studio E was the architect for the Grenfell Tower refurbishment … As architect, Studio E had primary responsibility for the design of the facade of Grenfell Tower, among other aspects of the refurbishment. We have concluded that Studio E fell well below the standard to be expected of a reasonably competent architect in respect of that work. Its failures relating to the design of the external wall and the selection of materials to be used in its construction had catastrophic consequences. Studio E therefore bears a very significant degree of responsibility for the disaster.[72]

Exova

Exova, a fire safety company, was employed as a consultant by Studio E for the KALC project. It was retained by the TMO to advise on the Grenfell Tower refurbishment. There was no procurement exercise for its fire engineering services on the Grenfell Tower project.[73]

Exova was expected to deliver a fire safety strategy for the refurbishment. In 2012, Cate Cooney produced a first draft. When she circulated the draft, she also made some blunt internal remarks to colleagues that expose some of the flaws with safety in the block and with the project. She wrote:

> We have just sent through the existing fire strategy for it, basically 1970s 24 storey residential tower with non-residential use to first 4 floors. They are now adding additional levels which merges uses around a single stair. Not great. Basically I have told him we can massage the proposal to something acceptable, with separation, lobbies etc but that there are approval risks to the project on the ff shaft / MOE front. James has been to site and given some advice, but I don't know what he's said, but it would appear not much. They are making an existing crap condition

> worse so it's a matter of working the worse bits out and making the new stuff work. No sprinklers wanted.[74]

The most serious criticism of Exova made was that it failed to produce a final version of the fire safety strategy and failed to warn the TMO, Studio E or others about the consequences. The public inquiry found that 'Exova's approach was to do the minimum required at the time and, when asked for advice, to adopt a narrow and blinkered approach to the questions it was asked'. The inquiry concluded that 'Exova bears considerable responsibility for the fact that Grenfell Tower was in a dangerous condition on completion of the refurbishment'.[75]

Rydon

The TMO appointed Rydon as principal contractor, with responsibility for all aspects of the refurbishment project, including its design, compliance with the building regulations and other statutory requirements. It subcontracted most of the work on the refurbishment, notably to Harley, J S Wright & Co Ltd, S D Plastering Ltd and S D Carpentry Ltd.[76]

The public inquiry made numerous criticisms of Rydon in its Phase 2 report. It accused Rydon of failure to investigate the competence of sub-contractors, including Exova's work on fire safety, and to appoint a fire engineer on the Grenfell Tower project. Similarly, Rydon failed to properly evaluate and co-ordinate design work. The inquiry highlighted Rydon's failure to respond to concerns about fire safety, including the message from the TMO's Claire Williams about her 'Lacknall moment' and her subsequent inquiries about the fire rating of the cladding. Rydon was also accused of failures in site supervision, notably to detect serious defects in workmanship.[77] The inquiry's Phase 2 report came to a damning conclusion:

> Rydon failed in a number of important respects properly to perform its role as primary contractor for the Grenfell Tower refurbishment. It promised the TMO that when completed the refurbishment would comply with the Building Regulations, but it did not. When co-ordinating, supervising and monitoring the

work it did not give sufficient importance to the safety of the building's occupants and it displayed a casual attitude to fire safety throughout the project. As a result, Rydon bears considerable responsibility for the fire at Grenfell Tower.[78]

Harley Facades

In 2014 Rydon, appointed Harley as a sub-contractor to carry out the design and construction of the overcladding of Grenfell Tower. The public inquiry was scathing, arguing that 'Harley failed to achieve the standard of a reasonably competent cladding contractor in several different aspects of its work'.[79]

The inquiry found that Harley bears a significant degree of responsibility for the decision to use Reynobond ACM PE panels on the tower, despite the awareness of its staff of the risks of ACM from industry presentations and real fire reports on projects it had worked on. The is well summed up by an email from Daniel Anketell-Jones to Harley's founding executive Ray Bailey. Anketell-Jones wrote: 'Just that it's ridiculous. There is no point in 'fire stopping', as we all know; the ACM will be gone rather quickly in a fire! The whole point is to stop 'unseen' fire spreading in the cavity and moving to other parts of the building.'[80]

The inquiry pointed to other Harley failures. Harley was responsible for the use of Celotex RS5000 insulation, as well as Kingspan K15 as a last-minute substitute for RS5000, when there was a delay in obtaining supplies of that product. Harley failed to play an active part in the design of the cavity barriers. The inquiry found that 'Harley did not concern itself sufficiently with fire safety at any stage during the refurbishment'.[81] The inquiry Phase 2 report concluded:

> In the light of the evidence as a whole, we consider that Harley's work on the refurbishment was characterised by a failure to take its responsibilities seriously, ignorance, complacency and a failure properly to manage its staff. As the specialist contractor responsible for the external wall of the tower, the standard of Harley's work fell well below that to be expected of a reasonably competent cladding contractor and it must therefore bear a significant degree of responsibility for the fire.[82]

TOTAL BUILDING FAILURE

The public inquiry's Phase 1 report concluded that after the refurbishment the external walls of the building did not comply with requirement B4(1) of Schedule 1 to the Building Regulations.[83] The installation of the ACM rainscreen cladding put at risk the safety of the residents of Grenfell Tower and the safety of firefighters responding to the incident.

The inquiry's Phase 2 report, Volume 4, described the tortuous path to this disastrous choice. In 2012–13, Studio E, Max Fordham, Leadbitter and Artelia collaborated to produce cost estimates for the project, which included discussions about 'value engineering'. These estimates were used by RBKC and the TMO for the procurement of the principal contractor, Rydon. Studio E found CEP Architectural Facades Ltd, which triggered the initial proposal of zinc panels to aluminium. The saving was estimated at £300,000. In early 2014, there were extensive discussions between Harley, Arconic, Studio E, Rydon and CEP about the use of ACM rainscreen cladding. Rydon was under pressure to use ACM panels to make up a shortfall in its costing errors, and the opportunity to generate additional profit.[84]

The exact liability will no doubt be the subject of lengthy court proceedings in the coming years. Stephanie Barwise, counsel for one group of residents, stated at the close of inquiry hearings:

> In our first group, those responsible for the selection of ACM PE, we split the protagonists into two groups and rank them in order: first, Arconic, manufacturer of the ACM panel material; second, Studio E, as lead designer and architect; third, Exova, as fire engineer. Those bearing secondary responsibility are Harley, as cladding design subcontractor; Rydon, as design and build contractor; RBKC building control; and government, as custodian of the statutory regime.[85]

Other building failures contributed to events on the night of the fire, because they caused the breakdown of compartmentation. These include failures relating to doors and lifts, the absence of a wet riser, and no alarm system. Inquiry expert Barbara Lane established robust evidence of multiple fire safety failures within the building, which she described as a 'culture of non-compliance' among the owners and managers responsible for safety.

Flat entrance doors, crucial fire safety protection, had multiple defects. At the time of the fire, 13 of the flat entrance doors dated from when the tower was built, while 104 were installed by Manse Masterdor Limited in 2011–12, as part of the TMO's replacement programme. Three had been replaced since 2014 and nine fitted to new flats on the lower floors. The flat doors tested by BRE achieved only 15 minutes integrity fire resistance, half the required duration for compliance with Approved Document B. Nearly two-thirds (77 out of 120) of the self-closing devices were either not installed, disconnected or not maintained, so flat doors did not close automatically when residents left the building.[86]

The stair doors, which do not seem to have been replaced during the refurbishment, achieved a fire resistance as low as 12 minutes integrity. Dr Lane concluded that 'none of the stair doors from Level 4 upwards complied with the design guidance used for the original design of the building'. She added that these non-compliances 'would have contributed to the failure to prevent the spread of smoke to the stair'.[87]

Grenfell Tower contained only a dry fire main (dry riser) instead of a wet fire main. Lane argued that this was non-compliant with the design guidance in force at the time of original construction and is also non-compliant with current standards. On the night of the fire, firefighters were 'unable to get adequate water for firefighting from the dry main on the upper levels due to the lower capacity of the dry main system compared to a wet main system'. Additionally, the location of the main directly outside 'Flat 3s' (i.e. flat numbers ending in 3) 'posed serious problems for the firefighters, once conditions deteriorated within the lobbies'.[88]

The smoke ventilation system had not worked properly for years before the refurbishment, which led to LFB imposing a deficiency notice in 2014. It took until 2016 for work to get under way. Lane concluded that 'the design of the lobby smoke control system was substantially non-compliant with the performance requirements of the relevant British Standard'. The smoke control system was intended to operate on one floor only. Therefore the system could not 'operate on multiple lobbies simultaneously, and so could not prevent smoke entering the stair in circumstances where there was smoke on multiple floors'.[89]

The Grenfell Tower lifts were not firefighting lifts. Before 2014, the TMO's policies required they should be tested by its own lift engineer, but the inquiry found 'it was not done regularly or, it seems, at all'. After PDERS became the maintenance provider, none of its service visit reports recorded 'testing of the fire control switch and there is no other written record of its having tested the switch'. The PDER's engineer who visited the tower in April and May 2017 told the inquiry the fire control switch was in good working order. However, CCTV subsequently came to light showing that no checks were made during the May visit. The inquiry concluded, 'there is no reliable evidence of when the fire control switch was last tested by PDERS before the fire. In fact, the weight of the evidence suggests that the fire control switch was not regularly tested before 14 June 2017'.[90]

The inquiry also revealed that an automatic fire recall function was installed in 2006. Although it found evidence that the system was tested in 2013 and 2014, correspondence suggested that this had been disconnected by 2015. The inquiry was unable to discover exactly when or who disconnected it. Investigations carried out after the fire also showed that there was no connection between the fire alarm, the smoke detection system and the lifts.[91]

Finally, Grenfell Tower had no automatic or manual means of raising an alarm or providing voice alarm announcements. The absence of such systems would inevitably hamper any effort to evacuate or rescue residents from the building in the event of fire.

The neglect of building safety extended to the attitude towards vulnerable residents. Some information was gathered during the refurbishment. In 2014, a Rydon report identified 57 residents as having a sensory, cognitive or mobility impairment. Of the 297 people in Grenfell Tower on the night of the fire, 67 were children and 37 were adults with sensory, mobility or cognitive impairments. There were another 17 residents who had a sensory, mobility or cognitive impairment that was not recorded in other documents.

Grenfell Tower did not have a premises information box, despite the request from LFB to install one. The list of residents that the TMO produced on the night identified only ten residents with mental or physical impairments, only half the number recorded as vulnerable by the TMO in tenancy documents. The TMO was unable to provide the LFB with an accurate list of vulnerable residents until those who died in the tower had already lost their lives.[92]

GRENFELL TOWER RESIDENTS WARN

Grenfell residents did not passively sit back in their homes before and during the refurbishment of the tower. They organised to raise their concerns with the council and the TMO in the years before the fire. It was the residents who best represented their own interests.

Between 2010 and 2017, there were four groups representing the residents of Grenfell Tower. They were the Lancaster West Residents' Association, the Grenfell Action Group, the Grenfell Tower Leaseholders' Association and the Grenfell Tower Compact.[93]

In 2010, the Grenfell Tower Leaseholders' Association wrote to Robert Black, chief executive of the TMO after the recent fire in the block. They quoted the TMO's own local *Link* magazine, which had recently admitted that 'some properties in the portfolio appear to have had no investment in them for a considerable amount of time'. Grenfell residents chastised the TMO for treating 'the defects in the building exposed by the fire as a minor fault', when they had 'potentially fatal consequences'. Residents issued a chilling warning:

> If the fire alarm system is not functioning and the vents are not working then it should be considered no doubt as a major fault. They are used as measures to save lives; so if they are not working then obviously you are endangering the lives of residents of the building. What's more, we are certain that out of 120 families living in the block, no-one is aware of the evacuation procedure. We have never had an evacuation procedure booklet sent to us for the past 36 years … The staircases of the surrounding high-rise buildings are exposed to open air and natural light and so,

> in case of a fire, the smoke can easily escape. But Grenfell Tower, with its interior staircase, malfunctioning ventilation system, there is certainly a high probability that in the event of another fire, the whole building can become an inferno.[94]

Around the same time, the Grenfell Action Group was formed to oppose the Kensington Academy and Leisure Centre development. The founder members were Edward Daffarn and Francis O'Connor. In 2012 they started the Grenfell Action Group blog, which exhaustively documented the failures of the refurbishment process.

In 2012, the TMO refused to recognise the Grenfell Action Group. Daffarn tried again in 2014, with support from the Leaseholders' Association, but TMO declined to recognise the Grenfell Action Group, claiming that a residents' association covering the area already existed. In 2015, Daffarn and others organised a meeting of Grenfell Tower residents, attended by over a hundred people from more than fifty households. Soon afterwards, residents held another meeting and agreed to form a group which they called Grenfell Community Unite.[95]

In 2012, at the beginning of the refurbishment, Grenfell residents attended a meeting of the Lancaster West Estate Management Board, along with TMO and Studio E staff. Daffarn asked whether Studio E had experience of working on tower blocks and, if not, why it was proposed that it should be appointed as architect for the refurbishment.[96] Six months before the Grenfell Tower fire, Daffarn posted a devastating warning on the blog:

> It is a truly terrifying thought but the Grenfell Action Group firmly believe that only a catastrophic event will expose the ineptitude and incompetence of our landlord ... Unfortunately, the Grenfell Action Group have reached the conclusion that only an incident that results in serious loss of life of KCTMO residents will allow the external scrutiny to occur that will shine a light on the practices that characterise the malign governance of this non-functioning organisation.[97]

In its Phase 2 report, the inquiry chastised the TMO for its relations with residents. It concluded that between 2011 and 2017, 'relations between the TMO and many of the residents of the tower were increasingly characterised by distrust, dislike, personal antagonism and anger'. Many residents of Grenfell Tower 'regarded the TMO as an uncaring and bullying overlord, which belittled and marginalised them, regarded them as a nuisance or worse, and simply failed to take their concerns seriously'.[98]

The treatment of Grenfell residents was worse than that. Had RBKC, the TMO and other bodies listened to residents, consulted with them about key decisions and acted on their legitimate concerns, the refurbishment would have been carried out differently. Perhaps the fire might have been prevented.

8
The 'impossible' fire

The Grenfell Tower fire on 14 June 2017 led to the deaths of 72 residents and the devastation of a whole community. NHS England reported that 74 were hospitalised. Some 845 residents from surrounding streets were evacuated on the night of the fire and prevented by the police cordon from returning to their homes. The residents of Grenfell Walk were never able to return home.[1]

This chapter examines the events on the night of the fire, within the context of deregulation that had caused the entire building to fail. It looks at conditions inside the block during the first hour, from the perspective of residents and expert reports from the Grenfell Tower Inquiry (GTI).

The chapter examines the emergency intervention by firefighters, their officers and control staff. It looks at conditions inside the tower from the firefighters' point of view. Finally, it challenges some findings made by the inquiry chair, who claimed an alternative evacuation strategy was possible within the first hour.

CONDITIONS INSIDE GRENFELL TOWER IN THE FIRST HOUR

The public inquiry's Phase 1 report contained a very useful synthesis of the evidence concerning conditions during the early stages of the fire. This combined evidence from resident and firefighter testimony, CCTV footage, firefighters' thermal imaging cameras, phone calls and expert analyses, helps to reconstruct the origin and spread of the fire.

The fire began in Flat 16 and originated in the large fridge-freezer. The fire was accidental and Behailu Kebede, the occupant of Flat 16, bears no blame for what occurred.[2]

LFB responded swiftly to the first call, with ten firefighters on scene within five minutes. Despite their efforts, by the time a crew wearing breathing apparatus (BA) entered the Flat 16 kitchen, the fire had already begun to escape into the cladding and further up the building.

The available video evidence showed that some time before 01.14 the fire entered the cladding. Professor Luke Bisby suggested the most likely ways the cladding was ignited were:

> The impingement on the ACM panels immediately above the kitchen window of flaming and hot gases, either through an open window or through the extractor fan or the extractor fan panel, and subsequent ignition of the external ACM panels; the failure of the uPVC window jamb and attached insulation board allowing fire to penetrate into the back of the cladding cavity where it could ignite combustible materials.[3]

The ACM panels contributed to the rapid fire spread, given the polyethylene core of those panels and its particular properties. The inquiry concluded that flames accelerated up the east face of the tower, reaching the top by 01.30. The architectural crown of the building played an important role in increasing the rate and extent of horizontal spread of fire around the building. The extensive vertical cavities in the columns and the longer ACM cassettes within the columns contributed to the rate at which the fire spread downward.[4]

There were three principal routes by which the fire is likely to have penetrated the building from the outside: failure of the window glazing, failure of the kitchen extractor fans and failure of the uPVC window surrounds.

The failure of fire doors contributed to the spread of smoke and flames. Inquiry expert Dr Barbara Lane concluded this occurred through gaps between the door leaf and the door frame, by the presence of untested components (including, in a large proportion of the doors, glazing) and doors failing to self-close effectively after the residents had left. Professor José Torero argued that the early spread of smoke through the tower was most likely to have been a consequence of flat doors having been left open, rather than having failed while closed due to exposure to heat or flame.[5]

With fire outside their windows, the occupants of 'Flat 6s' were forced to leave. A number of the doors to those flats appear to have been left open, due to the absence of effective self-closing devices. This may have been the case for Flat 36 on floor 6; Flat 76 on floor 10; Flat 86 on floor 11; Flat 96 on floor 12; Flat 116 on floor 14; Flat 136 on floor 16; and Flat 146 on floor 17. As a result, smoke from those flats was able to get into the lobbies.[6]

Firefighters' activities in the first hour did not play a significant role in fire and smoke spread. The inquiry Phase 1 report acknowledged that smoke was 'limited to the floors on or adjacent to which active firefighting operations were being conducted'.[7]

Conditions inside the building

The public inquiry collected an extensive set of witness statements from residents who survived the fire and from firefighters who entered the building. Some residents and firefighters also gave oral testimony, elaborating on the conditions they faced inside the building. The inquiry also assessed transcripts of phone calls between people inside Grenfell Tower with the emergency services and other persons outside.

This evidence paints a harrowing picture of ever-worsening conditions, particularly half an hour after the fire started and from the time the fire had spread from floor 4 to floor 23. This evidence has also been subject to analysis by three experts appointed by the inquiry: Lane, Torero and Professor David Purser.

The evidence from residents about smoke, heat and poor visibility, as well as the interpretation offered by the experts, demonstrates total building failure within the first hour.

Lane's analysis

Lane's report provides a valuable analysis of smoke reported in lobbies and stairs throughout the building at various times, particularly during the period from 01.19 to 01.38. Lane found that smoke was reported in 14 out of 20 lobbies (floors 4–23) by this time. The smoke reported in these lobbies is described as ranging from hazy and light on floor 22 to thick and black on floor 16. The first evidence of thick black smoke flowing into the stair at floor 4 was reported by residents between 01.19 and 01.38. Residents who escaped from the upper floors during this period 'describe the smoke thickening progressively within the stair as they descended'.

Between 01.19 and 01.38, some residents walked up the stairs as a result of conditions lower down on the stairs, either because it was 'too smoky' or because they heard shouts to 'go back'. Lane's analysis found thick smoke in the lobbies on floors 6, 10, 11, 12, 15, 16 and 20; as well as thick smoke on the stairs at floors 4 and 5, which affected anyone coming down from the floors above.[8]

Between 01.39 and 01.58 conditions worsened. The number of lobbies affected by smoke increased to 15 out of 20; in 10 of these the smoke was described as thick and black. There are limited resident observations in this time period, with no evacuations from above floor 11 between 01.41 and 02.25. The situation worsened even further by 01.49 with no evacuations above floor 3 between 01.49 and 02.18. Firefighter evidence described thick black smoke in the stairs, from floor 3 up to floor 21 during this time.[9]

Lane's conclusions are worth quoting extensively:

> The conditions in the lobbies created intense fear amongst the residents which is likely to have affected the ability of many of them to leave their flat and descend the stair. As the fire progressed, and conditions worsened in the lobbies, but also directly on the external wall of their own flat, and adjacent flats, it was even more difficult to overcome this fear, even when they were eventually instructed to do so.
>
> The evidence from the residents has emphasised this stark dilemma for them all too clearly.
>
> The residents were left in conditions that appeared life threatening to them. So much so that even with a flame front entering their home or neighbour's home, entering the staircase was believed to be a fatal option. In some cases, this belief appears to have seriously impacted their decision making process with respect to self-evacuation. It is my opinion they required very specific advice tailored to overcome their fear of the lobby

conditions, and to be informed, for example, that there was a concerted effort to meet and rescue people in the stairs.

Their experiences created a belief that entering the staircase was a fatal option ... For some residents they had already experienced conditions in the stairs and considered them to be life threatening and so turned back. For other residents, they had entered the stairs or approached the stairs, and heard instructions not to go down the stairs at all, and again had turned back ...

There were substantial signals of danger to residents, and to firefighters. This included large quantities of thick smoke impacting sight and breathing immediately outside flat entrance doors, intense heat outside flat entrance doors, heat and smoke within the stair itself; rapidly advancing fire and smoke entering flats from the external wall, and ultimately horrific and rapidly increasing numbers of fires for the residents to attempt to escape away from within their own flats.[10]

Torero's analysis

Torero created a useful smoke movement timeline for the first hour of the fire, based on the calls made by residents inside the building to LFB control and other emergency services.[11] The comments made by residents are indicative of rates of internal smoke spread (Table 8.1).[12]

Table 8.1 Residents' comments on smoke.

Time of call	*Evidence*	*Caller*
01.21	'No, we can smell smoke from the – this side.'	Flat 195, floor 22
01.24	'I can't breathe ... Yeah, the fire in the kitchen (?)!'	Flat 96, floor 12
01.25	'Smoke. I can't get out. I'm tried to open the door and there's a lot of smoke.'	Flat 111, floor 14
01.26	'Yes, it's coming through the floor – from our main door because it's outside.'	Flat 95, floor 12

01.28	'There seems to be smoke, like … outside the in the flat I guess but it's – the smoke is coming into the house.'	Flat 73, floor 10
01.28	'If I open the door there's smoke on the landing.'	Flat 82, floor 11
01.29	'There's like smoke on our floor. I think it's the building, like right next, the house right next to us. We don't know what to do.'	Flat 142, floor 17
01.29	'It's completely smoky outside.'	Flat 201, floor 23
01.30	'There's smoke everywhere. You need to get right to the top.'	Flat 205, floor 23
01.30	'You can't see a hand in front of ya.'	Flat 194, floor 22
01.30	'Yes, and there's all smoke now.'	Flat 195, floor 22
01.30	'Oh, it's below us? Okay, because the smoke's … coming into my flat. What do I do?'	Flat 175, floor 20
01.32	'There's a lot of smoke in the flat and in the building and …'	Flat 155, floor 18
01.33	'It's inside of the room.'	Flat 81, floor 11
01.33	'I tried to get out to go through the fire escape and there's just thick black smoke.'	Flat 152, floor 18
01.33	'It's just getting worse outside.'	Flat 82, floor 11
01.34	'We couldn't get down the stairs, because the stairs is full of smoke.'	Flat 192, floor 22
01.37	'But there was so much smoke in the, in the corridor, we just ran back inside and close the door.'	Flat 133, floor 16
01.37	'It's coming from this corridor, the whole corridor, the whole corridor's black, we tried to run out and there's smoke …'	Flat 113, floor 14
01.38	'Not safe to go outside. So – No, it's all smoke.'	Flat 95, floor 12
01.38	'We tried to go downstairs, I just think it's too smoky.'	Flat 182, floor 21
01.38	Operator: 'Where is the smoke coming in?' Caller: 'Yeah, it's under the door. Yeah.'	Flat 115, floor 14
01.38	'Smoke is coming in because I smell it under [inaudible] … it's not much come in, but I can't go outside because I can't see outside at all.'	Flat 204, floor 23

Purser's analysis

Purser also highlighted the barriers faced by residents in leaving the building:

> During the fire rapid smoke filling of the lobbies was reported on many floors over a short period of a few minutes. Although the timing and filling rate varied somewhat on different floors, my preliminary analysis indicates that rapid smoke filling of the lobbies most likely occurred over a period from approximately 01.20–01.35 hours ...
>
> From my analysis of witness statements by flat occupants so far, my preliminary view is that that rapid filling of the lobbies by dense smoke from around 01.30 hours was a major deterrent and obstacle to occupants attempting to escape from their flats. Some decided not to enter the smoke and remained in their flats. Others felt their way to the stair entrance door through dense smoke, some returning to their flats and succeeding only after more than one attempt.[13]

Purser also explained the impact of carbon monoxide and hydrogen cyanide:

> Based on this assessment it is my opinion that if as little as 5 per cent of the combustion products from the burning PIR outside each flat penetrated the flat after the flames reached the flat exterior but before the windows failed, then the flat would be filled with very dense smoke and almost zero visibility. This would result in some immediate distress and breathing difficulties. If the flat occupants did not evacuate immediately, then after a few minutes exposure (between approximately 2–25 minutes depending up on the exact conditions), they would collapse unconscious due to the combined asphyxiant effects of inhaling CO and HCN.[14]

Residents' testimony

Even before the fire in Flat 16 was extinguished, residents left the tower coughing, spitting and covered in soot. Residents themselves described the scene graphically as they exited the building (Table 8.2).[15]

Table 8.2 Residents' comments on conditions early in the fire.

Exit	*Residents' evidence*
01.19	'When I got out of the building, I was spitting black stuff. I was coughing as I went down the stairs but I covered my mouth with my clothes and covered my sister's face with my robe.'
01.20	'I think I went into shock very soon after getting out of the building … I started crying and … decided that we should both get away from the area.'
01.26	'I was crying and shouting and calling for my father … as you can see, my face was full of marks of the smoke and it was black … and even inside my mouth … [clothes] were a bit smoky from the smoke.'
01.26	'When I got out of the building I started coughing. I think this was due to the smoke … The cough was a very deep cough. I felt smoke in my throat and when I spat out the spit was dark.'
01.29	'I had no shoes or slippers on my feet and that I was in my nightdress. I was so very upset and distressed. I could not quite believe what I was looking at and all the people still trapped inside. My daughter took us to hospital as we had inhaled a lot of smoke; my son is also asthmatic.'
01.31	'My wife became hysterical due to what we had been through and she started to scream. My daughter was now awake having woken up whilst we were coming down the stairs.'
01.32	'As we got out of the Tower, my daughters started crying and screaming as they saw the fire. They started saying "Our building is burning", "Our home is burning". It took a few minutes to calm them down and reassure them that everything would be fine. They were terrified.'
01.35	'I walked around in a daze … I was very, very dirty with soot and I was talking complete rubbish.'
01.35	'My father was really out of breath when we got out of the Tower so I tried looking for somewhere to sit him down … He sat down on a concrete chair. He was shaking, out of breath, sweating and looked completely exhausted.'
01.35	'I saw [my husband] coming out of the door. He was covered with soot, he was barefoot. He was disoriented and didn't seem to know where he was. He was going from side to side he couldn't walk …'

Smoke overcame a number of residents in the lobbies early in the fire. Residents who used the lift and escaped the building at 01.26 explained how it had stopped at floor 10 and become stuck. Tragically it seems that three residents who were also travelling in the lift, stepped out into the lobby. Their bodies were later recovered from floor 10 by firefighters.[16]

The resident from Flat 134 on floor 16 tried to reach the stairs via his lobby, using a wet towel to cover his face. He described the situation vividly:

> I was now in sheer panic. I started to use both hands to try and find the way out, I was running my hands along the wall but not finding the door … I started to inhale the smoke. I thought to myself 'shit man, this isn't going to end well for me'. I thought I was about to die. Just then I felt someone tapping on the right side of my leg, I looked down and that's when I realised that the smoke was much thinner on the floor. I could see a fire fighter, lying on the floor. He was lying face down across the threshold of the doorway with his legs out in the stairwell … I think I was in the hallway outside my flat for less than fifteen seconds, probably more like five seconds. I don't think I would have survived for fifteen seconds … I feel the firemen must have saved me as I was taking my last breaths. I think he was lying on the floor when he grabbed me.[17]

Having been assisted to the stairs, he was then able to leave the building by 01.34.

At around the same time residents from Flat 44 on floor 7 made it across their lobby and onto the stairs. However when they reached the fire floor they reacted to the smoke by turning around and returning to their flat. As the adult woman resident explained candidly in her witness statement:

> There was so much smoke. I could see thick, black smoke pouring out of the door from the fourth floor landing into the stairwell, as the fourth floor landing/fire door was being held open by the firefighter and his hose. The smoke hit me in the throat; it had a powerful and poisonous smell. When I saw the

> smoke, I expected fire to also be there. I panicked thinking that there might be fire coming into the stairwell ... I called ahead to my husband. I shouted at him, three times, 'Come back! Come back! Come back!' He turned around immediately and then we began to run to back up the stairs to our flat.[18]

This was confirmed by the adult male resident:

> Eventually, I came to the landing between the 5th and the 4th floors. By this stage there was a large amount of smoke in the stairwell and it was heavy and coloured black ... There was thick, acrid black smoke pouring out of the door he was holding open. It was filling the stairwell at that level. It was unbelievable. I heard my wife shout behind me 'Stop! Come back!' or similar words. She shouted about three times ... We ran back to our flat in a rapid time frame.[19]

Fortunately, firefighters knocked on their door and directed the family to leave the building, which they were able to do by 01.48.

Evidence provided by the residents themselves would indicate strongly that their means of escape was compromised very early in the fire. Some of those who subsequently died and some who later did escape had already had contact with the emergency services. A number had already told control staff, the police and their relatives that they had attempted to leave the building, only to be put off by smoke in the lobbies or on the stairs.

People inside the building

The inquiry Phase 1 report stated that there were 297 occupants of the tower at the time the fire started. Of those, 112 had left the building by 01.30. A further 36 successfully left in the following 10 minutes.

By 01.40, nearly half of the 297 people who had been in the tower at 00.50 had left. A total of 152 occupants remained inside the building. A further 20 occupants left the tower between 01.40 and 01.50. After 01.50 there was a period of 29 minutes during which no one from above floor 4 left the tower. By around 02.00, 129 people remained in the tower.

With the exceptions of Flat 9 on floor 3 and Flat 23 on floor 5, which were shortly to be evacuated, all the flats on floors 1–8 were empty. People remained in flats on floors 9–12 and 14–23.[20]

In the early stages of the fire, firefighters had very little intelligence about where exactly people were located in the building. An hour after the fire started a significant number of people were still on the upper floors of Grenfell Tower.[21] The inquiry found:

- Twenty-nine people sheltering in five flats on floor 23, some of whom had walked up from lower floors.
- Fourteen people in three flats on floor 22.
- Twelve people in three flats on floor 21.
- Nine people in three flats on floor 20.
- Two adults in one flat on floor 19.
- Nine people in two flats on floor 18.
- Five adults in one flat on floor 17.

Firefighters had very little knowledge about the particular needs of vulnerable people still in the tower. Subsequently, the inquiry identified:

- Floor 23, women and men in their sixties and seventies, a woman with breathing and mobility difficulties, another woman who also used a walker and five children.
- Floor 22, two people in their sixties as well as six children.
- Floor 21, a woman in her seventies and five children.
- Floor 20, a woman in her seventies and three children.
- Floor 19, a frail woman with dementia.
- Floor 18, five children.
- Floor 17, two adults in their sixties and seventies.

On floor 16 there was a man with dementia and mental health problems, on floors 15 and 14 men with emphysema, and on floor 11 an elderly blind man. Shortly after 02.00, firefighters were able to rescue a disabled woman and her family from the third floor.

In hindsight, many residents trapped on the upper floors faced a very difficult route to safety by themselves. Only three people escaped from the top floor and only two from floor 22. Many of those more able to escape by themselves had caring responsibilities for older adults and/or young children. Understandably, they were not prepared to abandon them in order to escape.

EMERGENCY INTERVENTION

On 14 June 2017, firefighters and other emergency services faced unique and unprecedented conditions at Grenfell Tower, especially given the role of the cladding. Lane concluded:

> I do not consider it reasonable that in the event of the installation of a combustible rainscreen system on a high rise residential building, the fire brigade should be expected to fully mitigate any resulting fire event. That is particularly so in circumstances where the fire brigade had never been informed that a combustible rainscreen system had been installed in the first place.[22]

Nevertheless, firefighters had to intervene. Control staff received calls from members of the public and mobilised crews from fire stations. Fire appliances (mostly) crewed by five firefighters were dispatched to an uncertain and risky incident, tasked with saving life. This was a heavy responsibility for professional staff.

On 14 June 2017, after a call at 00.54 (12.54 a.m.), initially three fire engines were sent to a single flat fire, with personnel consisting of two watch managers (WM), three crew managers (CM) and 11 firefighters (FF). The inquiry Phase 1 report describes firefighters' intervention to tackle the fire in Flat 16 (Table 8.3).

The public inquiry praised the intervention by firefighters:

> There was no suggestion that the response to the fire in the kitchen of Flat 16 could have been materially quicker … Thereafter, there was no significant delay in the crews' reaching floor 4, setting in a hose and entering Flat 16 … In short, CM Batterbee and FF Brown acted as swiftly as they reasonably could …[23]

This was supported by Lane, who stated: 'The fire and rescue services arrived at Flat 16 and successfully dealt with the internal flat fire – they controlled the internal flat fire using the internal firefighting equipment provided to them.'[24]

Table 8.3 Firefighters' intervention in Flat 16.

01.01	WM Dowden, CM Batterbee, FF Brown, FF De St Aubin, FF Dorgu and FF Badillo entered the building via the main entrance.
01.03	CM Secrett established the bridgehead on the second floor. FF De St Aubin set up the Breathing Apparatus Entry Control Point.
01.04	FF Dorgu, FF O'Beirne and FF Badillo set up the fire hose on the fourth floor.
01.04	BA Team One (CM Batterbee and FF Brown) tallied out at entry control and went to floor 4.
01.08	BA Team One entered bedroom number one in Flat 16, searched the bedrooms and attempted to enter the kitchen.
01.20	CM Batterbee and FF Brown entered the kitchen and put the fire out inside the flat.

Incident command

Watch manager Mike Dowden was the officer in charge at the Grenfell Tower for most of the first hour. He made professional decisions to tackle the fire and the unanticipated way in which it spread, as indicated by the LFB timeline and public inquiry Phase 1 report (Table 8.4).[25]

Table 8.4 Early incident command.

Time	*Incident command decisions*
00.59	WM Dowden examined operational risk information.
01.01	WM Dowden discussed the situation with Mr Kebede at ground floor level. WM Dowden instructed CM Secrett to set up the bridgehead on the second floor.
01.05	WM Dowden confirmed by radio to WM O'Keeffe, who was en route, the fire was on floor 4 and that two BA wearers would be required.

01.06 WM Dowden informed CM Secrett by radio that the fire had breached Flat 16's kitchen window and that he wanted a covering jet.

01.12 WM Dowden asked CM Davies to formulate an informative message, to explain to Control and anyone monitoring the Airwave radio about the incident.
WM Dowden noted that the external cladding was burning.
WM Dowden tasked firefighters to lay out a ground monitor at the East elevation.
WM Dowden ordered 'Make Pumps Six' and one Hydraulic Platform.

01.13 WM Dowden detailed WM O'Keeffe to manage the bridgehead on 2nd floor.

01.19 WM Dowden ordered 'Make Pumps Eight'.

01.24 WM Dowden ordered 'Make Pumps 10' after radio communication with WM O'Keeffe.

01.27 WM Dowden ordered 'Make Pumps 15', Aerial Ladder Platforms 2.

01.28 WM Dowden ordered a 'Persons Reported' message to control.

01.29 WM Dowden noticed a large quantity of debris falling from the tower and ordered the crew working the covering jet (FF Murphy and FF Cornelius) to move back.
WM Dowden realised that the jet was having no effect on the fire. He ordered the crew to turn off the covering jet and report to the bridgehead wearing BA.
WM Dowden and WM Watson discussed the incident resourcing, ordered 'Make Pumps 20' and two FRUs.

01.31 WM Dowden ordered 'Make Pumps 25'.

01.33 SM Loft and WM Dowden discussed incident command. They agreed that the FSG calls took priority and that SM Loft would manage the FSG calls.

01.36 WM Dowden instructed CM Wigley (Paddington FRU) to get a line operations system working from the roof to establish a drencher system to put the fire out from the outside.
WM Watson began to establish a BA staging area within the ground floor lobby, after receiving a briefing from WM Dowden.

01.42 Paddington's TL pitched outside the South elevation. This is only possible because WM Dowden had previously tasked CM Davis to secure a separate hydrant to connect to a fire engine that only supplies water to the turntable ladder.

01.50 WM Dowden discussed incident command with SM Walton, before handing over the IC tabard.

WM Dowden was subjected to intense questioning over three days by the inquiry, often asked about LFB policy matters well above his rank. He was also questioned minutely about his decisions on the night. The inquiry chair acknowledged he had given his evidence 'with courage and candour and without shying away from the difficult questions'.[26]

WM Dowden emphasised that his primary purpose as incident commander was to save life. He explained how his decisions were informed by his experience, LFB policy and training, and his situational awareness on the incident ground. He also made it clear that as a watch manager, he had planned and trained for a four-pump fire, and would have expected far more senior officers to take over incident command beyond that stage.[27]

WM Dowden laid out the constraints facing firefighters at Grenfell Tower: the failure of the lift override to allow firefighters to control the one remaining lift that was working, the limitations of the dry riser in terms of its placement in the lobbies rather than the stairs and the limited water it could provide, the limits of the automatic opening vent, the single, narrow stairwell and other building failures.[28]

WM Dowden was asked about the situation in front of him. He had a clear memory of people exiting the block and people subject to smoke inhalation.

WM Dowden was right to describe the Grenfell Tower fire as an 'almost impossible situation'. With situational awareness, he would have seen residents leaving the building in such a state as to suggest that the means of escape were not secure. Such warning signs would mitigate against any hasty decisions.[29]

Counsel to the inquiry asked WM Dowden about evacuation. He explained that to evacuate the building at 01.30 would have been 'very, very difficult'. He stated:

> I would say not at that point, but I think it's important to clarify, I think around that sort of time I only had six – from looking back at the Vision log, we had six fire appliances in attendance at that time. From my understanding, most of them, you know, were consumed in terms of the BA resource at the bridgehead. For me, at that moment in time, to facilitate and change a stay-put policy

> to a full evacuation was impossible. I didn't have the resource at that time. We're looking at 20 floors above the fire floor with just six fire engines in attendance, one central staircase. It's something I've never experienced as an incident commander before.[30]

Instead, his strategy as more firefighters began to arrive was 'to try and get as many people into that tower as we can as BA wearers to perform as many rescues as possible'.[31] WM Dowden did command a partial evacuation of the building, by directing BA crews to rescue FSG callers, as these were perceived to be the persons at greatest risk from the unprecedented and erratic fire.

On arrival, SM Andy Walton was briefed by WM Dowden and took over incident command for a very short time. Although SM Walton had more resources to commit, he faced a worsening situation, particularly with regard to the means of escape. SM Walton relinquished command minutes after taking over, with DAC Andy O'Loughlin becoming the officer in charge. (GM Richard Welch had assumed command at this time without knowing more senior officers had arrived. He made pumps 40 and declared a major incident.) DAC O'Loughlin was officer in charge until AC Andy Roe took command, after his arrival at 02.31.

The incident commanders in the first hours of the fire faced what WM Dowden described as an 'impossible situation'. SM Walton captured the dilemma they faced:

> So we were in a catch 22. There was no escape route for the people to use themselves, they had to be rescued, and we had to try and maintain that pathway for us to carry out those rescues, let alone those people to try and use it themselves. So that meant the firefighting was essential.[32]

Faced with this terrible situation, incident commanders and other officers had to improvise as best they could in entirely unprecedented circumstances. Incident commanders sent crews into the building to establish the conditions for escape and assist residents to leave. They deployed 133 separate breathing apparatus teams in the course of the intervention. More than 200 firefighters were sent into the building in breathing apparatus – some multiple times – to extinguish the fire and rescue people.[33]

Emergency control staff

On the night of the Grenfell Tower fire, 11 LFB control room operators (CROs) were on duty at Stratford, London's back up control room. They took hundreds of calls on the night, including more than 150 FSGs. Control staff in North West Fire Control, Essex, Kent, Surrey and Merseyside also played a valuable role.

The inquiry's Phase 1 report praised their role: 'It cannot be doubted that CROs saved the lives of many, and some of the residents of Grenfell Tower have been able to express their gratitude to the CROs who helped them.'[34]

LFB control staff carried out their professional duties diligently throughout the duration of the fire. In the early stages they mobilised firefighters and alerted other agencies (Table 8.5).

Table 8.5 Early control staff decisions.

Time	*Control staff action*
00.54	CRO Pam Jones took a call from Behailu Kebede reporting a fire at Grenfell Tower. CRO Jones confirmed the address and asked how many floors there were in the building, to which Mr Kebede replied 'four'.
00.55	CRO Jones entered the relevant details from the caller onto a call collection form on the Vision system. The PDA was automatically selected for a fire in a residential dwelling: three fire engines.
00.57	CRO Christine Howson took a call from a remote monitoring company Tunstall Response. The operator confirmed that an automatic fire alarm had actuated at Grenfell Tower.
00.59	AOM Peter May at brigade control saw the incident on his Vision screen and observed that the address was given as a tower. He amended the incident code to a fire in a high rise building, which triggered an additional fire engine.
01.00	SM Andrew Walton was paged by brigade control and informed about the fire at Grenfell Tower as the closest officer at this rank on duty to the incident address.

01.15	Brigade control paged WM Matthew Leaver, a fire investigation officer, to inform him there was a fire in progress at Grenfell Tower.
01.23	AOM Deborah Real phoned Thames Water Authority to inform them of the fire in progress at Grenfell Tower and ordered a water services technician.
01.27	Brigade control request best approach road for officers. SM Walton had difficulty finding a route to the incident due to road closures.
01.29	AOM Real called the London Ambulance Service and asked for their attendance.
01.50	CRO Yvonne Adams called on a landline to the mobile phone allocated to CU8 in order to pass on FSG calls.

Within half an hour of the first call, the control room was overwhelmed with calls from the public, including residents inside the tower. This was clear from the number of calls that began to be diverted to other fire control rooms and to other emergency services. The inquiry reports acknowledge the long duration of some calls taken by control staff:

> By this point, there were three CROs in the LFB control room who were on long FSG calls. CRO Russell had started a call with Jessica Urbano Ramirez in Flat 201 on floor 23 at 01.30 which lasted for 55 minutes until 02.25. CRO Jones had started a call with a member of the El Wahabi family in Flat 182 on floor 21 at 01.38.38, which lasted approximately 59 minutes, until 02.49. CRO Duddy had started a call only three minutes earlier, at 01.54.14, with Roy Smith in Flat 95 on floor 12, which lasted for 40 minutes until 02.24.[35]
>
> At 01.41, a BT operator connected to North West Fire Control said that a caller for the LFB had hung up after waiting for about five minutes. That caller was Debbie Lamprell. At 01.41 CRO Aisha Jabin's call back to Debbie Lamprell was connected. The call lasted for over 40 minutes, until 02.21.[36]

However, the public inquiry was far too critical of control staff communications with residents on the night.

The Phase 1 report criticised control staff for not following national guidance. Phase 2 found that they acted in accordance with the LFB policy in force at the time (PN539), which hadn't been amended to reflect national guidance on false reassurance. Control staff were trained to give callers reassurance, both to help them make rational decisions in very frightening circumstances and out of basic humanitarian decency towards people in distress. The inquiry failed to properly absolve control staff of the initial criticism, despite accepting that they followed policy and training.[37]

The inquiry was wrong to claim control staff 'failed properly to assess escape routes on the night of the Grenfell Tower fire'. No matter how well trained, nobody working from a remote control room could judge whether escape routes were safe or not. To expect control staff to do so would be to invite them to offer potentially fatal advice. The inquiry's stance reflected its lack of knowledge of the profession and skills of control staff.[38]

Firefighters

The inquiry Phase 1 report praised the intervention firefighters made on 14 June 2017:

> The accounts given by many of the firefighters demonstrate that they displayed a remarkable degree of courage and devotion to duty. In many cases individual firefighters entered the burning building on several occasions in disregard of their own safety in an attempt to rescue those who were trapped.[39]

The Phase 2 report echoed that finding. It added that 'the firefighters involved in the firefighting operations outside the tower did all that they reasonably could to extinguish the fire and to protect the lives of those inside the building'.[40]

Firefighters did their professional duty, often putting their own lives on the line to make some significant rescues.

The inquiry Phase 1 report was clear that firefighters had not told residents to return to their flats. It stated: 'Although some witnesses appear to have assumed that instructions to that effect had been given by the firefighters, there is no evidence that they had.'[41]

There is testimony from residents that on encountering firefighters on the stairs or the lobbies, the firefighters gave terse instructions to go down and leave the building. There is also evidence of firefighters knocking on doors early in the fire to give these instructions (Table 8.6).[42] Firefighters also recalled some interventions during the first hour or so (Table 8.7).[43]

Table 8.6 Early interactions between residents and firefighters.

Exit	*Residents' comments about firefighters*	*Floor*
01.23	'I walked in front and opened the door to the stairwell, where I met a firefighter who was going up the stairs, quite quickly. He stopped for a moment and just said "run, get out". We started running down. We met a second firefighter who also said: "run, get out".'	7
01.26	'I then heard a female firefighter tell me to go downstairs. She motioned for me to keep walking downstairs past her.'	5
01.26	'I woke my dad who was still sleeping, and soon after I remember that a firefighter knocked on our door. He had no mask or breathing apparatus, and simply said: "do you guys want to start coming down?"'	7
01.26	'We saw another fireman on the eighth floor. This fireman told us to go down.'	10
01.27	'One firefighter then turned to me and said that I had two seconds to get out … I tried to put my daughter in her push-chair but the firefighter saw me do this. He had his helmet on and said that there was no time and that we just needed to leave.'	5
01.27	'When I got to the stairs, the door was held open by a fireman with an oxygen mask on. [My wife] and the kids were already going down the stairs. The fireman took off his mask and was shouting for people to get out, hurry up … Shortly before arriving at the mezzanine floor I believe I saw two firemen in the corridors telling people on the floor to get out.'	11
01.35	'I was still in the communal area at this point just staring at the smoke. One of the firemen looked at me and told me to get out and to not take anything with me.'	5
01.43	'I asked a fireman "shall I knock on more people's door", he said, "get out of the building now".'	6

Table 8.7 Firefighters' efforts to assist residents.

Time	*Firefighter witness statements*	*Floor*
01.30	'It wasn't until I opened the 16 floor lobby Oh, "Oh shit" alright definitely we need to make a rescue here because that smoke's pretty bad … So when I first went in I went as low as possible I was literally on my belly, I fully went into the foyer when I felt a body that was kneeling over, so I stood up, he was quiet, he was light so I put my hand right round him and picked him up. He felt light but he wasn't a dead weight so I thought he might still be conscious, brought him out and he was actually conscious, his eyes were wide open and he was in a state of shock.'	16
01.45	'We moved up to the 6th floor, knocked on, I can't remember which flat it was but one of the doors was answered … I knocked on the door and it was answered by an adult male. I asked if we could come in, we were wearing our breathing apparatus he was in the flat with an adult female who I am assuming it was his partner as well and child which was a little boy about 4 or 5 years old … The man said to me "Do we have to get out". I replied "Yes we have to get out". The man then said "Through that smoke?" It took me back a bit, I took my breathing apparatus off, it was clear in the flat. That comment threw me a bit, I had been thinking that the best thing to do was to get these people out and now I was looking at the smoke. I said "Yes you have to get out now, if you don't you won't get out".'	6
01.55	'This point the temperature just soared. It went from what I would call normal hot to unbearable. I dropped to my knees and I think I actually lay down on the floor. I knew we couldn't stay there. I crawled out and called to FF Badillo that we had to get out of there. We went out of the flat but the temperature was like nothing I have ever experienced before and I've been to enough fires to experience heat. I knew we were in trouble; it was just too hot and I was running out of air. We were also really high up in the building and no one was coming to get us. We just had to get out. I shouted for FF Chris Dorgu and he shouted back but we couldn't see each other. It took a while for him to find us. I grabbed his arm and told him I was running out of air so he was to stay with me and we needed to get out. I remember one other low pressure whistle sounding but I was not sure who it belonged to.'	20

02.15	'Eventually CM Gallagher and CM Tillotson returned to us. They came into the flat and took their masks off. Their ADSU alarms were going off. We discussed how we were going to work this to get everyone out safely. They had brought up 2 new BA sets … We put one of the new sets on the mum so she was wearing it on her back. Then got a spare mask set out and I hooked this up to my spare hose so the little girl would be breathing my air … CM Tillotson was virtually out of air, he only had 10 bar left which is nothing, probably a minute at most. So he attached his mask to the other new set and carried it. We said we had to go and quickly so I picked up the little girl and held her in my arms against my chest. We knew we needed to get down as fast as we could as we were low on air between us and the whole place was being consumed by the smoke …'	9

Almost every resident who left the building after 01.50 required some physical assistance from firefighters and often received irreplaceable advice from emergency control staff. Residents were very clear in their appreciation of these efforts (Table 8.8).[44]

Table 8.8 Residents describe their rescue by firefighters.

Exit	*Residents' comments about firefighters*	*Floor*
02.19	'The firemen helped my daughter put on her mask. I had an oxygen tank and plastic mask that covered my entire face. My glasses did not fit underneath, so I had to take them off, so was not able to see very well … One of the firemen carried my daughter out and I followed … I continued to hold onto the fireman with my right hand just above his elbow.'	9
02.21	'A firefighter came up to the top of the ladder and told us we would have to descend one by one. He gave some direction about how we should leave the flat and to get onto the ladder.'	5
02.25	'After about half an hour I saw a light coming towards me and I heard a fireman's voice. The fireman had a light on his forehead and I could see it through the smoke. I don't remember speaking to him. He wanted to hold my hand to help me down the stairs but I was too dizzy to walk very far and he began to carry me. I remember very little from this point. I remember saying thank you. I remember that he said that we needed to go downstairs. I could not continue walking and he soon had to carry me down because I couldn't walk.'	23

02.41	'I remember all four of us standing by the staircase and the firefighter gave us each a deep breath of oxygen from their breathing apparatus.'	12
02.53	'I started to pass out someone grabbed my left arm and said "casualty". It was a complete coincidence, it just felt like I was blessed in that moment. I was being passed from person to person as I went down the stairs because I kept feeling hands on and off of me. I remember there was a firefighter that forced his hand over my hand on my face to stop me from talking because I was inhaling too much smoke.'	15
03.07	'The firefighter I was holding on to was encouraging me to keep going. We were walking down the stairs relatively quickly … I just remember the firefighter I was with say "we made it". I could hear a lot more noise now.'	12
03.53	'There were two firefighters, I think one was black and one was white, one of them grabbed my arms and the other grabbed my legs. I was feeling dizzy and weak, I could feel myself going. They carried me down to the ground floor.'	15
04.13	'I went downstairs with a firefighter walking alongside me and helping me along but I can't recall if he was actually physically holding me. He wasn't carrying me at first but after going down about 2 floors I fell to the ground completely exhausted and struggling to breathe. I felt one of the firefighters lift me up from the ground and then place me over his shoulder before carrying me down the remaining floors to the ground level.'	10
04.20	'As we left the flat it looked like there was a wall of firemen between our door and the fire exit. This was in addition to the firemen accompanying each of us … We crossed the landing area to get to the stairwell, it was pitch black other than the firemen's lights that they had on them … As we ran down the staircase I remember as we reached each floor, being aware of a fireman there guiding us down.'	10
04.47	'The fireman shouted "can you see the torch, walk towards the torch". I followed [my partner] and he followed the firefighters through the door to the stairwell … One of the firefighters took [my daughter] … and another steadied me and we continued down the stairs.'	11
06.05	'I relied on the two firemen to guide me down. I was holding onto the fireman's jacket in front of me with my left hand … I do recall catching my foot on something, but I do not know what this was. The firemen from behind me helped to free my leg and we continued down the stairs.'	10
08.07	'The firefighters gripped me either side under my armpits to take me down the staircase. They just whisked me out of the flat.'	11

The care with which firefighters intervened was well summed up by one firefighter:

> I went round to the ambulance bit to check if the lady we had rescued from the twentieth (20th) floor was alright. She was there, sat up and she was talking. She was alive so that was cool. She recognised me straight away and she said 'thank you, thank you'. We gave each other a hug. I said 'you're out now, you're fine' and she said 'thank you, thank you'. It was really quick. I just wanted to make sure she was alive ... We managed to get her back, the CPR had worked.[45]

Firefighters faced huge uncertainties about the number of residents long into the fire. Some flats were empty, with some residents at work, on holiday, visiting family, away for leisure or religious commitments. As late as 05.50, incident commanders still believed that 115 people were unaccounted for. In fact by then there were still 67 residents in the building, but only two could still be rescued after that time.[46]

Shortly after the Grenfell Tower fire, the LFB estimated that firefighters had rescued 65 people from the building. The evidence provided by residents who survived the fire suggests that figure is about right. An additional 30–40 residents also received direction from firefighters and emergency control staff to leave the building.

WAS 'MASS EVACUATION' POSSIBLE ON THE NIGHT?

The central thread running through the inquiry's Phase 1 report was the claim that Grenfell Tower should have been evacuated. The report stated:

> Once it was clear that the fire had spread out of control, that compartmentation had extensively failed, but that evacuation remained possible, a decision should have been made to evacuate the tower ... prompt evacuation would have resulted in the saving of many more lives ... That point had been reached by 01.30 at the earliest and by 01.50 at the latest.[47]

The FBU does not accept the inquiry's conclusion that a decision to 'evacuate' should have been taken at 01.30 (or at least by 01.50). Inquiry lawyers did not make sufficient allowance for the actual conditions inside the building, when it wished for a unique intervention.

The public inquiry used the term evacuation too loosely in its Phase 1 report. Evacuation in plain language often means where residents are able to leave of their own volition. However, evacuation has a precise meaning. The Home Office defines an evacuation as 'the direction of people from a dangerous place to somewhere safe', while a rescue is 'where a person has received physical assistance to get clear of the area involved in the incident'.[48]

When the inquiry wrote of 'evacuation', in reality it proposed mass rescues. Firefighters would have had to clear floors and physically assist many residents to leave their flats, cross their smoke logged lobbies and descend smoky stairs.

Means of escape

The inquiry's assumptions ignored how swiftly the means of escape had been compromised by smoke for many residents. Although the stairs remained passable, the public inquiry underestimated the barriers over the entire route of escape that residents faced. For most, the means of escape consisted of two steps: leaving their flats to enter the lobby and then reaching the stairs through that lobby.

Those residents who managed to reach the stairs were able to leave the building. However it is clear from the witness evidence that many residents attempted to do this but still turned back because of conditions in their lobbies. Even those who took precautions, such as placing wet towels over their faces, experienced difficulties before and immediately after 01.30.

In her first Phase 1 report, Barbara Lane argued that any prospect of evacuation was earlier than suggested by the inquiry Phase 1 report. Lane wrote: 'In analysing these figures, after the event, it is clear to me that the window from 00.58 to 01.40 was when the total evacuation of Grenfell Tower needed to occur.'[49]

The inquiry accepted David Purser's distinction between conditions up to about 01.49 and those thereafter. He considered that 'until about 01.49 it was still possible to descend the stairs without danger of collapse'. After that 'it was still possible to escape by the stairs, but was more hazardous due to the dense smoke and absence of visibility in both the lobbies and the stairs'.[50]

By 01.40, conditions had deteriorated significantly and were extremely arduous. At the time, the building still contained more than 150 people and as far as firefighters would have known, potentially another one hundred people. After 01.50, no residents were able to exit the building unaided for the next half an hour. Almost all of those leaving after that required some assistance from firefighters.

Communication

The inquiry's evacuation scenario ignored the difficulties of communication with residents, including the most vulnerable and distant from the exit. Grenfell Tower had no alarm or public address system serving the whole building. At 01.43, firefighters used a loudhailer to urge residents to leave the building: 'This is the fire service. If you are able, exit the building.' Unfortunately very few residents were able to act on the advice, even if they had heard it.[51]

Although some residents within Grenfell Tower had managed to speak to LFB control staff or other emergency services, this was not sufficient for a mass evacuation. The transcript of a call at 01.28 between the occupants of Flat 73 on floor 10 and the Metropolitan Police illustrates the difficulties. The last exchange was:

> MPS Operator: 'Okay. Do you want to evacuate. Evacuate the building, please.'
> Male Caller: 'Evacuate the building?'
> MPS Operator: 'Yeah. Evacuate. Get everybody out. Get everybody out. And get everybody out.'[52]

The residents of the flat did not evacuate at that time. Another occupant called LFB at 01.41 and explained 'obviously, the thing is we can't evacuate because it's pitch-black outside'.[53]

The inquiry's evacuation proposal effectively boiled down to firefighters ascending the building to knock on doors. SM Daniel Egan explained to the inquiry what this meant: firefighters 'would systematically go through a couple of floors at a time, with crews going along, banging on doors, giving people a chance, you know, trying to cajole them out if they were in there'.[54]

Resources

Any approach going floor by floor would inevitably be very resource intensive. Some people may still be asleep. Others would have mobility or other vulnerabilities that make swift movement in smoky conditions far harder. The presence of older people and young children would be a major consideration in smoky conditions. The first firefighters into the building advised residents to get out, knocked on doors and in some cases, assisted residents to leave the building. As conditions became more arduous, firefighters faced unenviable decisions about whether they could risk moving people through hot and smoky conditions.

At 01.30 there were only 30 firefighters on the fireground. Only four BA teams (eight firefighters) had entered the building, two of those to extinguish the fire in Flat 16 and then withdraw. By 01.40 there were still only 61 firefighters present.

At 01.30 there were no firefighters with extended duration breathing apparatus (EDBA), the first would arrive at 01.35. No command unit had arrived that might have facilities to organise an evacuation – the first would arrive just after 01.30 (and in any case would take several minutes to set up). There was no turntable ladder that might be used to limit the spread of fire in certain parts of the building and thus provide some temporary place of safety for those on the upper floors. The first turntable ladder arrived at 01.32 and again inevitably took time to set up safely. By the time these resources were in position and operational, the window for evacuation had effectively closed.

Inquiry contradicts itself

The public inquiry Phase 1 report made a number of qualifications to its mass evacuation proposal that effectively undermined it. It admitted that no expert firefighting evidence was received on the approach of the LFB at the Grenfell Tower fire. The inquiry doubted that 'there was a sufficient number of firefighters at the scene by 01.30 to have allowed a safe and efficient assisted evacuation of all of the tower's occupants' and admitted there was 'very little practical guidance' on how to go about a mass evacuation. Yet the chair concluded:

> I fully recognise that, even if an order to evacuate (whether total or partial) had been given by 02.00, some lives might still have been lost. I also recognise that the mechanics of carrying out an evacuation of any sort in rapidly deteriorating conditions would have presented its own risks to the lives of residents and firefighters.[55]

These caveats, along with substantial evidence from residents and firefighters, undermine the speculation about mass evacuation. There was no prior planning to carry it out. The LFB had not developed standard operating procedures for carrying out this type of mass evacuation. The resources necessary for such a strategy were not worked out. Firefighters were not trained for mass evacuation, nor to undertake a risky manoeuvre in the middle of a rapidly spreading fire. In such circumstances, inventing such tactics in the heat of the moment would have been a dangerous gamble, not a practical strategy.

In its Phase 2 report, the public inquiry recognised the limitations of its earlier speculation. The chair wrote:

> It must also be acknowledged, however, that the LFB was not alone in this failing. At the time of the Grenfell Tower fire there was no national operational guidance on how to evacuate a residential high-rise building and it does not appear that any other fire and rescue service in the United Kingdom had included in their operational policies or training any guidance on the practical aspects of carrying out an evacuation, beyond saying that it should be considered …
>
> The evidence suggests that before the Grenfell Tower fire evacuations of high-rise residential buildings had been partial rather than total. (At any rate, we have not been provided with any evidence of a total evacuation of a residential high-rise building in London or elsewhere in the United Kingdom.)[56]

The real counterfactual at Grenfell Tower was that more lives would have been saved had the cladding not been installed, nor the building failed on fire safety grounds in other significant respects, including windows, doors, the ventilation system, lifts, stairwell and other failures. No fire of this magnitude would have taken hold of almost the entire building without those failures. The inquiry's verdict to blame firefighters, before it subjected the owners, managers and contractors to serious scrutiny, was unfair and unreasonable.

Many residents expressed their gratitude for firefighters' efforts to rescue them:

> I have nothing but praise for the ordinary firefighters of the London Fire Brigade who rushed in to that Tower and risked their lives to save people like us. Two of them saved my daughter's life ... Words cannot express my gratitude to them.[57]

> With regard to the firefighters. I can only say that without them and their extreme bravery and courage my daughter would not be alive.[58]

> I was beginning to lose consciousness. I was mentally exhausted from the trauma. The fireman was still with me, I was leaning on him. Without the fireman helping me I could have not made it out of the building.[59]

> The two firefighters who came for us, saved our lives. I did not meet those two firefighters afterwards. For us they were angels.[60]

> I want to thank the firefighter who saved my life. I am so grateful and owe him my life. He risked his own life to save me and for that I will be forever grateful.[61]

> I have no doubt that if the firemen hadn't knocked on my door, my daughter and I would have slept through until it was too late and died. The firemen were amazing. They saved my daughter's life and mine. I cannot thank them enough for what they have done.[62]

After the fire I visited Kensington Fire Station in Old Court Place. I had gone there to meet and thank a firefighter called Jamal [Stern] who I had been told was the firefighter who pulled me out of my landing on floor 16.[63]

9

Deregulation never stopped

In the eight years since the Grenfell Tower fire, there have been five different administrations at Westminster, four of them led by Conservative politicians. Theresa May was prime minister at the time of the fire, but only lasted two more years, deposed after failing to negotiate Brexit. In 2019, Boris Johnson became prime minister with the pledge to 'get Brexit done'. He duly won the December general election, but was hoisted on the petard of his incompetent handling of the Covid-19 pandemic, among other failures. In 2022, Liz Truss lasted as prime minister for 49 days, shorter than the shelf-life of a lettuce, defeated by economic illiteracy. Rishi Sunak managed less than two years, routed at the general election. He passed the baton to Labour's Keir Starmer.

Deregulation never ceased to be Westminster government policy after the Grenfell Tower fire. Although Conservative ministers were less bombastic in their open zeal for deregulation, it remained the guiding principle throughout their administrations.

This chapter examines the steps ministers took in the aftermath of the Grenfell Tower fire, particularly on building safety and fire safety, while still attached to deregulation. It further evaluates the Grenfell Tower Inquiry (GTI), especially its final, Phase 2 report. The public inquiry only superficially got to grips with deregulation, despite finding significant evidence of it. The chapter also describes the safety campaigns by the FBU and other organisations.

WESTMINSTER – DEREGULATION CONTINUED

Although the 2017 Conservative manifesto included the pledge for 'one in, two out' deregulation, for the first period after the Grenfell Tower fire, it did not apply, at least as far as building safety and fire safety were concerned.[1]

However deregulation never really went away. In the last days of Theresa May's premiership, the Department for Business, Energy and Industrial Strategy published a White Paper, *Regulation for the Fourth Industrial Revolution*. It claimed:

> The government ... ensures that alternatives to regulation (such as voluntary standards or incentives) are considered before regulation is introduced, and that regulation is regularly reviewed to minimise unnecessary burden to business.[2]

In 2021, prime minister Boris Johnson convened the Taskforce on Innovation, Growth and Regulatory Reform. It claimed the UK's exit from the EU presented new opportunities to redesign regulation. It sought to 'ensure that our markets are open and competitive and that businesses can scale up unencumbered by any unnecessary administrative burdens'. Within months, the taskforce published its report, which made over 100 recommendations. The first was to 'reimpose the 'one in, two out' regulatory duty on all government departments'.[3]

Johnson's *Build Back Better* growth plan included pledges was 'to ease burdens and cut red tape'. The business department consulted on *Reforming the Framework for Better Regulation*. Business secretary Kwasi Kwarteng, extolling the virtues of the UK's approach to regulatory reform, promised: 'Where markets achieve the best outcomes, we will let them move freely and dynamically. We will pursue non-regulatory options where we can ... where regulation does not achieve its objectives or does so at unacceptable cost, we will ensure it is revised or removed.'[4]

The FBU made a submission to the consultation, arguing that it indicated 'the Westminster government's desire to impose more deregulation and privatisation, to create the conditions for market competition and profitable opportunities for businesses within public services'.[5]

Although Johnson's government was committed to 'cutting red tape and minimising burdens' and considered reintroducing the 'one in, two out' rule, it hesitated due to Covid-19 and net zero plans.[6]

Liz Truss revived hyper-deregulation. Her business secretary, Jacob Rees-Mogg, drew up detailed plans for red tape budgets, setting a ceiling on the overall cost of regulation, with no exemptions. Despite his own enthusiasm for tackling bureaucracy, Rishi Sunak did not proceed with Rees-Mogg's proposals.[7]

But deregulation refused to go away. In April 2024, the Centre for Policy Studies, the old Thatcherite think tank, demanded that the government 'establish a new regulatory budget to replace the one in, one/two/three out rules ... This should cover the whole regulatory state, with no exemptions.'[8]

Building safety

The Westminster government implemented a wide range of building safety measures in the aftermath of the Grenfell Tower fire. Ministers commissioned Judith Hackitt to conduct an independent review of building regulations and fire safety. Hackitt's interim report concluded that 'the whole system of regulation, covering what is written down and the way in which it is enacted in practice, is not fit for purpose, leaving room for those who want to take shortcuts to do so'.[9]

In 2018, Hackitt published her final report. The FBU welcomed the direction of travel towards a new, more robust regulatory framework. However general secretary Matt Wrack argued that it was 'perverse that the Hackitt review does not recommend an outright ban on flammable cladding'.[10]

Cladding ban

In the immediate aftermath of the Grenfell Tower fire, ministers had to deal with flammable cladding found on hundreds of other high rise and other buildings. In 2018, MHCLG consulted on banning the use of combustible materials in the external walls of high rise residential buildings.

The FBU made a submission, arguing that ministers must impose a universal ban on these combustible materials on external walls of all structures of whatever type or height, irrespective of when they were constructed. As a precaution after the Grenfell Tower fire, only Class A1 materials should be used in wall construction for high rise buildings.[11]

In 2018, the Westminster government amended the building regulations and restricted the use of materials in an external wall to those achieving Class A2-s1, do or Class A1. The ban applied only to the use of combustible materials in and on the external walls of new blocks of flats, hospitals, residential care premises and student accommodation over 18 metres in height.

In 2020, ministers reviewed the ban and consulted on extending it to hotels, hostels and boarding houses, and whether to reduce the height threshold. The FBU's submission reiterated the demand for an outright cladding ban and the 11-metre height threshold.[12]

In 2022, ministers brought hotels, hostels and boarding houses within scope of the ban. They also promised to introduce a complete ban on the use of the type of composite material used on Grenfell Tower in the external walls of all new buildings and buildings undergoing building works, regardless of height or use. Although they retained the ban at 18 metres height, Approved Document B was amended to introduce new guidance for buildings between 11 and 18 metres.[13]

Building Safety Act

The Building Safety Act 2022 was the Westminster government's most significant response to the Grenfell Tower fire. In 2019, MHCLG launched a consultation, *Building a Safer Future: Proposals for reform of the building safety regulatory system*, based on Hackitt's recommendations. The FBU was disappointed that the proposals did not 'take the opportunity to evaluate the building regulations themselves or explore the balance between statutory proscription and voluntary guidance'. The union was also critical of some specific plans, which still left too much power in the hands of private businesses. The FBU argued that the proposals did not 'challenge the deregulatory, free market free-for-all that weakened fire safety and thereby contributed to the Grenfell Tower fire'. They did not 'embed in statute the role of the fire and rescue service in the new building safety regime'.[14]

In 2020, the Westminster government published its draft Building Safety Bill, covering new buildings of 18 metres or six storeys. They proposed to create a new Building Safety Regulator within HSE. It imposed new duties on building owners, known as the 'accountable persons', including the appointment of building safety managers. The bill renamed private approved inspectors 'building control approvers'. It abolished the existing Building Regulations Advisory Committee, replacing it with the Building Advisory Committee for England.

The Housing, Communities and Local Government Committee conducted an inquiry into the bill. The FBU's initial assessment was that the Building Safety Bill would create a more robust regulatory regime for high risk homes and some other sleeping accommodation. However, the FBU told the committee that the government had 'missed an opportunity to undertake a deeper, more systemic review of the building safety regime'. The fundamental shift during the 1980s towards deregulation, privatisation and contracting out was 'crucial to understanding what went wrong at Grenfell Tower and continues to hamper building safety'. The FBU also opposed the scheme to permit the Building Safety Regulator to seek private sector involvement if the fire authority could not assist. The bill's explanatory notes stated:

> It is expected that the Building Safety Regulator will work cooperatively with Fire and Rescue Authorities and local authorities to secure support from them. If the local authority or Fire and Rescue Authority in the area where the higher-risk building is located is unable to provide support, the Building Safety Regulator could seek support from other Fire and Rescue Authorities and local authorities whose capability is less stretched, or from the private sector.[15]

In 2021, the Westminster government published its Building Safety Bill. Matt Wrack gave evidence on behalf of the FBU to the bill committee. The FBU drew particular attention to the culture of complacency and lack of competence in the construction sector that led to tragedies like Grenfell, and to fire and rescue service cuts, which had led to fewer fire safety inspections. The FBU made a further written submission highlighting the need for more fire inspectors and the risks from private 'approved inspectors' undermining local authority building control.[16]

The Building Safety Act 2022 did not implement all the changes recommended by Hackitt. The building safety manager role, acting on behalf of building owners and as a necessary point of contact for residents, was removed late in the legislative process by communities secretary Michael Gove. The Building Safety Act created a new regulatory regime for 'higher-risk' buildings. It defined these as buildings that are 18 metres or seven storeys. The FBU, Royal Institute of British Architects and the Local Government Association (LGA) called for an 11m threshold.[17]

The devolved administrations also made changes to their building safety regimes. The FBU made submissions, generally praising these governments for going further than Westminster, while underlining the urgent need for investment in fire inspectors from within the firefighting workforce.[18]

Approved Document B

Only after the Grenfell fire did the Westminster government consult on tightening Approved Document B. In 2018, MHCLG consulted stakeholders. The FBU submission expressed the union's disappointment at the limited scope of the proposals, which were confined mostly to cosmetic changes to Approved Document B, rather than correcting the failings that led to the Grenfell Tower fire. The revised guidance still did not explain how to evacuate high rise residential buildings.[19]

MHCLG subsequently issued a call for evidence, to carry out a technical review of Approved Document B. The FBU submission warned that 'instead of reassessing the overall building safety regime, the current government seems to take an approach of more or less business as usual'. The government seemed 'happy to allow the construction industry and its lobbyists to continue to define the terms of regulation and guidance, which … puts profit above public safety'. The FBU demanded:

- Clear, baseline, prescriptive national standards for fire safety.
- Mandatory fire certification for certain designated premises.

- Properly resourced fire authorities to inspect and enforce fire safety legislation.
- Statutory national competency standards and accreditation for risk assessors.
- Scrapping private approved inspectors – bring all building control back into local authorities.
- A rolling review of Building Regulations and guidance, with new legislation and publications at least every five years in light of new developments.
- Statutory stakeholder committees that include the trade unions and other fire professionals, not secretive cabals of industry lobbyists and senior civil servants, should review and propose improvements to regulation and guidance.[20]

Fire safety

The Fire Safety Act 2021 was the first piece of legislation arising from the Grenfell Tower fire. In 2019, the Home Office put out a call for evidence on the Regulatory Reform (Fire Safety) Order 2005. The FBU submission warned:

> It should not have taken the Grenfell Tower fire... to prompt the Westminster government to review the regulatory system. This review should not be an excuse for more deregulation. It is deregulation that got fire safety into this mess.[21]

In 2020, the Westminster government introduced its Fire Safety Bill. It extended the Fire Safety Order 2005 to include the external walls and internal doors in the 'common parts' of buildings with two or more domestic premises, making them subject to audit and enforcement action by fire inspectors. The FBU briefed MPs for the second reading, made a submission to the Public Bill Committee and updated peers in the House of Lords. The FBU supported the modest clarification of the law, but argued would require significant investment in fire inspectors.[22]

In 2020, the Home Office also launched a wider consultation on fire safety. The FBU supported clarifications to the Fire Safety Order, regarding the 'responsible person' – building owners accountable for safety failures. The union supported the proposal for 'Approved Codes of Practice' into fire safety, like those that support the health and safety at work regime. However the FBU opposed introducing powers for building owners to issue notices on tenants and fire authorities to charge for enforcement activities and false fire alarms.

The FBU raised concerns about the Home Office task and finish group overseeing Grenfell Tower Phase 1 recommendations. The FBU was particularly unhappy that the industry-led competency steering group lacked trade union representation. Most of all, the FBU emphasised the need to recruit and train more firefighters as fire inspectors to tackle the additional responsibilities.[23]

White Paper

The FBU also had to face down efforts to impose changes to the fire and rescue service on the pretext of addressing the Grenfell Tower fire, when their proposals were nothing of the sort. The first challenge came in 2020, when HMICFRS published its first *State of Fire and Rescue* report. Chief inspector for England Thomas Winsor proposed scrapping the National Joint Council (NJC), the collective bargaining arrangement between the FBU and fire employers. He favoured imposing a pay review body instead. Winsor proposed tearing up the Grey Book of firefighters' conditions, giving a free hand to chief fire officers to decide contracts locally. He also wanted firefighters' roles expanded with no additional pay. The FBU challenged HMICFRS's independence and proposed instead investment, national standards and a statutory advisory body.[24]

In 2022, the Home Office published its White Paper, *Reforming Our Fire and Rescue Service*, parroting proposals made by the NFCC and HMICFRS. The FBU submission argued that the White Paper was flawed in many respects. It contained no provisions to improve the service firefighters provide to communities and promised no new investment in firefighters or equipment to improve the service. The White Paper threatened the legal rights of firefighters to collectively bargain with employers over pay, conditions, safety and other vital contractual matters. If implemented, it would have cut firefighters' pay, increase hours, roles and the intensity of work, introduced unsafe practices and stretched the service to breaking point. The White Paper threatened the right of firefighters to take lawful industrial action. It sought to give chief fire officers powers to dictate firefighters' pay, conditions, duty systems, safety and other matters.[25]

In 2023, the Home Office published its belated response to the White Paper consultation. It dropped almost all its draconian proposals, promising only to press ahead with a College of Fire and Rescue, and impose operational independence for chief fire officers. Neither were implemented before the general election. However the government did rush through minimum service levels, undermining the right of firefighters, control staff and other workers to take effective strike action.[26]

Ministers did not improve their reporting to parliament after the Grenfell Tower fire. In 2018, the revised National Framework simply added calls for efficiency, without central funding to back it up.[27] Ministers statutory reporting to MPs remained tardy and self-congratulatory. Ministers were late reporting to parliament.[28]

EVACUATION UNRESOLVED

The evacuation of high rise residential buildings understandably became a much-debated subject after the Grenfell Tower fire. The response from central government was totally inadequate.

In 2020, the Home Office consulted on the public inquiry's recommendation to introduce personal emergency evacuation plans (PEEPs) in high rise residential buildings. The FBU strongly supported the introduction of mandatory PEEPs for all residents who need them. The union commended disability rights organisations for their tireless campaigning.[29]

Despite the inquiry's recommendation and wide support, ministers rejected proposals for PEEPs. In 2022, Lord Greenhalgh, then fire minister, outraged many when challenged about the government's veto of PEEPs. He said:

> On practicality, how can you evacuate a mobility-impaired person from a tall building before the professionals from the fire and rescue service arrive? ... On safety, how can you ensure that an evacuation of mobility-impaired people is carried out in a

> way that does not hinder others in evacuating or the fire and rescue service in fighting the fire?[30]

Instead, the Home Office consulted on Emergency Evacuation Information Sharing (EEIS). The FBU's submission condemned the Home Office decision to sideline PEEPs. The FBU argued that 'the Westminster government's EEIS proposal waters down the responsibility on tower block landlords and gives the fire and rescue service responsibility for the emergency evacuation of all residents'.[31]

NFCC guidance

In 2017, the National Fire Chiefs Council (NFCC) published guidance on a temporary change to a simultaneous evacuation strategy in purpose-built block of flats. The irony of this 'temporary' guidance is that eight years on from the Grenfell Tower fire, it is still in place. The NFCC revised the guidance on three further occasions. Among other measures, it supported the use of waking watches. The FBU opposed the NFCC guidance.[32]

Three years after Grenfell, *Inside Housing* magazine revealed that more than 420 buildings across England had a 24-hour waking watch, with more than 300 fires in these blocks.[33]

Spiralling costs of waking watches, sometimes passed onto residents by landlords or levied on flat owners directly, led to widespread disquiet, with questions raised at Westminster. By 2023, DLUHC had spent more than £80 million on various waking watch relief and replacement funds.[34]

Similarly, in 2020, the previous GRA 3.2 high rise firefighting guidance was withdrawn, replaced with NFCC high rise guidance. However the FBU was unhappy with this guidance, particularly as it allowed incident commanders to 'follow local service procedure' in determining whether firefighters would go to the uppermost floors without having started their breathing apparatus sets.[35]

The NFCC's approach triggered a dispute with the FBU about high rise firefighting safety. The NFCC's high rise guidance proposed deploying firefighters above the bridgehead without their breathing apparatus started up. The FBU argued that is a hazardous procedure, putting firefighters and the public at greater risk and in breach of the duty of care fire employers have to their employees. Most chief fire officers, including in London, backed away from the procedure after the FBU intervened. Sadly, a small number of chief officers, backed by the NFCC, continued to promote the dangerous policy.[36]

MHCLG evacuation research

In 2020, MHCLG contracted OFR Consultants to research evacuation of high rise residential buildings. One of the OFR reports, *Means of Escape in Residential Buildings* (2023) ran abstract quantitative models for evacuation, based on restrictive assumptions. The heights selected did not reflect real worst-case scenarios, such as Grenfell Tower, Harrow Court, Shirley Towers or Lakanal House. Best case exemplar models did not help firefighters facing a number of worst case scenarios at high rise residential buildings.

The modelling recognised the difficulties people with vulnerabilities face in evacuating unaided, but the reports failed to take a position on PEEPs. They did not address the implications of very tall buildings for breathing apparatus wearers. The consultants argued against making second staircases mandatory, despite MHCLG secretary of state Michael Gove acceded to this demand in buildings over 18 metres. The priority seemed to be with the 'economics' of high rise residential buildings, not fire safety or firefighting intervention.[37]

EVACUATION GUIDELINES

In 2019, the public inquiry's Phase 1 report recommended that the government develop national guidelines for carrying out partial or total evacuations of high rise residential buildings. In response, the Home Office and MHCLG established a joint technical steering group to address the inquiry's recommendation. The FBU participated in the steering group, but it met infrequently and produced few results. It took the Home Office three years to publish *Evacuation from Fire in High-Rise Residential Buildings: A Rapid Evidence Review*.

In 2022, the Home Office, NFCC and LFB held a live testing exercise at a disused 17-storey tower block with two staircases, to run a series of evacuation simulations. FBU officials observed the proceedings. The exercises took place over 10 floors of the building. The most notable were a full evacuation using an alert system and a single staircase. This involved 80 evacuees and took more than 19 minutes to fully evacuate. Another full evacuation exercise used door knocking, but without an evacuation alert system, with a single staircase. This involved 68 evacuees and took nearly 29 minutes to fully evacuate. Both tests included far fewer people than in Grenfell Tower, in a smaller space in unrealistic conditions (without smoke), and yet still took a very long time to complete.

In 2024, more than four years after the inquiry's Phase 1 report, the Home Office published, *Evacuation Guidelines for Fire and Rescue Services during Fire Emergencies*, which contained nine guidelines to support operational guidance during a full or partial evacuation from high rise residential buildings. The guidelines, only nine pages in length, summarised self-evident truisms about evacuation. On behalf of the FBU, Matt Wrack wrote to home secretary James Cleverly to complain about the guidelines and their failure to meet the inquiry's recommendation.[38]

THE GRENFELL TOWER INQUIRY

Prime minister Theresa May announced the Grenfell Tower public inquiry just a day after the fire. On 28 June 2017, retired judge Sir Martin Moore-Bick was appointed to chair it. The terms of reference were set following a public consultation. On 15 August, the public inquiry was formally established.[39]

The inquiry divided their proceedings into Phase 1, the events on the night of 14 June 2017, and Phase 2, the causes of the events. The inquiry involved more than 600 people and organisations as core participants, including the FBU. The inquiry disclosed more than 300,000 documents.

The inquiry received 668 statements from firefighters, mostly from the LFB. It heard oral evidence from 88 firefighters, control staff, officers of the LFB and other brigades. Statements from another 262 fire and rescue personnel were read into the record.

FBU representatives attended police interviews with members and provided support to those giving testimony.[40]

The Phase 1 hearings took place over 88 days, from 21 May 2018 to 12 December 2018. The Phase 1 report was published on 30 October 2019. It consisted of four volumes, 900 pages and 46 recommendations. The Phase 2 hearings took place over 312 days, from 27 January 2020 to 10 November 2022. The Phase 2 report was published on 4 September 2024. It consisted of seven volumes, 1,700 pages and 58 recommendations. The inquiry formally closed on 10 February 2025, with its proceedings transferred to the National Archives.[41]

The FBU participated fully in the public inquiry. FBU officials attended in person to listen to the proceedings and to support members giving testimony. The union made more than 20 written submissions, some 50 pages long. The FBU's legal counsel Martin Seaward made oral submissions at the beginning and end of each module.

The benefits of a public inquiry

In September 2024, the public inquiry finally published its Phase 2 report, more than seven years since the fire. At the time, there were 17 public inquiries running in the UK. The Grenfell inquiry itself involved more than 200 legal professionals, at a cost of £178 million, mostly in legal fees.[42] At the close of the hearings, Imran Khan, counsel for one group of residents, cast doubt on the value of public inquiries. Khan argued:

> But for all of its advantages, what public inquiries do is they give the appearance of change without any change. They give the appearance of difference without making any difference ... It appears that those in power simply dither and dawdle, waiting for these events to dissolve from public consciousness ... so those in power can evade taking any remedial action to prevent future disasters.[43]

A strong case can be made for the value of the Grenfell Tower Inquiry. Its Phase 2 report was a damning indictment of central government failure over forty years. The key findings stated:

> We conclude that the fire at Grenfell Tower was the culmination of decades of failure by central government and other bodies in positions of responsibility in the construction industry to look carefully into the danger of incorporating combustible materials into the external walls of high-rise residential buildings and to act on the information available to them …
>
> In the years that followed the Lakanal House fire [2009] the government's deregulatory agenda, enthusiastically supported by some junior ministers and the Secretary of State, dominated the department's thinking to such an extent that even matters affecting the safety of life were ignored, delayed or disregarded.[44]

The public inquiry report traced deregulation to the Thatcher governments, notably through the weakening of building regulations, the introduction of ambiguous Approved Document B guidance, the part-privatisation of building control and the privatisation of BRE. The inquiry registered that deregulation had continued under the Blair administrations, notably through the Regulatory Reform (Fire Safety) Order. And the inquiry sharply admonished the failures of the Cameron administrations in the years before the fire.[45]

The Cameron government accelerated deregulation, despite denials from ministers when they were quizzed by the inquiry. Eric Pickles was responsible for building safety and fire, yet when he gave testimony, he urged counsel to 'use your time wisely' because he was 'extremely busy'. Challenged about supposed exemptions to deregulation, he retorted that he 'swore on the bloody Bible'. Pickles finished by referring to 'the nameless I think it was 96 people who were killed in the Grenfell fire'. The inquiry rejected his evidence and came to a withering verdict:

> We saw a significant number of documents that showed that DCLG saw itself as a deregulating department … Lord Pickles was not only aware of, but supported, that approach, including the application of the policies to the Building Regulations. While he was Secretary of State deregulatory considerations appear to have permeated every aspect of the department's development, assessment and implementation of policy.[46]

Brandon Lewis was twice fire minister and similarly committed to deregulation. The inquiry found that he 'expressed reluctance to pursue the idea of a national fire safety regulator because he was not attracted to the idea of introducing additional regulation'. Lewis was challenged by the FBU, about the need to regulate fire risk assessors, but remained unmoved. The inquiry supported the FBU's view.[47]

The public inquiry released a mountain of government evidence, which would have remained sealed away behind the 30-year rule or longer, before any of it would have come out. The BRE reports commissioned by central government, the minutes of BRAC and other committees, never mind the private correspondence between senior civil servants and their advisers were dragged into the light, exposing the inner dynamics of deregulation.

The Grenfell Tower Inquiry also deserves credit for its evisceration of manufacturers, construction industry lobbyists and private bodies, who were immediately culpable for making, selling, promoting and licensing materials that should never have been used on Grenfell Tower. As we saw in Chapter 8, the venal role of Arconic, Kingspan and Celotex was publicly exposed by the inquiry. The mountain of documentation, private correspondence and testimony will provide the mainstay of the police inquiry. If police and the courts do their jobs properly, then some of those responsible for the Grenfell Tower fire will go to prison. Justice, long overdue, may eventually be done.

The public inquiry also made searing criticisms of the private bodies such as BRE, BBA, NHBC and Building Control Alliance, which were supposed to test and certificate products as safe, but instead colluded with manufacturers to license flammable cladding and insulation for use on high rise buildings. The inquiry repeatedly identified the contradiction between private bodies undertaking public safety oversight, stating that there was 'the conflict between the need to act as a commercial organisation in order to attract and retain customers and the need to exercise a high degree of rigour and independence in its investigations'.[48]

The public inquiry carried out a detailed investigation into the immediate public bodies responsible for safety at Grenfell Tower. Both the council RBKC and the tenant management organisation were rightly subject to severe criticism, particularly for their roles in the refurbishment and for relations with the residents of Grenfell Tower.

The inquiry also subjected LFB to thorough scrutiny, drawing its senior management and policy making into sharp relief. The inquiry was careful to distinguish its criticism of LFB principal management from the work of firefighters and emergency control staff. Moore-Bick 'recognised that the firefighters who attended the Grenfell Tower fire displayed enormous courage and selfless devotion to duty'. By contrast, 'the LFB's failure was attributable to a chronic lack of effective leadership, combined with an undue emphasis on process and a culture of complacency'.[49]

The Grenfell inquiry generated some wider benefits for the fire and rescue service, mostly from expert reports. Luke Bisby's excellent report, *Grenfell Tower Inquiry: Regulatory Testing and the Path to Grenfell*, should serve as a primer on building safety regulation for years to come.

Water expert Ivan Stoianov's report, *The Provision and Use of Water for Fighting the Fire at Grenfell Tower on 14 June 2017*, also raised valuable problems with the provision of water for firefighting that deserve further discussion. Similarly, David Purser's insight that infants and children absorb asphyxiant gases at about twice the rate of adults has substantial implications for firefighter training, fire survival guidance and rescue efforts. In 2024, the FBU asked its officials to take up these issues with principal managers in brigades.[50]

Criticism of the public inquiry

Despite some undoubted virtues, the public inquiry also had flaws, which limit the lessons it took from the Grenfell Tower fire. An honest examination of these limitations is necessary.

The FBU supported the call for a public inquiry. But the union wanted a thorough investigation focused on central government policy, especially deregulation. Matt Wrack said:

> This inquiry needs to look not just at the immediate causes of the fire and the response to it, but also at who was responsible for the building and for any alterations made to it. But it also

> needs to look much wider at the regulations and the regime that now operates in building control, planning and fire safety. All of these have seen significant changes in the recent past as part of an agenda of de-regulation and cutting so-called 'red tape'. Those who took those decisions are going to have to start facing the consequences.[51]

The inquiry began with a consultation on its terms of reference, carried out by Martin Moore-Bick. The FBU made a submission, insisting residents must be central. The FBU's submission also demanded a focus on Westminster's policy of deregulation. It stated:

> There has been a long-running deregulation agenda, under the euphemisms of 'better regulation' or 'cutting red tape' as well as a 'soft touch' enforcement agenda that has emphasised the impact on business rather than compliance with safety standards. The inquiry should examine the impact of this on the robust application of fire safety provision.[52]

The consultation received 554 written responses. Sadly, neither the chair nor the prime minister took sufficient heed of the FBU. First, Moore-Bick did not explicitly commit the inquiry to investigating central government policy before the fire. Second, the judge discounted demands to examine social housing policy as part of the inquiry, despite the demands of Grenfell residents to do so. Third, Moore-Bick confined the inquiry's focus on fire matters solely to LFB, ignoring the political and industrial context of the fire and rescue service as a whole. Theresa May accepted Moore-Bick's draft without amendment. The FBU criticised the narrow terms of reference publicly.[53]

The narrow terms of reference were compounded by the chair's decision to divide the inquiry into two phases: the first dealing with events on the night and the second with the events that led to it. Moore-Bick never convincingly explained his motivation for starting with the night of the fire.[54]

Sadly, the two-phase division had a major impact on the conduct of the inquiry. It prolonged the inquiry's proceedings considerably, with several matters from the night the fire revisited in Phase 2. It took too long – seven years – to complete its work. While the Covid-19 pandemic undoubtedly delayed hearings, the choice of two phases, and to proceed back to front, hampered the process.

The structure of the inquiry had perverse outcomes. The inquiry hearings started and finished with criticism of firefighters, not politicians and business. Firefighters giving oral evidence had to endure a grilling on the stand, as counsel put the wrong questions to junior officers. Inquiry lawyers pursued the unfounded hypothesis that their vague evacuation strategy was an obvious choice for firefighters to make and that they were somehow hampered by stay put advice, rather than the actual conditions in the tower. Chapter 8 of this book, as well as the evacuation research discussed earlier in this chapter, shows that such a mass rescue is far harder in real life.

The inquiry process invited some lawyers to grandstand demagogically when giving their opening and closing statements, relishing the opportunity to attack LFB, firefighters or the FBU without the full right of reply (except indirectly, through the union's counsel). The final hearings offered counsel an opportunity to repeat tropes against firefighters that had been answered in the course of proceedings. Many firefighters, including many who attended the fire and rescued residents, were insulted by the haughty condescension of lawyers, who had never put themselves in danger to help others.

The public inquiry's decisions about who to call to give evidence were also baffling. The inquiry failed to call leading politicians to the stand. None of the living prime ministers – May, Cameron, Brown, Blair or Major – were called, despite their deregulatory policies and clear precedence in other inquiries. Nor was Boris Johnson called, despite his role as London mayor for eight of the nine years before the fire and architect of the damage to LFB. While lesser politicians like Pickles, Lewis, Barwell, Wharton and others appeared and were exposed as culpable, they still kept their titles.

The inquiry seemed extremely wary of political matters, avoiding occasions when politicians spoke about cladding, fire safety or other relevant issues in parliament or to other audiences. This reflects a weakness in all public inquiries. A clue was given by Luke Bisby's expert report, which contained an extensive discussion of warnings about cladding before the Grenfell Tower fire. Bisby quite rightly examined the Garnock Court fire in 1999 and the subsequent investigations, including by BRE and the Environment, Transport and Regional Affairs Committee. In the course of his narrative, Bisby felt obliged to state:

> However, I should make clear at this point that I have been advised by the Inquiry that the Committee's proceedings are, in its view, proceedings in Parliament within the meaning of Article IX of the Bill of Rights 1689 and thus may not be the subject of investigation or comment by the Inquiry. In those circumstances, I have been asked not to pass comment on the evidence which was given to the Select Committee.[55]

To his immense credit, Bisby did evaluate the select committee's work, including the written and oral submissions, along with the final report. Bisby also gave credit to the FBU's submissions.

By contrast, the Phase 2 report contained only cursory references to the select committee. It stated: 'The Select Committee heard evidence on 20 July 1999 from a variety of witnesses, including witnesses from BRE and the department. It also received memoranda from the department and several other organisations.'[56] It was hugely disappointing for the public inquiry to leave out any reference to the FBU, which had the foresight to warn about dangerous cladding right in the seat of power to an audience of politicians, 18 years before the Grenfell Tower fire.

The inquiry and the FBU

The attitude displayed by the public inquiry towards the FBU could be characterised as grudging tolerance, rather than genuine engagement. The FBU played a full part in the inquiry from beginning to end as a core participant, with only a small staff and legal team. Despite representing the overwhelming majority of firefighters who entered Grenfell Tower on the night of the fire, providing witness statements and written submissions, the inquiry failed to call any FBU official to give evidence. Despite frequent criticism aimed at the FBU by lawyers, the inquiry failed to call general secretary Matt Wrack to rebut those views.

The inquiry diminished itself by publishing Colin Todd's attack on the FBU. Todd had his own problems during the investigation. Initially regarded as an expert, he faced criticism as author of the LGA's *Fire Safety in Purpose Built Blocks of Flats*, censure for comments made about 'poor disabled people crawling on their hands and knees down smoke filled corridors' and ridicule for his bizarre defence of Carl Stokes' risk assessments. In his last submission dealing with recommendations, Todd chose to misrepresent the FBU's views on fire risk assessors and the role of firefighters. Todd didn't bother to seek clarification from the FBU, nor did he engage with the union's central demand for a statutory advisory body. His comments sneaked out with the last batch of inquiry paperwork. Todd's conduct demeaned himself and the inquiry.[57]

The inquiry's Phase 2 report expended more than a million words trying to get to the bottom of how building safety and fire safety was weakened. The FBU had played an open, public role in opposing deregulation from the beginning, against the Thatcher, Blair and Cameron administrations. The FBU had warned of cladding risks, problems with stay put, weaknesses with Approved Document B, poor enforcement of the Fire Safety Order and the need to mandate standards for fire risk assessors. Yet the inquiry made only three paltry references to the FBU, in two paragraphs, citing none of the evidence provided by the union or its interpretation of the failures that led to the fire. To find anti-union prejudice among lawyers charged with exposing the truth was disappointing, although not altogether surprising.

Inquiry versus fire and rescue service

The inquiry made a fundamental error by restricting its terms of reference simply to LFB and did not interrogate the failings of fire and rescue service principal management as a whole. It compounded its error by appointing Steve McGuirk as its firefighting expert – a decision opposed by the FBU. McGuirk was a retired chief fire officer and leading figure in the fire safety regime that failed before the fire. He was not independent of the organisations and individuals who led the fire and rescue service during that period.

The result was that McGuirk made a worthless contribution, adding nothing to a vital area of the inquiry's work. His long overdue report, published almost four years after the fire, consisted mostly of speculation, garnished with obnoxious attacks on individual firefighters. He endorsed the inquiry's view of mass evacuation, despite knowing there was no planning, training nor any precedent for making up such a policy on the night of the fire.[58]

The inquiry failed to interrogate the role played by CFOA/NFCC in the decades before the Grenfell Tower fire, giving the likes of Ken Knight an easy ride. Ministers took advice exclusively from chief fire officers during those crucial years, and no account of the events that led to the fire would be complete without examining their role. Chief fire officers implemented the deregulation agenda of successive governments, notably the Fire Safety Order and its weak enforcement policy. They imposed austerity and fragmentation, regardless of the risks to the public or to firefighters. CFOA/NFCC were responsible for failed operational guidance, such as GRA 3.2 on high rise firefighting. This was a glaring omission, in contrast with the inquiry's approach in other areas.

The inquiry made some gross errors with respect to the fire and rescue service. For example, it claimed that austerity cuts had not impacted on LFB. The Phase 2 report stated:

> Although we acknowledge the strength of opinion held by some that the approach to funding public services adopted by the government between 2010 and 2015 and by the Mayor of London between 2012 and 2016 constrained the LFB's operational effectiveness, none of the witnesses from whom we heard told us that insufficient financial or other resources had caused or contributed to the failings that occurred on the night of the Grenfell Tower fire. In that respect, it is telling that the LFB did not suggest that budgetary constraints had been responsible for any of its shortcomings and it is worth noting that the report of Her Majesty's Inspectorate of Constabulary and Fire and Rescue Services on the LFB, published after the Phase 1 report on 17

December 2019, stated that, although the brigade was inefficient in its spending, it was not under-funded.[59]

The passage is riddled with sophistry. The impact of cuts was never just about the response on the night, but on planning, training and risk management. Of course LFB principal managers would deny the cuts they imposed on behalf of Cameron and Johnson affected the service. An inspectorate signed up to Conservative fire policy would not criticise deregulation and austerity. The inquiry should have called the FBU to make the case about cuts.

Similarly, the inquiry expended much energy in Phase 2 on the inability of firefighters to override the lifts at Grenfell Tower on the night of the fire. The inquiry clarified that the fire control switch had not been tested before the fire. It heard abundant evidence that the switch was jammed with debris. The switch was tested after the fire. Arup's report identified wall plaster. André Horne's said the debris appeared to be dirt, mortar or sand. Another expert Roger Howkins believed the debris amounted to half to three-quarters of a teaspoonful. This seemed like a conclusive explanation. The inquiry sought to obtain the key used on the night, but could not be sure they had the original. Tests with different keys did not resolve it. Despite the weight of the evidence suggesting debris from the refurbishment had jammed the switch, the inquiry concluded that 'the wrong size of drop key is the most likely reason for the failure of the fire control switch to operate properly on the night of the fire'. This favoured lift manufacturers, ignored the refurbishment and put the onus on firefighters. Such a verdict made no sense.[60]

The public inquiry's recommendations

The public inquiry's Phase 2 report made 58 recommendations. Most will make incremental improvements to the building safety regime.

Probably the most significant was the proposal to create a single regulator for the construction industry, which would bring certification and testing facilities of building materials under public ownership and control. After the failures of BRE, the BBA, NHBC and other private industry bodies, this was welcome. However the construction regulator will also require safeguards, to avoid industry capture. This includes a statutory advisory committee, with representation for trade unions in the construction industry. And fire risk assessment, which arises from the Fire Safety Order, should be overseen by fire professionals from the fire and rescue service, not the new construction regulator.[61]

The recommendations made by the inquiry for Approved Document B, beyond the need for regular review, were more problematic. The guidance should be strengthened, so that following it provides the best route to compliance with the regulations. Flexibility and ambiguity meant previous versions of Approved Document B were seen as something to get around, rather than follow. Similarly, the FBU cannot accept the recommendation to weaken the importance of compartmentation for fire safety matters within Approved Document B and other guidance.[62]

On building control, the inquiry made a convincing case about the failures of private approved inspectors. The FBU wants these private bodies removed, so building control reverts solely to a public endeavour. The FBU opposed the proposal to cede building control functions to a national authority. This would wreck local building control and create a bureaucratic entity, too weak to carry out the necessary supervision. Local authority building control, with sustained investment and national standards, working together with local fire and rescue service professionals, is the best way to ensure individual projects comply with building regulations.[63]

On fire safety matters, the inquiry made some important proposals, although it failed to establish a robust framework for ongoing national standards. The FBU supported the recommendation to bring responsibility for the functions relating to fire safety into one department under a single Secretary of State, as long as it meant all aspects of the fire and rescue service. The FBU argued that the right department and Secretary of State is MHCLG. Collaboration between building safety and fire safety is best within the same department. Building safety is mostly under MHCLG and should remain so. Fire and rescue service funding has continued within MHCLG for England (despite the Home Office transfer), because the sector is resourced through central and local funding. Fire and rescue service employers are mostly in local government. The Home Office police model is not appropriate for the fire and rescue service. Fire safety is integral to firefighting – splitting them would weaken resilience.[64]

The FBU supported the recommendation for mandatory accreditation to certify the competence of fire risk assessors. Ministers should task a fire statutory advisory body, involving key representative stakeholders, with overseeing this work as an urgent priority.[65]

The FBU could support the recommendation to create a College of Fire and Rescue, if it was part of a change of direction for fire and rescue on standards and consultation. The FBU asked the last government what a College of Fire and Rescue might look like, but ministers, civil servants and the NFCC never shared any concrete proposals. The FBU opposed the privatisation of the Fire Service College and argued that its status must be considered in discussions about any new facility.

A new College of Fire and Rescue cannot simply institutionalise the current role of the NFCC, which dominates fire policy and guidance, excluding the FBU and other stakeholders. The FBU opposed the suggestion to make the college a not-for-profit company. This would constitute deregulation, the same failure identified by the public inquiry at the root of central government mistakes that led to the Grenfell Tower fire. A College of Fire and Rescue alone is not sufficient to resolve the matters listed by the inquiry. A statutory advisory body has a crucial role in national standards, planning, research, guidance, procedures, training and related matters.[66]

At least three significant recommendations were missing from the report: the cladding ban, social housing and the statutory advisory body.

First, the FBU made the demand for a statutory advisory body central to its recommendations to the inquiry. For decades, the CFBAC had provided ministers with sound advice, overseeing the implementation of regulations and guidance to drive up standards in the fire and rescue service. The CFBAC was scrapped in 2004 and no adequate alternative put in place. Almost every other sector has such a statutory body: in fire safety it is a necessity. The inquiry simply ignored the recommendation, failing even to evaluate its efficacy. This was the flip side of its failure to examine the role of chief fire officers and ministerial advisers.

Second, after making important criticisms of the tenant management organisation's role in the fire, the inquiry failed to make any recommendations about social housing. This stemmed from the original mistake to omit social housing from the terms of reference. Yet having identified the role of deregulation in matters of building safety and fire safety, the inquiry failed to apply this to TMO's, which allow councils to contract out housing provision. The failure to make any recommendations about social housing was a serious omission, a missed opportunity to bolster tenant's voices in managing their own homes.[67]

Third, the inquiry consistently found that flammable cladding played the central role in causing the Grenfell Tower fire. The Westminster government introduced a ban on such cladding on the external walls of buildings over 18 metres in height, just as other governments in France, Germany, Hong Kong and China have done. Instead of endorsing this precautionary approach, the inquiry opened the door to relaxing it, arguing that the ban is 'potentially disadvantageous because the development of new materials and methods of construction is liable to require frequent legislative intervention'. This was a terrible error.[68]

Ministers' response to the inquiry's recommendations

On the day the public inquiry published its Phase 2 report, prime minister Keir Starmer spoke in the House of Commons to apologise for the failures of the British state. Starmer referred to the deregulatory agenda of previous governments, which MPs Jeremy Corbyn, Zarah Sultana and Nadia Whittome underlined in their contributions. The prime minister promised a full government response within six months.[69]

In February 2025, Starmer implemented a key recommendation from the public inquiry by moving responsibility for fire from the Home Office to MHCLG, effective from 1 April 2025. The FBU welcomed the decision, which should enable a more coherent approach to public safety.[70]

A fortnight later, the Westminster government published its full response to the inquiry's report. Deputy prime minister Angela Rayner gave a statement in parliament and MPs held a further discussion. Rayner said ministers had accepted 28 of the 37 recommendations aimed at central government 'in full' and the remaining nine 'in principle'. Labour MP Mary Kelly Foy criticised central government's 'obsession with deregulation'. The drive to scrap red tape was 'a key failing, which led to such a terrible incident and the avoidable loss of life'.[71]

The FBU agreed with ministers that certain recommendations should be accepted 'in principle'. The union was content with the single construction regulator, but unhappy ministers had not resolved what would happen to private bodies such as the BRE and BBA, which test and certificate products. They were criticised by the Inquiry for prioritising commercial interests above safety.

Ministers accepted in principle to establish a College of Fire and Rescue, but agreed to consult on proposals. The FBU said it would scrutinise any plans and contribute to the consultation process. The union argued that any new college must be a public body, not a private company. Firefighters and emergency control staff must be consulted about new training, research and national standards. The FBU was not consulted by the NFCC when it arrogantly accepted recommendations 'on behalf of all fire and rescue services'.[72]

The Westminster government agreed to establish a panel to examine building control. The FBU wanted local authority building control strengthened, an end to private building control approvers and close collaboration with local fire inspectors. The union also highlighted ongoing matters, such as the cladding crisis and PEEPs for vulnerable residents.[73]

CAMPAIGNING

No account of responses to the Grenfell Tower fire would be complete without reference to campaigners who took up the issues with central government, the public inquiry and in communities. Throughout the years since the fire, the FBU reached out to organisations within the Grenfell community, as well as wider society, to support their demands and find common ground for campaigning. The FBU worked closely with Justice for Grenfell and established good relations with some key figures within Grenfell United. More widely, the FBU supported disability campaign CLADDAG, which took up PEEPs. Similarly, the FBU supported End the Cladding Scandal, which fought for remediation for individual owners and residents of high rise blocks, facing bills for cladding removal, waking watches and other costs.

The FBU took its own initiative in campaigning, while seeking to work alongside others. The FBU immediately organised delegations to join the monthly silent walks that were organised by the Grenfell community. In autumn 2017, the FBU took motions to the TUC and Labour Party conference. The FBU's Firefighters 100 Lottery donated money to Grenfell organisations, including Kids on the Green and Dale Youth Boxing Club.[74]

Just after the first anniversary of the fire, the FBU supported the Justice for Grenfell solidarity march to Downing St, to demand urgent action from central government. In 2018, the union took another resolution to the TUC, seeking to build support across the labour movement. The FBU also published its blue pamphlet on the fire, providing some of the deregulatory background to the fire, which it had submitted as evidence to the inquiry.[75]

In 2019, the FBU added its weight to the #EndOurCladdingScandal campaign, launched by *Inside Housing* magazine and UK Cladding Action Group. The campaign focused on the slow pace of cladding removal and the exorbitant costs dumped on residents.[76]

On the second anniversary of the fire, the FBU launched the *Grenfell: Never Again* campaign. It was backed by the *Daily Mirror* newspaper and won support from Labour leader Jeremy Corbyn and London mayor Sadiq Khan. The campaign raised five key demands:

1. Remove flammable cladding from all tower blocks and public buildings.
2. Retrofit sprinklers in high rises and schools, wherever a risk assessment deems them necessary.
3. Ensure tenants are given a real voice in the running and upkeep of their buildings.
4. Reverse the cuts to firefighter numbers and fire safety officers.
5. Create a new independent national body to oversee standards and best practices in fire and rescue services across the country.[77]

In 2019, the FBU took the Grenfell campaign back to the Labour Party, publishing another pamphlet on the role of deregulation in causing the fire. The green pamphlet was launched at an event at Labour conference, featuring Labour leader Jeremy Corbyn, Emma Dent Coad (MP for Kensington) and Gill Kernick (a former Grenfell resident and building safety expert).

In 2020, the FBU published a red pamphlet, this time addressing the events on the night of the fire and evaluating the inquiry's Phase 1 report.[78] Although the Covid-19 pandemic made public campaigning more difficult, the FBU continued to take up the issues. The FBU published Grenfell survivor Nicholas Burton's account of his visit to 50 fire stations in 23 countries, to campaign for safe buildings and housing reform. The union seized on the National Audit Office report into the UK's flammable cladding scandal, condemning the government's action removing cladding as 'too slow and too weak'. The FBU called on the government to requisition any building that the owner would not make safe.[79]

The FBU also reacted to evidence from the public inquiry about the 'revolving door' between manufacturers and regulators. The union drew attention to Digby Harper, former chief executive of Celotex, who chaired BBA's board of governors from 2008 until 2016. Similarly, Michael Ankers, then chief executive of the Construction Products Association, sat on the BBA board from 1999 until after Grenfell Tower disaster. The FBU leapt on the revelation that just six weeks after the Grenfell Tower fire, Kingspan hired PR agencies Portland and Grayling communications to convince MPs that combustible materials were no more dangerous than non-combustible when properly installed.[80]

In 2021, the FBU supported the Labour Party's campaign to fix the building safety crisis, as well as direct action by the End Our Cladding Scandal campaign. The union organised delegations of firefighters from across the UK to attend the silent walks, which restarted after the pandemic abated. As Labour conference resumed, the FBU moved another motion on the cladding scandal.[81]

During 2022, the FBU allied with disability campaigners after the Westminster government rejected the public inquiry's recommendation to introduce PEEPs for vulnerable people living in high rise buildings. Matt Wrack wrote to fire minister Lord Greenhalgh: 'The government's decision is a negative, backward step, and the FBU stands with disability campaigners, the Grenfell campaign groups and the LGA in asking you to reconsider.'[82]

On the fifth anniversary of the fire, firefighters from across the UK participated in the silent walk, led by bereaved, survivors and residents of Grenfell. The FBU supported the Grenfell United banners with the hashtag #DemandCharges, demanding those responsible face criminal prosecution.[83]

The FBU also campaigned for justice for its own members, who suffered as a result of their intervention on the night of the fire. In 2024, the FBU announced that firefighters had settled claims for £20 million in the High Court. The 114 affected firefighters were given legal support through the FBU and its solicitors Thompsons. Firefighters suffered personal injury and loss caused by alleged negligence and breach of statutory duty. Some were left unable to work again due to severe trauma. The claims were brought against Arconic, Celotex and Rydon, RBKC and LFB.[84]

Over the eight years since the fire, the FBU campaigned alongside residents and others, to ensure justice for the Grenfell community, defend the interests of firefighters and emergency control staff, and hold politicians to account. Despite criticism and other battles, the FBU never relented, never gave up, never allowed Grenfell to fall from prominence. The FBU is proud that its campaigns have won victories and given other activists a platform. The union demonstrated that solidarity is at the heart of its mission.

10

Justice delayed, lessons unlearned

Grenfell Tower still stands eight years after the fire. An empty shell, covered with sheeting, it is a reminder of what robbed people of their lives, their homes and their community. That no long term solution for the site has been determined, despite ministerial announcements, is also a reminder: Grenfell Tower is unfinished, unresolved, still ongoing.[1]

Just a week before the Grenfell Tower public inquiry published its Phase 2 report, further tower block fires showed that the risks starkly demonstrated by the Grenfell fire have not disappeared.

In August 2024, a fire at the Spectrum Building in Dagenham, East London required firefighters to evacuate more than 80 people and rescue 20 others. Four people were treated on scene, with two taken to hospital for smoke inhalation. Control staff took 16 calls about the fire and gave vital fire survival guidance. The first crew arrived within five minutes and the second crew arrived within six minutes. An aerial appliance also arrived in under six minutes. The fire was declared a major incident and LFB said a full simultaneous evacuation was carried out.

Grenfell United said that the Dagenham fire was 'a scenario we have warned about for seven years' and constituted a 'near miss'. They added: 'It seems work was underway to remove non-compliant cladding and the building had a number of fire safety issues.' LFB had served an enforcement notice on the company managing the building a year earlier, demanding it review fire risk assessments and implement prevention measures. Matt Wrack, FBU general secretary, said after visiting the site that the fire exposed the 'national scandal of flammable cladding and deregulation in the building industry'.[2]

In the same week, a fire at the Mosaic apartments in Slough, Berkshire saw more than 50 firefighters evacuate nearly 300 residents. The block had similar cladding to the materials found on Grenfell Tower.[3] Yet one of two fire engines in Slough was removed just weeks after the fire. Berkshire Fire and Rescue Service had only 14 appliances available across the county at any time, but the FBU warned of longer response times on some nights.

Steve Wright, FBU vice-president, told the BBC: 'A cut to the frontline response is baffling me and rather alarming following the fire in Slough and the risks that are still present.'[4]

JUSTICE FOR GRENFELL

Eight years after the fire, there is still no justice for Grenfell. The bereaved, survivors and residents have demanded above all else that those responsible are brought to trial and prosecuted. But no trials are expected before 2027 – a decade after the fire.

Operation Northleigh, the police investigation, involves a team of 180 investigators. It has 27,000 exhibits, enough to fill a warehouse of 25 double decker buses. Police are investigating 58 individual suspects from 19 companies and organisations. Fifty people have been interviewed under criminal caution. Officers have compiled 20 early case files, of which they have submitted nine to prosecutors. Each file relates to one company or organisation. If printed, the evidence from just one file would be 17,000 A4 pages, standing 7ft tall.[5]

The FBU has been clear from the beginning that all those responsible, especially company directors and ministers, business owners and senior public servants, must be held to account. Where crimes have been committed and culpability established, those organisations and individuals have to face legal proceedings.

BUILDING SAFETY CRISIS

At present, there are 4.25 million residents living in 2.3 million homes over 11 metres tall in England. This included 1.3 million living in almost 700,000 homes of 18 metres or more, at least seven storeys tall. Almost three million people were living in 1.6 million homes between 11 and 18 metres in height. Overall, 8 per cent of the population in England live in high or mid-rise flats.[6] Eight years after the Grenfell Tower fire, the cladding crisis continues, with people living in high rise residential buildings still unsafe in their homes.

In January 2025, there were more than 5,000 residential buildings 11 metres and over in height identified with unsafe cladding in England. Half of those had still not started remediation, and less than 30 per cent had completed remediation. MHCLG had identified more 500 high rise residential and publicly owned buildings over 18 metres with ACM cladding systems and unlikely to meet Building Regulations. More than 2,500 social sector buildings 11 metres and over in height had been identified as having life-critical fire-safety cladding defects. Less than half were reported to have started or completed remediation works. A damning National Audit Office report estimated between 9,000 and 12,000 buildings of 11 metres or higher had unsafe cladding that required remediation.[7]

Eight years after Grenfell, the cladding crisis extended across the UK. In Scotland, only five of the 107 buildings within the government's pilot cladding remediation programme were undergoing work. Only one had been completed. Scotland had more than 5,000 buildings of 11 metres or higher with combustible cladding, affecting 25,000 people. In Wales, 407 buildings were identified with fire safety issues, including cladding. In Northern Ireland, an expert panel found 280 buildings over 11 metres, with 110 of those over 18 metres, but only one building with ACM cladding had applied for remediation.[8]

More than 15,000 residents had been ordered to leave their unsafe homes since Grenfell. Residents were left homeless or forced to pay rent on top of a mortgage, as well as charges on a flat that they cannot even live in, much less sell. The End Our Cladding Scandal campaign underlined that there was no end in sight for the building safety crisis. The FBU added its voice to the campaigns led by residents demanding the remedial work is accelerated and completed.[9]

The public inquiry argued that 'the way in which the Grenfell Tower refurbishment was handled raises serious questions for the whole of the construction industry'. Although the inquiry did not investigate the industry as a whole, it concluded that similar problems were 'widespread' across construction.[10]

The Grenfell Tower fire exposed the role of private sector organisations involved in the testing and certification of building materials. The FBU demands public ownership of the Building Research Establishment (BRE), with results made public, a system open to public and professional scrutiny. The FBU also wants an end to private 'approved inspectors' (now known as 'building control approvers'), with local authority building control departments properly resourced to enable them to carry out their duties effectively.

The FBU also wants a revolution in social housing, with tenants and residents fully consulted about all aspects of their homes. Housing is a basic human need and should not depend on the uncertainties of the market. Decent, safe homes for all is a basic human right. Ministers must build more affordable homes and give everyone who lives in them the democratic channels to collectively manage their own living.

FIRE AND RESCUE SERVICE

The Grenfell Tower fire demonstrated the best and the worst of the fire and rescue service. The firefighters and emergency control staff who intervened on the night of the fire were rightly praised for their courage and determination to save lives, often at personal cost to themselves. They were mostly FBU members and the union is immensely proud of them for what they did.

However the Grenfell Tower fire also revealed flaws at the heart of principal management leading the fire and rescue service, both in London and across the UK. For more than a decade before the Grenfell Tower fire, ministers only took advice from chief fire officers, through CFOA and its successor, the NFCC. Sadly, this arrangement continued after the fire, despite evident failings. This system of advising on fire policy obviously and very tragically failed. This failure must be acknowledged and the current system replaced.

In 2022, the FBU submitted recommendations at the request of the public inquiry. The FBU's key proposal was:

> The Westminster government and Secretary of State for the Home Department must create a new statutory advisory body to oversee standards and best practice in fire and rescue services across the UK. The new body must involve the FBU within its structures, including its leading committees. The statutory advisory body would have a wide remit, to include monitoring progress in meeting recommendations from inquiries, inquests, serious accident investigations, APPGs, select committees and other official bodies. The remit would review international best practice and seek to level up the UK to the highest global standards.[11]

The FBU demanded that the Westminster government and the devolved administrations must ensure there are UK wide standards and guidance across the fire and rescue service. The standards and guidance should be developed by the new statutory advisory body in consultation with fire sector stakeholders (including the FBU) and would include:

- UK-wide standards for recruitment and training of all competent firefighters
- a maximum response time standard of five minutes from the time of call to arrival of the first pumping appliance
- a maximum response time standard for the second pumping appliance
- UK-wide standards for pre-determined attendance at high rise fires
- a minimum of five crew members on all pumping appliances
- permanently crewed aerial appliances.[12]

The FBU demanded UK-wide standards across a range of key indicators. Attendance times are necessary for the first, second and further appliances. High rise residential fires require a pre-determined attendance, including appliances and aerial ladder platforms. National standards are also essential for recruitment, training, promotion and other matters, to ensure consistent, professional development across the whole workforce.

In 2023, the FBU made similar proposals in its *Firefighters' Manifesto*. In 2024, the Labour Party published its general election manifesto, titled *Change*. The Labour manifesto promised:

> Labour will improve resilience and preparation across central government, local authorities, local communities, and emergency services. This includes formally working with all stakeholders in the Fire and Rescue services to inform policy and establish national standards …
>
> Labour will also take decisive action to improve building safety, including through regulation, to ensure we never again see a repeat of the Grenfell fire.[13]

No doubt many changes are necessary for a resilient, integrated, well-resourced fire and rescue service. These are best delivered and implemented through consultation with the workforce, represented by the FBU.

In 2024, ministers in the newly formed Labour government convened a Ministerial Advisory Group (MAG) on Fire and Rescue Service Reform. It consisted of key stakeholders within the fire and rescue service, including the FBU, fire employers, NFCC, HMICFRS, senior civil servants with a range of other associate members. The FBU participated actively in the Ministerial Advisory Group, welcoming the high level coordination and consultation. The MAG has the potential to develop into a statutory advisory body, with FBU represented at all levels. This is crucial for transforming the fire and rescue service, away from deregulation and austerity, towards resilience and greater professionalism.

GOVERNMENT AND DEREGULATION

The FBU argued that deregulation was the root cause of the Grenfell Tower fire. This was not a popular or widely accepted view in the months immediately after the fire. The FBU was often told it was 'too political' an explanation. However the solid arguments and evidence the union provided convinced many sceptics that this was the best explanation. Even the public inquiry accepted that the Westminster government's deregulatory agenda dominated to such an extent that 'even matters affecting the safety of life were ignored, delayed or disregarded'.[14]

However, deregulation has not been scrapped. When the public inquiry's Phase 2 report was published, former prime minister and now Lord Cameron claimed that 'fire safety and building safety regulations were explicitly excluded from the coalition government's greatly-needed "red tape reviews"'. Grenfell campaigners rightly slammed Cameron for his talk of a bonfire of regulations, when his policies had turned people's homes to ashes.[15]

Similarly, former prime minister Tony Blair told Sky News just after the report was published that 'however good your system is and however well-intentioned it is, and however hard people work, they're going to make mistakes'. Matt Wrack's response on behalf of the FBU was blunt:

> Tony Blair's despicable comments are the remarks of a multi-millionaire who has lost touch with the reality of people's lives. The Grenfell fire was not the result of well-intentioned people making mistakes, but of a systematic disregard for the safety of residents – and the prioritisation of private profit over human life. As prime minister, Tony Blair was an enthusiastic supporter of the same agenda of deregulation that led to the Grenfell disaster.[16]

In October 2024, just a month after the public inquiry report was published, new Conservative leader Kemi Badenoch put deregulation at the heart of her political agenda:

> Moreover, more and more of those within the private sector will now be engaged on dealing with this regulatory burden … Such ever expanding regulation is seen in area after area. For example, UK building regulations are now 1,500 pages, despite the misleading and dishonest arguments that the sector is 'deregulated'. Indeed, the complexity now acts to make the limited genuine requirements (e.g. protecting us from unsafe cladding) obscured in a thicket of wider regulations.[17]

These politicians deny that their policies had anything to do with the fire. Their record in government, their public statements and the policies they implemented show that deregulation was the problem and can be traced all the way to Grenfell.

Tragically, deregulation remains at the heart of Westminster politics. In January 2025, Nigel Farage pledged that a Reform UK government would 'cut regulation' and 'unshackle' the country. Keir Starmer, speaking on the new government's growth plans, also endorsed deregulation. He said:

> In the 1980s, the Thatcher government deregulated finance capital. In the New Labour era, globalisation increased the opportunities for trade. This is our equivalent. For too long regulation has stopped Britain building its future. Today the chancellor will show how this government will sweep it away. And working people will benefit.[18]

The Grenfell Tower fire showed that far from helping working people, deregulation harms working class people and our communities.

The relationship between business and government deserves more scrutiny in light of Grenfell. In particular, the relationship between the construction industry and political parties cannot be avoided. A Transparency International UK report found that between 2010 and 2020, more than 10 per cent of all political donations came from individuals and companies related to substantial property interests. Most of that money went to the Conservative Party. Property-related contributions accounted for more than a fifth of the Conservative's reportable donations. Another report by Autonomy research, based solely on company data, also found construction and real estate had donated millions of pounds, the majority of it to the Conservatives.[19]

The FBU fought against deregulation and warned ministers about the folly of their actions. Many other organisations and campaigns agree that deregulation, when the pursuit of profit is elevated above public safety, must be stopped. It is up to the state to control market forces and promote public services. We must never forget how deregulation caused the Grenfell Tower fire and remind politicians of its consequences for future policy.

CLASS, RACE AND SOCIAL DIVISIONS

The Grenfell Tower fire raises some much wider questions, about the world we live in and the direction it is heading. The fire also raises questions of social divide that cannot be avoided, as Grenfell survivors themselves made clear.[20] The public inquiry dismissed these questions from the start, but still felt obliged to issue a denial in its Phase 2 report. It stated:

> Given the repeated urging by some of those representing the bereaved, survivors and residents to consider whether the race or social background of those who lived in the tower played a part in bringing about the disaster and the implicit assertion that it did, we think it right to make it clear that our investigations have not brought to light any evidence to support that conclusion.[21]

Imran Khan, representing some of the residents, made a powerful case to address these wider issues. He said:

> Those who died in the fire were largely from low income homes, at least 85% of them from minority ethnic backgrounds. The government's race disparity audit in 2017, the year of the disaster, said that those from minority ethnic communities were the most likely groups to rent social housing ... Official housing surveys have found that 40% of high-rise residents in the social rented sector are from black, Asian and minority ethnic communities, which make up 14% of the population.[22]

By contrast, the UK now boasted 165 billionaires, up from 134 at the time of the Grenfell Tower fire. Rishi Sunak, prime minister on the seventh anniversary, was rich enough to make number 245 on the *Sunday Times Rich List*.[23] The multi-million-pound mansions of Notting Hill are only a short walk from what remains of Grenfell Tower. The contrasts between wealth and poverty – power and exploitation – are class questions that cannot be avoided.

Notes

The book draws on many government, official, archive and FBU sources. References are listed in end notes. Most are by author, title, date and page, so the reader can find the original materials. Parliamentary materials are given in the standard format: HC Deb (House of Commons debate) and HL Deb (House of Lords debate), with date, volume and column in Hansard. Some of the documents can only be found in the National Archives. These have the box code for reference. From the public inquiry, individuals who gave testimony are quoted from transcripts, with column and line numbers (not pages). Witness statements are listed by name, date and page. The inquiry reports include the relevant section (§) number, as well as volume and page numbers.

Chapter 1 Housing as a social service

1. Grenfell Tower Inquiry, *Phase 1 Report*, vol. 1, §3.1, §3.9, §3.20, October 2019: 19, 21, 24.
2. Rebecca Tunstall and Nicholas Pleace, *Social Housing: Evidence Review*, Research Report, York: University of York, 2018: 8.
3. DLUHC, English Housing Survey data, Table FT1101 (S101). Trends in tenure (accessed 1 October 2024).
4. HC Deb 16 March 1949, vol. 462, c2221; Stuart Hodkinson, *Safe as Houses: Private Greed, Political Negligence and Housing Policy after Grenfell*, Manchester: Manchester University Press, 2019: 22.
5. Patrick Dunleavy, *The Politics of Mass Housing in Britain 1945–75*, Oxford: Clarendon Press, 1981: 1–3.
6. Ibid., 34–8.
7. Ida Danewid, 'The fire this time: Grenfell, racial capitalism and the urbanisation of empire', *European Journal of International Relations*, 26, 1, 2020: 297; Harry Mount, 'My great-grandfather, a Victorian den of poverty', *Daily Telegraph*, 17 June 2017; Grace Mae Bradley, 'From Grenfell to Windrush'. In Dan Bulley, Jenny Edkins and Nadine El-Enany, *After Grenfell: Violence, Resistance and Response*. London: Pluto, 2019: 135–6.
8. Jack Grahl, *Freedom from Fire*, FBU, 1943: 15.
9. Shane Ewen, *Before Grenfell: Fire, Safety and Deregulation in Twentieth-Century Britain*. London: University of London Press, 2023:

26; Scotland introduced national building regulations in 1959 and Northern Ireland in 1972.

10. CS Todd and Associates, *Legislation, Guidance and Enforcing Authorities Relevant to Fire Safety Measures at Grenfell Tower: Report for The Grenfell Tower Inquiry*, March 2018: 5, 36.
11. Luke Bisby, *Grenfell Tower Inquiry: Regulatory Testing and the Path to Grenfell*, 2022: 70–71; GTI, *Phase 2 Report*, vol. 1, §5.8, §5.13, September 2024: 49, 51.
12. Marian Hawkesworth and Rob Imrie, 'Organisational change in systems of building regulation and control: illustrations from the English context', *Environment and Planning B*, vol. 36, 2009: 554.
13. British Board of Agrément, Written opening statement, GTI Phase 2, Module 2, 12 October 2020: 2; HC Deb 10 November 1965, vol. 720, cc311–40.
14. Bisby, *Regulatory Testing*, 20–21.
15. Roger Courtney, 'Building Research Establishment past, present and future', *Building Research & Information*, vol. 25, no. 5, 1997: 286–7; HC Deb, 22 December 1971, vol. 828, c354; Ewen, *Before Grenfell*, 61–72.
16. NHBC, Request for review and release of NHBC structural warranty services undertakings due to change of circumstance: Submission to the Competition and Markets Authority, 13 January 2017: 4.
17. GTI, *Phase 2 Report*, vol. 1, §6.10, 70.
18. Joint Committee of the Building Research Board of the Department of Scientific & Industrial Research and of the Fire Offices' Committee, *Fire Grading of Buildings Part I General Principles and Structural Precautions*, Post-War Building Studies no. 20, 1946; *Fire Grading of Buildings Part II: Fire Fighting Equipment; Part III: Personal Safety; Part IV: Chimneys and Flues*, Post-War Building Studies no. 29, 1952.
19. British Standards Institution, BSI code of practice, CP3: Chapter IV: Part 1: 1962. Code of Basic Data for the design of buildings. Chapter IV Precautions against fire. Part 1. Fire precautions in flats and maisonettes over 80ft in height, 1962: 8.
20. BSI, Code of practice, CP3: Chapter IV: Part 1: 1971. Code of Basic Data for the design of buildings. Chapter IV Precautions against fire. Part 1. Flats and maisonettes (in blocks over two storeys), 1971: 5, 8, 34.
21. S. Melinek and R. Baldwin, *Evacuation of Buildings: Some Effects of Changes in Performance Standards*, BRE, 1975: 1, 6.
22. Richard Read, *Fire Risks of High-Rise Buildings*, BRE, January 1979: 7–8.

23. Grahl, *Freedom from Fire*, 15.
24. FBU, *Fire – Protecting Britain: Report of a Public Conference on Fire Protection, convened by the Fire Brigades Union*, London, February 1945: 3, 40.
25. John Horner, *A Service for the Sixties*, FBU, May 1960: 18.
26. FBU, *Fire Safety – Public Issue*, 1980: 12; FBU, *Cutting the Lifeline*, 1994: 7–9.
27. FBU, *Executive Council's Annual Report*, 1961: 24.
28. Richard Sharples, HC Deb 20 November 1970 vol. 806 cc1590–91.
29. Fire Precautions, Draft of a Bill, 20 November 1964.
30. FBU, 'Fire safety – a national concern. Fire safety in Britain: The role of fire brigades. Memorandum submitted by the FBU to the TUC local government advisory committee', *Report of Proceedings*, 1965: 29–30, 32.
31. FBU, *Backing Britain's Fire Service*. January 1968: 26.
32. Ian Macdonald QC, 'FBU final submission'. In FBU, *Without a Chance*, 1969: 18–19.
33. Ronald Holroyd, *Report of the Departmental Committee on the Fire Service*, May 1970: 17, 164–5.
34. Sharples to Morris, Confidential: Fire Precautions Bill, National Archives HLG/118/1221, 28 October 1970: 1, 3.
35. HC Deb 20 November 1970, vol. 806, cc1594–5.
36. Channon to Sharples, National Archives HLG/118/1221, 19 November 1970: 1.
37. Sharples to Channon, National Archives HLG/118/1221, 16 December 1970: 1.
38. CFBAC, Fire Precautions Act 1971: Note from the Home Office, National Archives HLG/118/1221, August 1971: 2–3.
39. FBU, 'TUC and Fire Safety', *Firefighter*, October 1971: 1; 'Prospects for the seventies', *Firefighter*, January 1972: 4.
40. Hugh Griffiths, *Report of the Inquiry into the Collapse of Flats at Ronan Point, Canning Town Presented to the Minister of Housing and Local Government*, 14 October 1968: 58, 60.
41. After campaigning by the Newham Tower Blocks Tenants' Association and architect Sam Webb, matters came to a head in 1984 when the local authority evacuated Ronan Point. Questions were raised at Westminster. In 1985, BRE carried out a fire test. It concluded that it was extremely unlikely that collapse could be caused by fire, but recommended remedial works at Ronan Point and the appraisal of all Taylor Woodrow Anglian buildings. In 1986 Ronan Point was demolished.

42. 'Summerland: Why 50 people died', *FIRE Special Supplement*, June 1974: i, v, vii; Joseph Cantley, *Report of the Summerland Fire Commission: Inquiry into Fire at Summerland Leisure Centre, Douglas, Isle of Man*, 2 August 1973, May 1974: 78–9.
43. Terry Parry, 'How to prevent another Summerland disaster', *Firefighter*, September 1974: 11.
44. CFBAC, 'Fire precautions in high-rise blocks of flats', July 1975: 2–3; Kenneth Holland, *Report of Her Majesty's Chief Inspector of Fire Services*, 1976: 26.
45. CS Todd and Associates, *Legislation, Guidance and Enforcing Authorities*, 2018: 30.

Chapter 2 Thatcher's deregulation unleashed

1. Colin Hay, 'Whatever happened to Thatcherism?', *Political Studies Review*, vol. 5, 2007: 185.
2. FBU, 'Wrecker', *Firefighter*, July 1979: 1.
3. FBU, 'A message to Mrs. Thatcher: Cut out the cuts', *Firefighter*, September 1979: 4.
4. HC Deb 15 May 1979, vol. 967, cc78–9.
5. John Hoskyns, Government Strategy, National Archives PREM19/24 f11, 12 June 1979; Note of MT-Ministers meeting, National Archives PREM19/25 f156, 18 June 1979; Michael Heseltine, Minute to MT, National Archives PREM19/25 f104, 22 June 1979.
6. John Hoskyns and Norman Strauss, *The Stepping Stones*, November 1977: 7.
7. Thatcher, Speech to the Conservative Political Centre Summer School, Thatcher Archive CCOPR 921/79, 6 July 1979. The Margaret Thatcher Foundation has reproduced thousands of internal government documents from various sources on its website.
8. Geoffrey Howe, Priority Strategy Proposals, Memo to E Committee, National Archives CAB134/4336, 24 September 1979.
9. John Redwood, Deregulation and Simpler Government, National Archives PREM19/1312 f225, 17 April 1984.
10. Andrew Turnbull, No. 10 record of conversation, National Archives PREM19/1203 f8, 24 July 1984.
11. Robert Armstrong, Deregulation, National Archives PREM19/1517 f270, 28 June 1985.
12. HL Deb 16 July 1985, vol. 466, cc610.
13. Lord David Young, *Lifting the Burden*, White Paper, July 1985: 1, 3.

14. HC Deb 16 July 1985, vol. 83, c172; Shane Ewen, *Before Grenfell: Fire, Safety and Deregulation in Twentieth-Century Britain*, 2023: 34.
15. Young, Minute to MT, National Archives PREM19/1518 f117, 3 October 1985.
16. Cabinet Office, Letter to Lord Young, National Archives PREM19/1679 f19, 29 October 1985.
17. HC Deb 6 November 1985, vol. 86, cc18–19.
18. HL Deb 26 March 1986, vol. 472, cc1493–4WA.
19. HC Deb 22 May 1986, vol. 98, cc542–56.
20. HC Deb 13 June 1986, vol. 99, cc665–731.
21. HC Deb 25 November 1987, vol. 123, cc208–9W.
22. Ewen, *Before Grenfell*, 30–36.
23. Housing and Building Control Bill, HC Deb 23 November 1982, vol. 32, cc716–800.
24. Central Policy Review Staff, Strategy note circulated to E Committee, National Archives CAB 134/4336, 16 July 1979; Heseltine minute to MT, National Archives PREM19/245 f228, 22 August 1979; Howe, Priority Strategy Proposals, 24 September 1979.
25. 'Controversial amendments to the building regulations', *FIRE*, March 1980: 556; 'Changes in building regulations', *FIRE*, August 1980: 146; 'Heseltine demands debate on building regs', *The Architects Journal*, no. 170, 1979: 51.
26. DoE, *The Future of Building Control in England and Wales*, February 1981: 4, 7, 15–16; HC Deb 26 February 1981, vol. 999, cc438 9W.
27. HC Deb 5 July 1983, vol. 45 c169, cc226–7.
28. FBU, 'Summerland', *Firefighter*, December 1983: 2.
29. HC Deb 29 November 1979, vol. 974, c796W; HC Deb 25 January 1980, vol. 977, c392W.
30. HC Deb 8 April 1981, vol. 2, c302W; HC Deb 21 July 1982 vol. 28 c204W.
31. HC Deb 8 April 1981, vol. 2, cc301–2W.
32. Lord Christopher Soames, Letter to John Nott, National Archives PREM19/772 f78, 27 January 1981.
33. Heseltine, Letter to Soames, National Archives PREM19/555 f67, 5 February 1981; HC Deb 3 April 1981, vol. 2, c152W.
34. HC Deb 5 July 1983, vol. 45, cc158–241.
35. Peter Robinson, 'New building controls: A giant step, or just a pace, in the right direction?' *FIRE*, October 1985: 13; 'November date set for new building controls', *FIRE*, September 1985: 53; DoE, The Building Regulations 1985: Mandatory Rules for means of escape in case of fire, HMSO, 1985: 1, 3.

36. 'Abolition: New authorities are Home Office guidelines', *FIRE*, November 1985: 27.
37. Jim Fitzpatrick and Del Vaux, 'Talking to the people', *Firefighter*, June 1984: 3; Greg Bluestone, *Report of Proceedings*, 1984: 126.
38. DTI, *Burdens on Business*. Draft report, National Archives PREM19/1516 f120, 22 February 1985.
39. DoE, *Action Document: Building Control: Annex A: Building Regulations*, National Archives CAB130/1298, 30 May 1985.
40. HC Deb 17 July 1985, vol. 83, cc169–70W.
41. Ibid.; HC Deb 11 November 1985 vol. 86 c26W.
42. Roger Courtney, 'Building research establishment past, present and future', *Building Research & Information*, vol. 25, no. 5, 1997: 288.
43. HC Deb 23 January 1987, vol. 108, cc779–80W.
44. HC Deb 24 October 1988, vol. 139 ,cc87–8W; HL Deb 28 March 1990, vol. 517, cc961–2WA.
45. Courtney, 'Building research establishment', 287–8.
46. Home Office, *Review of Fire Policy*, June 1980: 355.
47. Ibid., 4, 105.
48. Ibid., 110, 128, 125, 427–8.
49. Ibid., 143–4.
50. Home Office, *Future Fire Policy: A Consultative Document*, Green Paper, 1980: 32.
51. Ken Cameron, 'No U-turns on pay formula', *Firefighter*, October 1980: 3; Mike Fordham, 'Further attack on the service', *Firefighter*, September 1980: 3.
52. FBU, *Fire Safety – A Public Issue*, August 1980: 10, 12–13.
53. HC Deb 18 January 1982, vol. 16, c12W.
54. F. Clayton, 'Government assault on the fire precautions! It's now time to sound safety alarm', *Firefighter*, December 1982: 7.
55. Nicholas Owen, 'Administrative and legislative burdens on small firms', Minute to MT, National Archives PREM19/1203 f53, 29 June 1984.
56. FBU, *The Battle for Britain's Fire Service: Report of the Joint Committee on Standards of Fire Cover*, 1984: iii.
57. Ibid., 11, 22, vii.
58. Young, *Lifting the Burden*, 28.
59. HC Deb 23 July 1985, vol. 83, c465W; Home Office, A Review of the Fire Precautions Act 1971: A Consultative Document, July 1985: 7.
60. Dave Matthews, 'Review of Fire Precautions Act will lead to losses, damage and death', *Firefighter*, April 1986: 6.
61. HC Deb 6 December 1985, vol. 88, c356W.

62. Lord Young, Letter to David Waddington, National Archives PREM19/1772 f209, 14 March 1986.
63. Audit Commission, *Value for Money in the Fire Service*, September 1986: 1, 6; FBU, C6 Audit Commission, *Record of Decisions*, 1987: 11; FBU, 46 Audit Commission report, *Record of Decisions*, 1989: 3–4; FBU, *What Value a Life? Report of the Joint Working Party on Audit Commission Paper 'Value for Monday in the Fire Service'*, February 1990.
64. Michael Simmonds, *The Burning Question*, Adam Smith Institute, 1989: 28, 42; Ken Cameron, 'NJC/Home Office Working Party Adam Smith Institute report', *Firefighter*, November 1989: 12; FBU, 49 Privatisation, *Record of Decisions*, 1989: 8.
65. Bickerdike Allen Partners, *Fire and Building Regulation*, Enterprise and Deregulation Unit, 1990: 1, 15, 17, 20, 23, 25, 41–2.
66. Bickerdike Allen, *Fire and Building Regulation*. 30–31, 35, 25.
67. FBU, ER 12 Fire Safety, *Record of Decisions*, 1990: 19; FBU, *Report of Proceedings*, 1990: 195–6; FBU, 'Building threat to fire prevention', *Firefighter*, June 1990: 9.
68. Glyn Evans, 'Bickerdike Allen Partners review fire and building regulation: A warning', *Firefighter*, December 1990: 16.
69. HC Deb 12 February 1992, vol. 203, cc967–8.
70. HC Deb 8 February 1994, vol. 237, cc147–245.
71. Dick Pearson, 'Review aims to "water down" fire safety', *Firefighter*, May 1994: 6; Glyn Evans, 'Union's Deregulation Campaign Begins', *Firefighter*, March 1994: 12.
72. HC Deb 6 July 1994, vol. 246, c224W; HC Deb 13 May 1996, vol. 277, cc625–6.
73. HC Deb 14 June 1995, vol. 261, cc785–6.
74. HC Deb 21 January 1994, vol. 235, cc863–7W; GTI, *Phase 1 Report*, vol. 1, §3.18, October 2019: 20; GTI, *Phase 2 Report*, vol. 3, §31.1, §31.2, September 2024: 9.
75. DTI, *Deregulation – Cutting Red Tape*, January 1994: 39; FBU, *Cutting the Lifeline*. April 1994: 2.
76. Alex Galloway, Sandra Caldwell, Peter Edmundson and Geraldine Mahon, *Fire Safety Legislation and Enforcement: Report of the Interdepartmental Review*, London: DTI, June 1994: xix.
77. FBU, 'Deregulation disastrous', *Firefighter*, October 1994: 11.
78. Lord Falconer, HL Deb 11 April 2002, vol. 633, cc124–5WA.
79. Mike Fordham, 'Wider audience for safety', *Firefighter*, September 1995: 4–5.
80. FBU, *A Fighting Chance*, 1995: 2–3, 23.

81. HC Deb 3 July 1996, vol. 280, cc444–5W; DoE Circular 8/96: Changes to NHBC Building Control Services Ltd's Approval as an Approved Inspector.
82. DoE Circular 10/96: The Designation of a Body for the Approval of Inspectors, 1 July 1996; Graham Watts, The National Centre for Construction in the UK, Building Research & Information, 25, 5, 1997: 279–84.
83. HC Deb 27 June 1996, vol. 280, cc216–17W; DoE Circular 19/96: Approval of Three Corporate Bodies as Approved Inspectors by the Secretaries of State – Approval of Persons as Approved Inspectors by the Designated Body.
84. Courtney, 'Building research establishment', 289.
85. HC Deb 7 November 1995, vol. 265, c747W.
86. Courtney, 'Building research establishment', 289; HC Deb 2 April 1996, vol. 275, cc160–4W; HC Deb 24 October 1996, vol. 284, c2W.
87. Courtney, 'Building research establishment', 289; HC Deb 19 March 1997, vol. 292, cc602–3W.
88. Home Office, *A Review of the Fire Precautions Act*. PR Edmundson and GI Hubbard, December 1993: 1, 88, 102–4; HC Deb 17 February 1994, vol. 237, c909W.
89. DTI, 'Deregulation Task Forces Proposals for Reform', January 1994, in Galloway et al., *Fire Safety Legislation and Enforcement*, June 1994: Annex E, 98; FBU, *Who Will Pick up the Pieces?* 1994: 2.
90. FBU, *Cutting the Lifeline*, April 1994: 4.
91. Galloway et al, *Fire Safety Legislation and Enforcement*, 1994: xvi–xxi, 41, 98.
92. HC Deb 22 June 1994, vol. 245, c227W.
93. FBU, *Who Will Pick up the Pieces?* 1994: 57; Mike Fordham, 'Who will pick up the pieces?', *Firefighter*, December 1994: 2.
94. HC Deb 11 March 1996, vol. 273, c441W; Mike Fordham, 'Deregulation on hold', *Firefighter*, March 1995: 5; Ken Cameron, 'Government silent on Fire Safety Regulation and Enforcement', *Firefighter*, September 1995: 3; 'FBU early day motion on funding a deregulation', *Firefighter*, April 1996: 13.
95. FBU, 'Victory for FBU in three-year campaign', *Firefighter*, June 1996: 4.
96. Audit Commission, *In the Line of Fire: Value for Money in the Fire Service – the National Picture*, February 1995: 5–6.
97. HC Deb 9 January 1996, vol. 269, c190W.
98. FBU, *Executive Council's Annual Report*, 1997: 62.

99. Mike Fordham, 'FBU launches – Fire Safety Act 2000', *Firefighter*, May 1996: 4–5.
100. HC Deb 11 December 1996, vol. 287, c284.
101. Ian McCartney, 'Covert deregulation plans unearthed', *Firefighter*, December 1996: 4.

Chapter 3 Blair's 'better deregulation' unchecked

1. National Audit Office, *Regulatory Reform in the UK: Briefing for Regulatory Reform Select Committee*, February 2008; Eren Waitzman, *Deregulation: Government Policy since 1997*. House of Lords Library, 10 July 2017; Martin Stanley's Understanding Regulation website has useful analysis, insights and links to government documents.
2. Matthew Tempest, 'Mandelson: we are all Thatcherites now', *Guardian*, 10 June 2002.
3. New Labour, *Because Britain Deserves Better*, 1997.
4. HC Deb 4 June 1997, vol. 295, cc193–4W.
5. HC Deb 1 July 1997, vol. 297, cc88–9W; HC Deb 1 June 1998, vol. 313, c1W.
6. HC Deb 1 June 1998, vol. 313, c1W; HC Deb 3 July 1997. vol. 297. cc221–2W; HC Deb 5 February 1998. vol. 305. c732W.
7. HC Deb 23 July 2004, vol. 424, c761W.
8. HC Deb 21 October 1999, vol. 336, cc649–50W; HC Deb 15 December 1999, vol. 341, cc260–61; HC Deb 10 April 2000, vol. 348, c53W.
9. HC Deb 31 January 2000, vol. 343, c465W; HC Deb 3 February 2000, vol. 343, cc718–9W.
10. HL Deb 21 December 2000, vol. 620, cc850–902.
11. Labour Party, *Ambitions for Britain: Labour's Manifesto 2001*, April 2001.
12. Office of Public Services Reform, Memorandum to the Select Committee on Public Administration, July 2002.
13. Tony Blair, *Reforming our Public Services: Principles into Practice*, March 2002: 10.
14. Ibid., 19, 20, 24.
15. Philip Hampton, *Reducing Administrative Burdens: Effective Inspection and Enforcement: Interim Report*, December 2004; Philip Hampton, *Reducing Administrative Burdens: Effective Inspection and Enforcement*, March 2005: 8.
16. Gordon Brown, 'How to lighten the regulatory burden on UK business', *Financial Times*, 23 May 2005, in Steve Tombs and David

Whyte, 'Transcending the deregulation debate? Regulation, risk, and the enforcement of health and safety law in the UK', *Regulation & Governance*, vol. 7, 2013: 67; Hannah Furness, 'Regulating the banks: What politicians used to say about the City', *Daily Telegraph*, 4 July 2012, in Tombs, '"Better Regulation": Better for whom?', *Briefing*, vol. 14, April 2016: 2.

17. BTRF, *Regulation – Less is More: Reducing Burdens, Improving Outcomes*, March 2005: 3.
18. Ibid., 6.
19. HC Deb 24 March 1998, vol. 309, c85W.
20. HC Deb 11 March 1998, vol. 308, cc192–3W; HC Deb 20 April 1998, vol. 310, c427W.
21. HC Deb 21 April 1998, vol. 310, c551W.
22. HC Deb 22 April 1998, vol. 310, cc792–800.
23. HC Deb 22 July 1999, vol. 335, cc585–7W.
24. HC Deb 3 February 1998, vol. 305, c637W.
25. HC Deb 16 December 1998, vol. 322, cc544–5W.
26. HC Deb 7 November 2001, vol. 374, c292W.
27. HC Deb 8 November 2001, vol. 374, c338W.
28. FBU, Memorandum, Select Committee on Environment, Transport and Regional Affairs (ETRA) Committee, Potential Risk of Fire Spread in Buildings via External Cladding Systems: Minutes of Evidence and Appendices, 20 July 1999; Glyn Evans, Testimony to the ETRA Committee, 20 July 1999.
29. Mike Fordham, 'Developing a fire safety policy in the UK and the European Community', *Firefighter*, May–June 2001: 20–23.
30. FBU, *Report of Proceedings*, 2002: 24–6.
31. FBU, *Office of the Deputy Prime Minister, Proposals for Amending Part B (Fire Safety) of the Building Regulations: A Response*, 18 November 2005: 4.
32. Ibid., 5.
33. Ibid., 16.
34. Ibid., 24.
35. Ibid., 25.
36. Ibid., 34.
37. HC Deb 23 June 1997, vol. 296, c362W.
38. HC Deb 7 July 1997, vol. 297, cc600–601.
39. HC Deb 27 November 1997, vol. 301, cc609–10W.
40. HC Deb 8 April 1998, vol. 310, cc254–5W.
41. FBU, 'Fighting fire and the causes of fire', *Firefighter*, June 1998: 8.

42. FBU, 'Fire Safety Development Group', *Firefighter*, June 1998: 8; Jim Fitzpatrick, 'Fire Safety All Parliamentary Group', *Firefighter*, May 1999: 2.
43. FBU, *Record of Decisions*, 1999: 16; FBU, *Report of Proceedings*, 1999: 31; FBU, 'New Fire Safety Bill must be enacted', *Firefighter*, June 1999: 14.
44. HC Deb 6 May 1999, vol. 330, c463W.
45. FBU, *Executive Council's Annual Report* 2000: 41–2.
46. FBU, *Executive Council's Annual Report* 2001: 48.
47. Mike O'Brien, 'Speech to the LGA Fire Conference', 8 March 2000.
48. FBU, *Executive Council's Annual Report*, 2002: 65–70; HC Deb 4 April 2001 vol. 366 cc213–14W.
49. FBU, *Report of Proceedings*, 2001: 108.
50. HC Deb 2 July 2001, vol. 371, c21W.
51. HC Deb 3 July 2001, vol. 371, c121W; HC Deb 4 July 2002, vol. 388, cc563–4W.
52. HC Deb 15 October 2002, vol. 390, cc829–31W.
53. HC Deb 2 December 2002, vol. 395, cc627–8W.
54. HC Deb 16 December 2002, vol. 396, cc552–67; George Bain, Michael Lyons, Anthony Young, *The Future of the Fire Service: Reducing Risks, Saving Lives*, The Independent Review of the Fire Service, December 2002: vii–ix.
55. HC Deb 19 December 2002, vol. 396, c90WS; HC Deb 7 March 2003, vol. 400, cc1251–2W.
56. FBU, *Executive Council's Annual Report*, 2004: 44–5.
57. HC Deb 8 May 2003, vol. 404, cc856–924; HL Deb 12 November 2003, vol. 654, c1520.
58. HC Deb 30 June 2003, vol. 408, cc21–36; ODPM, Our Fire and Rescue Service White Paper, 30 June 2003: 60–61.
59. Memorandum by The Fire Brigades Union (FBU) (FIR 30) to the Select Committee on Office of the Deputy Prime Minister: Housing, Planning, Local Government and the Regions Written Evidence, 15 October 2003.
60. HC Deb 12 January 2004, vol. 416, c530; HC Deb 26, January 2004, vol. 417 cc40–129; HL Deb 22 July 2004, vol. 664, c333.
61. HC Deb 11 December 2003, vol. 415, cc97–8WS; Mott MacDonald, *The Future of Fire and Rescue Service Control Rooms in England and Wales: Update*, 2003; HM Fire Service Inspectorate, *Analysis of the Best Value Reviews of Control and Communications*, November 2003.
62. HC Deb 30 June 2005, vol. 435, c1655W.

63. House of Commons ODPM: Housing, Planning, Local Government and the Regions Committee, *The Fire Service Third Report of Session 2003–04, Volume I: Report*, 23 January 2004.
64. Sharon Peverett, 'The future of Fire and Rescue Controls', *Firefighter*, April 2004: 6.
65. HL Deb 16 October 2001, vol. 627, cc86WA.
66. ODPM, 'Minister announces fire safety reform proposals', press release 048, 30 July 2002.
67. ODPM, The Regulatory Reform (Fire Safety) Order: Statement by the ODPM, 19 April 2004: 1–2.
68. Ibid., 14.
69. Ibid., 13, 19.
70. FBU Memorandum to the Regulatory Reform Committee, (May 2004) in Eleventh Report, 20 July 2004: Ev 2.
71. Glyn Evans, Select Committee on Regulatory Reform, Minutes of Evidence, 15 June 2004.
72. Regulatory Reform Committee, Draft Regulatory Reform (Fire Safety) Order 2005, 30 March 2005: 4, 11; House of Lords Delegated Powers and Regulatory Reform Committee, Draft Regulatory Reform (Fire Safety) Order 2005, Sixteenth Report, 24 March 2005: 3–4.
73. HC Deb 12 January 2006, vol. 441, c13WS; HC Deb 6 March 2006, vol. 443, c47–8WS.
74. HC Deb 10 October 2005, vol. 437, c361W.
75. Ibid.
76. FBU, Memorandum by the Fire Brigades Union (FBU) (FRS 63), House of Commons ODPM: Housing, Planning, Local Government and the Regions Committee The Fire and Rescue Service Session 2005–06 Volume II Oral and Written evidence, 13 March 2006: Ev 256–9.
77. Ibid., Ev 259.
78. Matt Wrack, ODPM Committee – The Fire and Rescue Service: Evidence, 6 February 2006; Ev 41.
79. Ruth Winters, ODPM Committee – The Fire and Rescue Service: Evidence, 6 February 2006; Ev 35.
80. HC Deb 25 January 2006, vol. 441, cc421–42WH.
81. Glyn Evans, 'Regulatory reform order', *Firefighter*, September 2006: 8–9.
82. HC Deb 2 November 2009, vol. 498, c756W.
83. HC Deb 26 March 2007, vol. 458, c326W.
84. NAO, *Regulatory Reform in the UK*, February 2008: 13.

85. BRAC, Minutes, 28 February 2008: 3–4.
86. HC Deb 27 March 2008, vol. 474, c394W; DCLG, Future of Building Control, Consultation, March 2008.
87. HC Deb 11 Nov 2009 vol. 499 c526W.
88. Mike Wood, 'Fire safety disconnect', *Firefighter*, January–February 2009: 5.
89. HC Deb 24 October 2007, vol. 465, c374W.
90. HC Deb 20 October 2008, vol. 481, c6W.
91. HC Deb 26 January 2009, vol. 487, c120W.
92. DCLG, Initial Evaluation of the Effectiveness of the Regulatory Reform (Fire Safety) Order, March 2009: 5–7.
93. HC Deb 10 December 2009, vol. 502, c591W.
94. House of Commons Communities and Local Government Committee, FiReControl, Fifth Report of Session 2009–10, 1 April 2010: 12, Ev1; Memorandum from the Fire Brigades Union (FBU) (FIRE 27), January 2010: Ev 101–9; Fire Brigades Union (Supplementary) (FIRE 27A) Ev 110; 'FBU speaks truth to power', *Firefighter*, April 2010: 10–13.
95. John Gummer and Zack Goldsmith, *Blueprint for a Green Economy*, Submission to the Shadow Cabinet, September 2007: 71–2.
96. Conservative Party, *Regulation in the Post Bureaucratic Age: How to Get Rid of Red Tape and Reform Quangos, A Policy Paper on Better Regulation*, October 2009: 3–4.
97. David Cameron, 'David Cameron pledges health and safety clear-out', *Daily Telegraph*, 1 December 2009.

Chapter 4 Cameron's deregulation accelerated

1. The Coalition, *Our Programme for Government*, 20 May 2010: 9–10, 29.
2. BIS, Action plan announced to end excessive regulation, 2 June 2010; NAO, The NAO's Work on Regulatory Reform, 15 October 2010.
3. Prime Minister's Office, 'David Cameron's speech to the Federation of Small Businesses', press release, 27 January 2014.
4. Prime Minister's Office, 'Transcript of a speech by the Prime Minister on the Big Society', press release, 19 July 2010.
5. HC Deb 17 November 2010, vol. 518, c41WS.
6. HC Deb 11 July 2011, vol. 531, c25.
7. Matt Wrack, 'Emergency fire services cannot be built on the sands of privatisation', *Guardian*, 6 September 2011.
8. HC Deb 3 June 2010, vol. 510, c575.

9. BIS, 'Speech: BCC annual conference, Central Hall, Westminster', press release, 15 March 2012.
10. HC Deb 19 November 2012, vol. 553, c16WS.
11. BIS, 'Cutting the burden and costs of regulation', press release, 27 February 2012.
12. Prime Minister's Office, 'Red Tape Challenge', press release, 7 April 2011.
13. BIS, 'Speech to British Chambers of Commerce', press release, 7 April 2011.
14. HC Deb 14 July 2011, vol. 531, c450.
15. HC Deb 14 May 2012, vol. 545, c283.
16. Cabinet Office, 'Government unveils Deregulation Bill', press release, 1 July 2013.
17. Prime Minister's Office, Supporting small businesses: David Cameron's speech to the Federation of Small Businesses, press release, 27 January 2014.
18. Matt Wrack, 'Clear and present danger', *Firefighter*, August-September 2010: 14.
19. Prime Minister's Office, 'PM announces review of health and safety laws', press release, 14 June 2010; 'Lord Young restores common sense to health and safety', press release, 15 October 2010.
20. Prime Minister's Office, 'Business boosting measures announced', press release, 5 January 2012.
21. Conservative Party, *Strong Leadership: General Election Manifesto*, April 2015: 19.
22. Queen's Speech 2015: background briefing notes, 27 May 2015.
23. HC Deb, 20 November 2015, vol. 602, cW.
24. BIS, 'Javid launches new drive to cut red tape', press release, 16 July 2015.
25. BIS, Getting government off your back: our commitment to cutting red tape, press release, 3 March 2016.
26. FBU, *A Service to Be Proud of – a Service Worth Defending: FBU Submission to the Comprehensive Spending Review*, September 2010: 8.
27. 'Fire Brigades Union warns of 10,000 job losses in Fire and Rescue Service', press release, 20 October 2010; Dave Green, '10,000 job cuts nightmare', *Firefighter*, October 2010: 7.
28. 'FBU tell governments: no fire cuts', *Firefighter*, January–February 2011: 10–11.
29. FBU, 'Voice of the professionals', *Firefighter*, November–December 2012: 4.

30. FBU, *Facing Reality – the Need for a Fully-Funded Fire and Rescue Service: FBU Submission to the Spending Review 2013 and Initial Response to Ken Knight's Review*, June 2013.
31. House of Commons Communities and Local Government Committee, Knight Review of Fire and Rescue Services, Oral and written evidence, 31 March 2014: Ev28; 'Knight proposals are rubbished', *Firefighter*, October 2013: 10.
32. Matt Wrack, 'A magnificent response from all members', *Firefighter*, November–December 2013: 2; Helen Hague, 'A magnificent show of solidarity', *Firefighter*, November–December 2013: 10.
33. FBU, *Sounding the alarm: the future of our fire and rescue service*. September 2014: 8–9.
34. Building Regulations in Northern Ireland, Scotland and Wales are the responsibility of the devolved administrations in those jurisdictions.
35. DCLG, 'Council workers to help in radical plan to cut red tape. A radical plan to banish red tape and repeal unnecessary laws was unveiled by Communities Secretary Eric Pickles today', press release, 7 July 2010.
36. HC Deb 13 December 2010, vol. 520, c64WS; HC Deb 17 January 2011, vol. 521, c558, 560.
37. HC Deb 28 March 2011, vol. 526, c77.
38. DCLG, Eric Pickles speech to the Confederation of British Industry annual dinner 2011, The London Hilton, original script, press release, 21 March 2011.
39. DCLG, Eric Pickles speech to the British Chambers of Commerce annual conference, Church House, Westminster, original script, press release, 7 April 2011.
40. DCLG, 'Council workers to help in radical plan to cut red tape', press release, 7 July 2010.
41. HC Deb 16 December 2010, vol. 520, c114WS.
42. DCLG, Future changes to the Building Regulations – next steps, December 2010: 7.
43. Ibid., 16.
44. HC Deb 31 January 2012, vol. 539, c38–39WS.
45. DCLG, 'Independent panel to help government cut housebuilding red tape and boost growth', press release, 31 October 2012.
46. HC Deb 18 December 2012, vol. 555, c83WS.
47. Bob Ledsome, Building Control by Approved Inspectors under Part II of the Building Act 1984, 21 December 2012.
48. HC Deb 5 February 2015, cW.
49. HC Deb 6 January 2015, vol. 590, c5WS.

50. Eric Pickles, GTI Phase 2: Transcript Day, 6 April 2022: 10/13, 52/2–13, 78/14; GTI, *Phase 2 Report*, vol. 1, §10.21, 10.50, §10.52. 2024: 150, 159.
51. DCLG, Cutting Red Tape review will give construction industry the foundations to get Britain building, press release, 2 December 2015.
52. HC Deb 20 April 2016, cW.
53. HC Deb 20 July 2015, vol. 598, c1341–3.
54. DCLG, Greg Clark: NHBC speech, original script, press release, 26 November 2015.
55. HC Deb 11 May 2016, vol. 609, c341–4WH.
56. Sarah Morgan, Building control review – meeting with JW follow up actions, email, 23 October 2015; Privatisation discussions confirmed in Richard Harral, GTI witness statement, 16 November 2018.
57. Alex Murphy to James Wharton and Greg Clark, Simplification of Building Regulations and the building control system, email, 10 November 2015: 23.
58. Jeff Ord, 'Advisory body begins work', *FIRE*, October 2003: 8; FBU, *Executive Council's Annual Report*, 2011: 29, 33.
59. DCLG, 'Leading a lean and efficient fire and rescue service', draft speech, press release, 29 June 2010; 'New government promise 'local' future', *FIRE*, September 2010: 17.
60. DCLG, Fire Minister Bob Neill responds to claims the government plans to scrap sprinkler requirements for industrial buildings, press release, 19 November 2010.
61. HC Deb 24 November 2010, vol. 519, c304W.
62. DCLG, 'Local Government Association annual fire conference 2011: the future of fire', transcript of the speech, press release, 9 March 2011.
63. HC Deb 16 March 2011, vol. 525, c333W.
64. DCLG, Fire Futures Reports: Government response. April 2011: 17.
65. FBU, 'What does the future hold for the fire and rescue service?' *Firefighter*, June–July 2011: 14.
66. HC Deb 22 March 2012, vol. 542, c67WS.
67. Jack Ford, 'Time to think again about the Fire Service College sell-off', *Firefighter*, May 2012: 9.
68. HC Deb 28 February 2013, vol. 559, c33WS; DCLG, Sale of the Fire Service College completed, press release, 28 February 2013.
69. HC Deb 10 January 2012, vol. 538, c43W.
70. Neil Connor, Pre-consultation letter, 21 November 2012.
71. Andy Dark, Letter to Neil O'Connor, 28 January 2013.

72. Brandon Lewis, Letter to James Duddridge, chair of the Regulatory Reform Committee, 23 January 2013.
73. James Duddridge, Letter to Brandon Lewis, 14 February 2013.
74. Andy Dark, Letter to James Duddridge, 8 February 2013.
75. Brandon Lewis, Letter to Matt Wrack, 15 March 2013.
76. Matt Wrack, 'Fighting on three fronts', *Firefighter*, March 2013: 2; 'Contracting out plans will cost lives – FBU', *Firefighter*, March 2013: 7.
77. HC Deb 5 March 2013, vol. 559, c931W.
78. FBU, 'Mutual plan is "back door privatisation"', *Firefighter*, April 2013: 5.
79. FBU, 'We still need to combat bids to privatise the fire service', *Firefighter*, August–September 2013: 7.
80. FBU, 'Cleveland firefighters reject mutualisation proposals', *Firefighter*, October 2013: 16.
81. FBU, 'Privatisation creeps and sneaks but still fails', *Firefighter*, March 2015: 16–17.
82. HC Deb 7 January 2014, vol. 573, c221W; HC Deb 17, November 2014, cW.
83. DBIS, *Focus on Enforcement Reviews: Regulatory Reform (Fire Safety) Order*, August 2013: 9, 21.
84. HC Deb 3 November 2014, cW.
85. NAO, *Financial Sustainability of Fire and Rescue Services*, November 2015: 20.
86. Andy Dark, 'An appeal for professional standards [letter to Ken Knight]', *Firefighter*, November-December 2011: 16.
87. House of Commons Communities and Local Government Committee, Knight Review of Fire and Rescue Services. Oral and written evidence, 31 March 2014: Ev28.
88. Andrew Watterson, *Firefighter Fatalities at Fires in the UK: 2004–2013: Voices from the Fireground*, January 2015.
89. FBU, *Submission to the Consultation: Enabling Closer Working between the Emergency Services*, 19 October 2015.
90. DCLG, Legislation to allow Police and Crime Commissioners to take responsibility for their local fire service, press release, 26 January 2016.
91. Home Office, Theresa May: Home Secretary speech on fire reform, to Reform think tank event in London, 24 May 2016.
92. FBU, 'Firefighter job cuts put public safety at risk', *FRS Matters*, July 2015.
93. FBU, *Submission to the Comprehensive Spending Review 2015*, September 2015: 3.

94. FBU, 'Local government finance settlement: fire and rescue service slashed again', *FRS Matters*, April 2016.
95. Prime Minister's Office, The new role for business in a fairer Britain: article by Theresa May, press release, 20 November 2016.
96. Prime Minister's Office, CBI annual conference 2016: Prime Minister's speech, press release, 21 November 2016.
97. Conservative Party, *Forward Together: General Election Manifesto*, May 2017.
98. APPG Built Environment, *More Homes, Fewer Complaints*, July 2016: 21.
99. Ibid., 23.
100. HC Deb 24 October 2016, vol. 616, c16.
101. HC Deb 31 October 2016, vol. 616, c751.
102. HC Deb 1 March 2017, cW.
103. Home Office, 'Fire Minister speaks at CFOA conference', press release, 13 September 2016.
104. Home Office, 'Fire Minister Brandon Lewis speaks at Fire Sector Summit 2016', press release, 18 October 2016.
105. HC Deb 23 January 2017, vol. 620, c14.
106. FBU, *Oldham Street Incident July 2013: The Death of Stephen Hunt*, October 2016: 2, 81–2.
107. FBU, *Give the FBU a Role in Setting Professional Standards*, parliamentary lobby, November 2016; Matt Wrack, 'Our fight for standards continues', *Firefighter*, December 2016–January 2017: 2; 'Lobby to save a service going backwards professional standards', *Firefighter*, December 2016–January 2017: 4.
108. HC Deb 4 November 2016, cW.
109. HC Deb 9 February 2017, cW.
110. David Wibberley, 'Private Mon£Y Public Mayhem: Privatisation Special Report', *Firefighter*, February 2017: 11–13.
111. FBU, 'More than 9,600 firefighter jobs cut since 2010', *FRS Matters*, September 2016.
112. FBU, 'Local Government Finance Settlement', *FRS Matters*, March 2017.
113. FBU, 'Almost one-in-five frontline firefighter jobs cut since 2010', *FRS Matters*, July 2017.

Chapter 5 Building safety downgraded

1. This chapter draws on Luke Bisby, *Grenfell Tower Inquiry: Regulatory Testing and the Path to Grenfell*, 2022; Peter Apps, *Show Me the*

Bodies, London: Oneworld Publications, 2022; as well as primary sources published by the Grenfell Tower Inquiry (GTI).

2. H.W. Harrison, J.H. Hunt and J. Thomson, *Overcladding External Walls of Large Panel System Dwellings*, BRE, 1986: 25.
3. Ibid., 118.
4. B.F.W Rogowski, R. Ramaprasad and J.R. Southern, *Fire Performance of External Thermal Insulation for Walls of Multi-Storey Buildings*, BR 135 1/e, 1988: 6.
5. Paddy Shennan, 'Towering Inferno', *Liverpool Echo*, 5 April 1991.
6. BRE, Assessment of Overcladding to Knowsley Heights, Liverpool, Investigation of the Fire at Knowsley Heights, Huyton, Liverpool, 5 April 1991 National Archives April 91 BRE 180/2/89, Knowsley fire AT 66/389; BRE, *Summary of fires investigated*: April 1991 to March 1992, CR176/92, November 1992: 19–20.
7. 'Fire News', *Private Eye*, 21 June 1991.
8. Bisby, *Regulatory Testing*, 98–9.
9. The FBU, along with Apps and Bisby, found National Archives materials useful in clarifying the weaknesses in the investigation of Knowsley Heights. FBU, *The Grenfell Tower Fire: A Crime Caused by Profit and Deregulation*. September 2019: 31.
10. Bisby, *Regulatory Testing*, 101–2.
11. Peter Apps, 'Special investigation: how the government missed the chance to prevent the cladding crisis in the 1990s', *Inside Housing*, 13 June 2021; Apps, *Show Me the Bodies*, 35; Bisby, *Regulatory Testing*, 104–5.
12. Raymond Connolly, *Investigation of the behaviour of external cladding systems in fire. Report on 10 full-scale fire tests*. Fire Research Station, CR 143/94, April 1994: 42.
13. HC Deb 20 January 1997 vol. 288 c440W.
14. Bisby, *Regulatory Testing*, 111.
15. Ibid., 112.
16. Ibid., 113.
17. FBU, *A Fighting Chance*, 1995: 18, 20–21.
18. Ken Cameron, 'Hazards that a humanitarian service should not have to face', *Firefighter*, September 1992: 1, 3; FBU, 'Heroic firefighters decorated for rescue', *Firefighter*, November 1993: 19; Eleanor Lawson, 'Hero fireman aged 22 who died while tackling tower block blaze remembered on anniversary of death', *Express and Star*, 28 July 2023.
19. Mike Fordham, 'New Labour Government delivers: Victory on Fire Safety', *Firefighter*, September–October 1997: 7.

20. FBU, *Executive Council's Annual Report*, 1999: 77.
21. FBU, Memorandum, ETRA Committee, *Potential Risk of Fire Spread in Buildings via External Cladding Systems: Minutes of Evidence and Appendices*, 20 July 1999: 2.
22. Ibid., 3.
23. Ibid., 4.
24. Glyn Evans, Testimony to the ETRA Committee, 20 July 1999, in ibid., 12.
25. ETRA Committee, Report and Proceedings: Potential Risk of Fire Spread in Buildings via External Cladding Systems, First Report HC 109, 5 January 2000: x–xi.
26. DETR, Government Response to the First Report of the Committee: Potential Risk of Fire Spread in Buildings via External Cladding Systems, 6 April 2000: 1.
27. Ibid., 1.
28. HL Deb 16 October 2001, vol. 627, cc85–6WA.
29. Penny Morgan, Brian Martin and Tony Morris, *Fire at Garnock Court, Irvine on the 11 June 1999*, BRE Client Report 79902, Prepared for North Ayrshire Council, August 1999; Penny Morgan, *Fire at Garnock Court, Irvine. Phase 2 Fire Tests on GRP cladding*, Prepared for North Ayrshire Council. Fire Protection Systems Centre, April 2000; Penny Morgan, *DETR Framework Project Report: Investigation of Real Fires*, Project report number 76572, August 2000.
30. An informal fee proposal letter from J.N. Smithies of BRE to G.D. Wallace of North Ayrshire Council, 26 July 1999, explicitly noted that, 'BRE is now fully privatised and is owned by the Foundation for the Built Environment. Any work we do for non-government customers is confidential'. Bisby, *Regulatory Testing*, 133, n. 432.
31. Morgan et al., *Fire at Garnock Court, Irvine*, 2–3; Morgan, *Fire at Garnock Court*, 9–10; Bisby, *Regulatory Testing*, 134–6.
32. Sarah Colwell, Jason Foster and Brian Martin, *Fire Spread in External Cladding – A Literature Review*, BRE client report 80415 for DETR, 21 July 2000: 3, 7–8; Bisby, *Regulatory Testing*, 143–4.
33. Colwell, *DETR Framework Project Report: Survey Summary and Options Report*, Project report number Milestone – 80417, 24 July 2000: 4; Bisby, *Regulatory Testing*, 145.
34. BRE, DETR Contract number CC1924; Bisby, *Regulatory Testing*, 147–51; BRE, *Analysis of ISO 9705, European and British Standard Fire Test Data for BR135 Project*, Client report number 209984, For ODPM, 19 September 2002.

35. Andy Dark, Letter to Carole Whale, Sustainable Buildings, Communities and Local Government, 24 October 2007.
36. FBU, *Report of Proceedings*, May 2005: 81.
37. FBU, *Health and Safety Investigation Report: Harrow Court*, 2007: 233–34.
38. Ibid., 240.
39. Ibid., 235, 239.
40. Edward Thomas, Harrow Court Fire, Coroner's Rule 43 Letter, Harrow Court, Hertfordshire, 8 March 2007: 2.
41. FBU, 'HSE Notices have national implications', *Firefighter*, June 2009: 4.
42. Ken Knight, *Report to the Secretary of State by the Chief Fire and Rescue Adviser on the Emerging Issues Arising from the Fatal Fire at Lakanal House, Camberwell on 3 July 2009*, 30 July 2009: 5.
43. FBU, 'We must have a public inquiry', *Firefighter*, August–September 2009: 12–13.
44. FBU, *Executive Council's Annual Report*, 2010: 96.
45. David Crowder, Richard Chitty, Martin Shipp and Róisin Cullinan, *Lakanal House Fire Investigation - Computer Modelling and Reconstruction Fire*, Prepared for Metropolitan Police Service, BRE client report number 259441, 17 December 2010.
46. Matt Wrack, 'Alan Bannon and James Shears: devastating tragedy in Southampton', *Firefighter*, May 2010: 2–3; FBU, 'Firefighters die at tower block fire', *Firefighter*, May 2010: 4.
47. Antonia Crawford, David Crowder, Luke Ellis, Phil Clark, Martin Shipp and Róisin Cullinan, *Communities and Local Government Report: BD 2786. Investigation of Real Fires July 2010 – July 2011*. BRE. Prepared for Brian Martin, 27 July 2011: 72–4.
48. Ibid., 121–2.
49. Ibid., 126–7.
50. Ibid., 137–9.
51. David Crowder, Amaia Harries, Phil Clark, Martin Shipp, Carl Sherwood, Emma Warren and Antonia Crawford, *Department for Communities and Local Government Report: BD 2786 Investigation of Real Fires July 2011–July 2012*, Prepared for Brian Martin, 26 July 2012: 21.
52. GTI, *Phase 2 Report*, vol. 1, §8.12, §8.13, September 2024: 124.
53. Andy Dark, Letter to Brian Martin, 30 March 2011; Andy Dark, Standards in Building Regulation Compliance, Executive Council paper 44/11AD, 13 April 2011: 2–3.
54. Dave Sibert, GTI witness statement, 27 April 2018: 7.

55. Dennis Davis, GTI witness statement, 19 November 2020: 7, 9.
56. LGA, *Fire Safety in Purpose Built Blocks of Flats*. May 2012: 9–11.
57. Eric Pickles, GTI witness statement, 16 January 2019: 12.
58. HC Deb 4 November 2013, vol. 570, c21W.
59. LGA, *Fire Safety in Purpose Built Blocks*, 18.
60. Ibid., 28.
61. Ibid., 120 (with redactions); GTI, *Phase 2 Report*, vol. 1, §14.17, 222.
62. Steve Hull, Letter from Health and Safety Executive to Hampshire Fire and Rescue Service, 10 February 2012; Hampshire Fire and Rescue Service, Fatal Fire Investigation, 2013: 163.
63. FBU, *Shirley Towers: FBU Health and Safety Interim Investigation Report*. May 2012: 51–2 (unpublished); Hampshire Fire and Rescue Service, *Fatal Fire Investigation*, 2013.
64. 'FBU reaction to Shirley Towers' inquest verdict – death by misadventure, with narrative verdict', press release, 10 July 2012; 'FBU satisfied with Shirley Towers verdict', *Firefighter*, August–September 2012: 5
65. Keith Wiseman, Inquest into the deaths of Alan Bannon and James Shears, Coroner's Rule 43 Letter – Shirley Towers, Hampshire, 4 February 2013: 2–3.
66. FBU, 'Lessons must be learned from the Lakanal House fire', *Firefighter*, 28 March 2013: 7.
67. Frances Kirkham, Lakanal House fire, 3 July 2009, Coroner's Rule 43 Letter to Eric Pickles, Secretary of State for Communities and Local Government, 28 March 2013: 2–3.
68. Eric Pickles, Reply to Frances Kirkham: Coroner's Rule 43 Letter – Lakanal House, 20 May 2013: 2.
69. Bisby, *Regulatory Testing*, 220; Brian Martin, Email to Tony Baker, Sarah Colwell, Stephen Howard, November 2013.
70. Bisby, *Regulatory Testing*, 224–6.
71. David Amess, Letter to Stephen Williams, 5 August 2014; Stephen Williams, Letter to David Amess, 9 September 2014; Bisby, *Regulatory Testing*, 223.
72. Nathan Cole, Clara Holland, Martin Shipp and David Crowder, *Department for Communities and Local Government Research Report: BD 2890 Investigation of Real Fires – External Fire Spread in Multi Storey Buildings*, Prepared for Brian Martin, 9 January 2015 [misdated 2014]; Clara Holland, David Crowder and Martin Shipp, *BRE Report on External Fire Spread – Part 1 Experimental Research*, April 2016; Clara Holland, David Crowder, Martin Shipp and Nathan Cole, *BRE*

Report on External Fire Spread – Part 2 Experimental Research, April 2016.

73. HC Deb 3 March 2015, vol. 593, c248WH.
74. HC Deb 24 October 2016, vol. 616, c16.
75. Building Regulations: Fire Prevention: Written question – 6319406, 9 February 2017.
76. Damien Gayle, 'Southwark council pleads guilty over worst ever tower block fire', *Guardian*, 24 February 2017.
77. Peter Apps, 'PM's chief of staff did not act on multiple warnings about fire safety in months before Grenfell, new letters show', *Inside Housing*, 13 June 2019; Gavin Barwell, GTI Phase 2: Transcript Day 260. 5 April 2022: 257/9–12.
78. This section draws on Peter Apps and other journalists at *Inside Housing* magazine; Andrew Chapman, River of Life blogs on Grenfell Tower; Bisby, *Regulatory Testing*.
79. Peter Robinson, 'New building controls: A giant step, or just a pace, in the right direction?' *FIRE*, October 1985: 13; 'November date set for new building controls', *FIRE*, September 1985: 53; 'Abolition: New authorities are Home Office guidelines', *FIRE*, November 1985: 27.
80. Department of the Environment and The Welsh Office, The Building Regulations 1985, Fire, Approved Document B: B2/3/4 Fire Spread, HMSO 1985: i.
81. GTI, *Phase 2 Report*, vol. 1, §5.25, 55.
82. Department of the Environment, Approved Document B. 1985: 13, 46.
83. GTI, *Phase 2 Report*, vol. 1, §6.22, 73.
84. Department of the Environment and The Welsh Office, The Building Regulations 1991, Fire Safety, Approved Document B, HMSO 1992: 72.
85. ODPM, The Building Regulations 2000, Fire Safety, Approved Document B, NBS, 2006: 90.
86. DCLG, The Building Regulations 2000, Fire Safety, Approved Document B, vol. 2 – Buildings other than Dwellinghouses, NBS, 2007: 93–4.
87. GTI, *Phase 2 Report*, vol. 1, §6.40, 77.
88. HL Deb 5 April 1984, vol. 450, cc823–54; Apps, *Show Me The Bodies*, 33–4.
89. H.L. Malhotra, *Fire Safety in Buildings*. Department of the Environment, Building Research Establishment, Fire Research Station, Borehamwood, 1986: 12; Bisby, *Regulatory Testing*, 90–91.

Chapter 6 Fire safety fragmented

1. HC Deb 2 November 2009, vol. 498, c756W.
2. Ronald Holroyd, Report for the Departmental Committee on the Fire Service, May 1970: 26–35.
3. HC Deb 19 December 2002, vol. 396, c90WS; HC Deb 7 March 2003, vol. 400, cc1251–2W.
4. HC Deb 13 March 2003, vol. 401, cc420–2W.
5. Home Office, FIRE1001: Average response times by location and fire and rescue authority/geographical category, England (accessed 25 July 2024).
6. Home Office, FIRE0101: Incidents attended by fire and rescue services by nation and population (accessed 25 July 2024).
7. Home Office, FIRE0501: Fatalities and non-fatal casualties by nation and population (accessed 25 July 2024).
8. Home Office, FIRE0904: Fatalities and non-fatal casualties in non-fire incidents by fire and rescue authority and non-fire incident type, England (accessed 25 July 2024).
9. FBU, 'Firefighters continue to rescue more people year on year', *FRS Matters*, February 2019.
10. National Audit Office, 'Financial sustainability of fire and rescue services', November 2015; FBU, 'Local Government finance settlement: Fire and rescue service slashed again', *FRS Matters*, April 2016.
11. Home Office, Fire Statistics Table 1101: Staff in post employed by fire and rescue authorities by headcount, for England, 31 March.
12. Home Office, FIRE1403: Fire stations and appliances, by fire and rescue authority; FBU, *Losing Control? Cuts, Closures and Challenges in UK Fire Controls*, April 2017.
13. HC Deb 2 November 2009, vol. 498, c756W; DCLG, 'New Chief Fire and Rescue Adviser appointed', press release, 22 January 2013.
14. Home Office, Theresa May: Home Secretary speech on fire reform, to Reform think tank event in London, 24 May 2016.
15. HC Deb 19 July 2017 vol. 627 c51–2WS.
16. Home Office, Fire and Rescue National Framework for England, July 2012: 7.
17. Home Office, National Framework, July 2012: 17.
18. Peter Murphy and Katarzyna Lakoma, 'The (mis)interpretation of Section 25 of the Fire and Rescue Services Act 2004', *FIRE* magazine, September 2020.
19. HC Deb 7 April 2003, vol. 403, c4WS.

20. HMICFRS, Fire and Rescue Service inspections 2018/19: Summary Tranche 1, 2018; HMICFRS, Summary Tranche 2, 2019.
21. CACFOA, *Whither the Future*, February 1981: 7, 50; Brian Fuller, 'CACFOA urged to support moves to greater self-regulation', *FIRE supplement*, September 1980: 23; 'Self controls would ease fire service's paperwork burden, says Lord Belstead', *FIRE supplement*, September 1981: 7.
22. Jeff Ord, 'Advisory body begins', *FIRE*, October 2003: 8; Richard Bull, 'Legislation – progress at last', *FIRE*, February 2002: 10–11; Alan Doig, 'Collaboration key to reform', *FIRE*, February 2004: 9; ODPM Committee, The Fire and Rescue Service: Evidence, 23 March 2006: Ev 45.
23. Jonathan Herrick, 'The Regulators Code – contributing to the economy', *FIRE*, January 2015: 36; Jonathan Herrick, 'Fire safety – who can you trust?' *FIRE*, March 2015: 48.
24. DCLG, Initial Evaluation of the Effectiveness of the Regulatory Reform (Fire Safety) Order, March 2009: 5–7.
25. GTI, *Phase 2 Report*, vol. 1, §12.23, §12.28, §12.33, September 2024: 210.
26. Ibid., §12.41, §12.43, 210.
27. Ibid., §12.49, 211; Tani Nisbet-Jones, email submission, Government Response to the Knight Review, 17 July 2013.
28. DBIS, Focus on Enforcement Reviews: Regulatory Reform (Fire Safety) Order, August 2013: 9, 21.
29. FBU, Executive Council's Annual Report, 2015: 58–9; GTI, *Phase 2 Report*, vol. 1, §12.53, 212.
30. DCLG, Operational Statistics, Appendix 15; MHCLG, Operational Statistics, Appendix 15; Home Office, FIRE1204.
31. FBU, 'Cuts to fire safety inspectors put the public at risk', *FRS Matters*, October 2017.
32. HMFSI, A Guide to Operational Risk Assessment, vol. 3, Generic Risk Assessment 3.2 Fighting Fire – High Rise Buildings. September 1998: 17–23.
33. HC Deb 7 July 2008, vol. 478, c1346–7W.
34. Peter Cowup, *National Guidance and London Fire Brigade Operational Policy for Fighting Fires in High Rise Buildings*, Report to the GTI, January 2019: 3.
35. Ibid., 7.
36. DCLG/CFRA, Generic Risk Assessment 3.2, 'Fighting fires – In high rise buildings', February 2014: 6–7, 16–17, 20.
37. Dave Sibert, 'The problem with PORIS', *FIRE*, May 2014: 12–14.

38. Ken Knight, GTI witness statement, 13 September 2018: 2; Ron Dobson, GTI witness statement: 28 January 2019: 3; Dany Cotton, GTI witness statement, 21 February 2018: 1.
39. Hélène Mulholland, 'London Fire chief says union officials are "thick" and "nasty"', *Guardian*, 25 November 2010.
40. FBU, 'Strike ballot over sack threat', *Firefighter*, October 2010: 4; 'First strikes over mass sackings – more planned', *Firefighter*, November–December 2010: 4; *Executive Council's Annual* Report, 2011: 19–20, 105–6.
41. HC Deb 30 November 2000, vol. 357, c929W.
42. AssetCo, Financial statements, 31 March 2007: 4, 6.
43. AssetCo, *The AssetCo Fire and Rescue Report 2008*, March 2008: 4–5; AssetCo, Financial statements, 31 March 2008: 8; AssetCo, Financial statements, 31 March 2010: 5.
44. Francis Beckett, 'Strikebreakers mow down a picket', *Firefighter*, March 2011: 14–15.
45. David Hencke, 'Profiting from the fire service', *Firefighter*, March 2011: 16–17; David Hencke, 'AssetCo shows the folly of privatisation', *Firefighter*, October 2011: 16.
46. Matt Wrack, Letter to Ron Dobson, 11 February 2011; Matt Wrack, Letter to Bob Neill, 22 March 2011; Matt Wrack, Letter to Bob Neill, 12 July 2011; FBU, 'Public safety in jeopardy as London's fire engine fleet is bought and sold', press release, 16 August 2012.
47. Peter Dominiczak, Michael Howie, 'Taxpayer set to foot bill as London fire engine contract stripped from colourful baronet', *Evening Standard*, 14 November 2012; Babcock, 'Babcock named preferred bidder for London Fire Brigade fleet management contract', press release, 1 April 2014.
48. Financial Reporting Council, *Particulars of Fact and Acts of Misconduct: Grant Thornton UK LLP and Robert Napper*, 24 April 2017; Bernard Eder, Pamela Ormerod and John Alexander, *Report of the Disciplinary Tribunal of the Financial Reporting Council*, 7 August 2018.
49. European Services Strategy Unit (ESSU), *Privatisation of London's Fire Service Training and Control Centre*, Report for FBU, Unison and GMB, October 2011: 6.
50. Matt Wrack, 'Emergency fire services cannot be built on the sands of privatisation', *Guardian*, 6 September 2011.
51. Andrew Dismore, Babcock training contract (1), Mayor's Question Time 20504, Greater London, 14 November 2019; FBU, 'Fire service on the table', *Firefighter*, June–July 2012: 10.

52. Ron Dobson, GTI witness statement, 28 January 2019: 13.
53. Dexter Whitfield, *Privatisation of London's Fire Service Training and Control Centre*. European Services Strategy Unit. October 2011; FBU, 'Who is in control?' *Firefighter*, May 2012: 17.
54. London Fire and Emergency Planning Authority, Minutes of the meeting of 21 June 2012: 9–11; FBU, 'Fire service on the table', *Firefighter*, June–July 2012: 10.
55. GTI, *Phase 2 Report*, vol. 5, §79.95, September 2024: 157.
56. Ibid., §79.45, §79.123, 144, 164.
57. Ibid., §79.99, §79.102, 158–9.
58. Ibid., §79.115, §79.119, 161–3.
59. Ibid., §79.41, §79.79, 143, 153.
60. HL Deb 18 March 1998, vol. 587, cc203–4WA.
61. Gordon Fielden, 'FBU wins victory in dispute over high-rise attendance', *FBU Organiser*, 41, July 2006: 10.
62. 'Boris Johnson takes £30m from fire brigade to boost Met', *Evening Standard*, 5 April 2012.
63. FBU, '7 out of 10 Londoners think Mayor's fire cuts will put safety at risk as firefighters take to the streets in protest', press release, 17 July 2013.
64. FBU London region, *The draft London Safety Plan Five LSP5: Final Observations*, 14 July 2013: 21.
65. Matthew Weaver, 'Boris Johnson's unused water cannon sold for scrap at £300,000 loss', *Guardian*, 19 November 2018.
66. FBU London region, *London Safety plan 2017: Submission to Consultation*, January 2017: 10.
67. Home Office, Fire Statistics Table 1101: Staff in post employed by fire and rescue authorities by headcount by role, 31 March each year, 6 September 2018.
68. LFB, Freedom of Information Act request – staff dedicated to inspecting and auditing fire safety by full time equivalent, FOIA3207.1, 14 August 2017.
69. Ron Dobson, Letter to London Borough Housing Departments and Associations, and other social housing providers, 9 July 2009; Dobson, Letter to Knight, 14 December 2009.
70. Francis Kirkham, Lakanal House fire 3 July 2009 – Coroner's Rule 43 Letter to the London Fire Brigade, 28 March 2013: 2–3; LFB, *Lakanal House – Monitoring Report and Action Plan – update*, March 2016.
71. Ron Dobson, Commissioners high rise presentation, RISCAuthority, 17 October 2016: 1, 10.
72. LFB, *Grenfell Tower Fire: Preliminary Report*, 2 April 2019: 44.

73. Cowup, *National Guidance and London Fire Brigade*, January 2019.
74. LFB, *Grenfell Tower Fire: Preliminary Report*, 2 April 2019: 28.
75. GTI, *Phase 1 Report*, vol. 4, §28.55. October 2019: 607.
76. GTI, *Phase 2 Report*, vol. 5, §83.1, §83.3, 207.

Chapter 7 Refurbishment botched

1. GTI, *Phase 2 Report*, vol. 1, §1.3, September 2024: 3.
2. Richard Millett, GTI Phase 1: Transcript Day 1, 4 June 2018: 106/19; Millett, GTI Phase 2: Transcript Day 1, 27 January 2020: 18/17; Millett, GTI Phase 2: Transcript Day 312, 10 November 2022: 31/22.
3. GTI, *Phase 1 Report*, vol. 1, §6.12, §6.17, October 2019: 35–6.
4. Sam Stein, GTI Phase 2: Transcript Day 67. 9 November 2020: 28/19; Stein, GTI Phase 2: Transcript Day 175. 15 September 2021: 157/21–5.
5. Stein, GTI Phase 2: Transcript Day 175. 15 September 2021: 168/11–16; 169/7–17.
6. GTI, *Phase 2 Report*, vol. 2, §17.4, §17.22, September 2024: 13, 18.
7. Ibid., §17.13, §17.14, §17.16, §17.21, 16–17.
8. Ibid., §20.1, §20.2, 35.
9. Ibid., §18.26, §20.7, 25, 36.
10. Ibid., §20.17, §20.24, 38, 40.
11. Ibid., §20.40, §20.42, 44–5.
12. Ibid., §20.38, 44.
13. Ibid., §16.5, §16.15, 10–11; Arconic, Overarching closing submissions by AAP SAS, 2022: 1–2, 4.
14. GTI, *Phase 2 Report*, vol. 2, §22.1, §22.9, § 22.10, 65, 67.
15. Ibid., §22.12, §22.17, §22.25, 68, 70, 72.
16. Ibid., §22.53, §22.54, 80.
17. Ibid., §22.60, §22.61, §22.62, 82–3.
18. Ibid., §22.93, §22.94, 91.
19. Ibid., §22.97, 92.
20. Ibid., §22.134, §22.135, 102.
21. Ibid., §24.1, §24.4, §24.6, 119–20.
22. Ibid., §24.12, §24.19, §24.39, 121–2, 123, 128.
23. Ibid., §24.53, §24.64, §24.76, 131, 134, 137.
24. Ibid., §24.107, §24.121, 145–6, 148.
25. Ibid., §24.1, 119.
26. Ibid., §24.134, 152.
27. Adrian Williamson, GTI Phase 2: Transcript Day 309. 7 November 2022: 68/22–5–69/1–2.

28. Sam Stein, GTI Phase 2: Transcript Day 175. 15 September 2021: 176/25–177/1–15.
29. GTI, *Phase 2 Report*, vol. 2, §22.20, 70.
30. Ibid., §22.120, 98–9.
31. Ibid., §24.76, 137–8.
32. Ibid., §29.13, §29.27, 215, 218.
33. Ibid., §20.19, §20.20, §20.24, 39–40.
34. Ibid., §21.13, §21.25, §21.26, 53–4, 56.
35. Ibid., §21.55, 63.
36. GTI, *Phase 2 Report*, vol. 1, §2.35, §2.36, September 2024: 34.
37. GTI, *Phase 2 Report*, vol. 2, §29.41, 221.
38. Ibid., §23.1, 103.
39. Ibid., §22.95, §24.134, §22.134, 92, 152, 102.
40. Ibid., §26.1, §26.2, 163.
41. Ibid., §26.7, §26.8, 164.
42. Ibid., §26.9, §26.30, §26.40, 164, 169, 171.
43. Ibid., §26.55, §26.72, 175, 178.
44. Ibid., §26.81, 181–2.
45. GTI, *Phase 2 Report*, vol. 3, §31.2, §31.12, September 2024: 9–10.
46. Hodkinson, *Safe as Houses*, 31–5.
47. RBKC, Phase 2, Module 1 Opening Statement, 20 December 2019: 8; RBKC, Module 3 Opening Statement, 19 March 2021: 9; GTI, *Phase 2 Report*, vol. 3, §35.4, 46.
48. GTI, *Phase 2 Report*, vol. 3, §31.35, §31.36, §38.2, 14–15, 65.
49. Ibid., §38.5, §38.6, §38.24, 66, 70–71.
50. Ibid., §38.35, §38.62, 73–4, 80.
51. Ibid., §38.63, 80.
52. Ibid., §39.51, §39.77, 98, 105.
53. Peter Apps, 'KCTMO project manager admits destroying evidence relating to Grenfell refurbishment after fire', *Inside Housing*, 19 October 2020; GTI, *Phase 2 Report*, vol. 4, §50.10, §55.87, September 2024: 28, 134.
54. GTI, *Phase 2 Report*, vol. 4, §66.3, §66.8, §66.11, §61.1, §66.15, 315–17, 239.
55. Ibid., §66.1, 315.
56. Ibid., §62.3, §62.45, 245, 258.
57. Ibid., §62.54, §62.55, 260–61; John Hoban, GTI Phase 2: Transcript Day 45. 30 September 2020: 107/1–15; 110/23–4.
58. GTI, *Phase 2 Report*, vol. 4, §62.64, 263.
59. Shane Ewen, *Before Grenfell*. 2023: 1.
60. RBKC, Chronology of Grenfell Tower, Version 2. 4 June 2018.

61. GTI, *Phase 2 Report*, vol. 3, §31.39, 16.
62. Matthew Ramsey, GTI witness statement, 24 January 2019: 7–8; GTI, *Phase 2 Report*, vol. 3, §31.41, §46.73, 16, 197.
63. GTI, *Phase 2 Report*, vol. 3, §38.73, §46.77, 82, 198.
64. Michele McHugh, GTI witness statement, 8 February 2019: 6–7, 10; GTI, *Phase 2 Report*, vol. 3, §31.53, 18.
65. LFB, *Grenfell Tower Operational Risk Database*. 15 February 2017: 4.
66. GTI, *Phase 2 Report*, vol. 4, §51.2, §51.4, §51.10, §51.11, 41–3.
67. Ibid., §67.10, 320; RBKC, Chronology of Grenfell Tower, 3–10; Peter Apps, 'Grenfell Tower refurbishment: a timeline', *Inside Housing*, 27 November 2020.
68. GTI, *Phase 1 Report*, vol. 1, §§6.2–6.6, 33.
69. GTI, *Phase 2 Report*, vol. 4, §51.6, §63.1, §63.5, 42, 265–6.
70. Ibid., §63.10, §63.11, §63.24, §63.27, 268, 272.
71. Ibid., §63.29, §63.30, 63.50, 273, 279.
72. Ibid., §63.1, 265.
73. Ibid., §50.26, 32.
74. Cate Cooney, Email to Andrew Martyn, 16 August 2012; GTI, *Phase 2 Report*, vol. 4, §54.34, §54.47, 75, 79.
75. GTI, *Phase 2 Report*, vol. 4, §54.165, §54.170, 110–11.
76. Ibid., §50.37, §50.46, 35–6.
77. Ibid., §64.16, §64.17, §64.29, §64.30, §64.37, §64.38, §64.39, 64.41, 284, 287–90.
78. Ibid., §64.1, 281.
79. Ibid., §65.1, §65.7, 293–4.
80. Ibid., §65.29, §65.22, §65.36, §57.46, 300–301, 298, 185.
81. Ibid., §65.44, §65.52, §65.70, §65.84, 303–4, 308, 312.
82. Ibid., §65.6, 294.
83. Ibid., §26.4. October 2019: 583–4.
84. Ibid., §53.1, §53.8, §53.46, §55.1, §55.11, §55.57, §55.59, 53–4, 63, 113–15, 126–7.
85. Stephanie Barwise, GTI Phase 2: Transcript Day 309. 7 November 2022: 10/12–21.
86. Barbara Lane, *Phase 1 Report (Supplemental)*. Section 2. 5 November 2018: 47–9; David Crowther, Ciara Holland and David Butler, *BRE Global Client Report: Grenfell Tower Fire Investigation – On-Site Investigation*. Prepared for: Metropolitan Police Service, P109378.1000. Issue:2. 20 February 2019: 76–9; GTI, *Phase 2 Report*, vol. 3, §40.1, 107.
87. Lane, *Phase 1 Report*, vol. 2, 5 November 2018: 57.
88. Ibid., 63.

89. GTI, *Phase 2 Report*, vol. 3, §43.52, §43.83, 158, 166; Lane, *Phase 1 Report*. 2. 2018: 64–6.
90. GTI, *Phase 2 Report*, vol. 3, §44.3, §44.9, §44.12, §44.24, §44.25, §44.27, §44.28, 167–9, 171.
91. Ibid., §44.32, 172.
92. Ibid., §46.71, §46.81, §46.88, 197, 199–200; GTI, *Phase 1 Report*, vol. 4, §30.102, 715.
93. GTI, *Phase 2 Report*, vol. 3, §33.9, 29.
94. Grenfell Tower Leaseholders' Association, Letter to Robert Black, 3 September 2010: 5–6.
95. GTI, *Phase 2 Report*, vol. 3, §33.22, §33.29, §33.32, 31–3.
96. GTI, *Phase 1 Report*, vol. 4, §66.6, 316.
97. Edward Daffarn, 'KCTMO – Playing with fire!' Grenfell Action Group blog, 20 November 2016. The public inquiry is churlish about Daffarn, suggesting he should have been more conciliatory, and petty about the notoriety of the blog post. GTI, *Phase 2 Report*, vol. 3, §33.49, §42.42, 36, 144.
98. GTI, *Phase 2 Report*, vol. 3, §33.67, 40.

Chapter 8 The 'impossible' fire

1. Metropolitan Police, 'Update: Number of victims of the Grenfell Tower fire formally identified is 70', 16 November 2017. In addition, Logan Gomes and Pily Burton were not included in the police update. NHS England, 'Statement on fire at Grenfell Tower', press release 14 June 2017; GTI, *Phase 2 Report*, vol. 7, §105.38, September 2024: 152.
2. GTI, *Phase 1 Report*, vol. 4, §21.2, §21.26, October 2019: 505, 514–15.
3. GTI, *Phase 1 Report*, vol. 4, §22.11, §22.36, 521, 537; GTI, *Phase 2 Report*, vol. 7, §110.7, 198.
4. GTI, *Phase 1 Report*, vol. 4, §23.21, §23.25, §23.54, 548, 549, 558.
5. Barbara Lane, *Phase 1 Report (Supplemental)*, Section 19, 24 October 2018: 18; José Torero, *Grenfell Tower: Phase 1 Report* (revised), 21 October 2018: 90–100.
6. GTI, *Phase 1 Report*, vol. 4, §24.31, §24.32, 569.
7. Ibid., §24.36, 570–71.
8. Lane, *Phase 1 Report (Supplemental)*, Section 2, 2018: 27.
9. Ibid., 27.
10. Ibid., 44.
11. Torero, *Grenfell Tower: Phase 1 Report* (revised), 2018: 107–10.
12. The comments in Tables 8.1–8.8 are reproduced exactly as they appear in the source documents and have not been edited.

13. David Purser, *Effects of Exposure of Grenfell Occupants to Toxic Fire Products – Causes of Incapacitation and Death*, Phase 1 Report, 5 November 2018: 44–6.
14. Purser, *Effects of Exposure of Grenfell Occupants to Toxic Fire Products*, 2018: 76.
15. Zakariya Chebiouni, GTI witness statement, 9 September 2018: 5; Emma O'Connor, GTI witness statement, 17 May 2018: 7; Nadia Jafari, GTI Phase 1: Transcript Day 54, 8 October 2018: 56/15; Van Quang Ho, GTI witness statement, 11 July 2018: 6; Nida Mangoba, GTI witness statement, 17 September 2018: 5; Richard Fletcher, GTI witness statement, 20 May 2018: 12; Meron Mekonnen, GTI witness statement, 23 May 2018: 5; Nagawa Nalukwago, GTI witness statement, 13 March 2018: 5; Mohammed Rasoul, GTI witness statement, 6 June 2018: 5; Rashida Ali, GTI witness statement, 2 March 2018: 10.
16. GTI, *Phase 1 Report*, vol. 2, §10.215, §10.221, October 2019: 141, 144; GTI, *Phase 2 Report*, vol. 6, §86.14, September 2024: 23.
17. Edward Daffarn, GTI witness statement, 15 May 2018: 6.
18. Turufat Girma, GTI witness statement, 6 June 2018: 5–6.
19. Abraham Abebe, GTI witness statement, 12 June 2018: 4.
20. GTI, *Phase 1 Report*, vol. 2, §11.25, §12.32, §14.124, 175, 215, 284.
21. Ibid., §14.125, §14.151, §14.156, §14.166, §14.173, §14.180, §14.188, 285, 289–90, 292–5.
22. Lane, *Phase 1 Report (Supplemental)*, Section 2, 2018: 14.
23. GTI, *Phase 1 Report*, vol. 4, §28.12, 597.
24. Lane, *Phase 1 Report (Supplemental)*, Section 2,. 2018: 15.
25. LFB, *Grenfell Tower Fire Preliminary Report*, 2 April 2019: 9–10.
26. Martin Moore-Bick, GTI Phase 1: Transcript Day 11, 27 June 2018: 113/25–114/1.
27. WM Mike Dowden, GTI Phase 1: Transcript Day 10, 26 June 2018: 159/22.
28. Dowden, GTI Phase 1: Transcript Day 10, 26 June 2018: 56/4, 67/9, 132/13.
29. Dowden, GTI Phase 1: Transcript Day 11, 27 June 2018: 28/4, 59/20.
30. Dowden, GTI Phase 1: Transcript Day 10, 26 June 2018: 160/12; 161/18–19.
31. Dowden, GTI Phase 1: Transcript Day 11, 27 June 2018: 24/4–6.
32. SM Andrew Walton, GTI Phase 1: Transcript Day 46, 20 September 2018: 198/18–23.
33. LFB, *Operational Response to Grenfell Tower*, vol. 1, version 1.0, July 2020: 489; LFB, *Operational Response to Grenfell Tower*, vol. 2, version 1.0, September 2021: 146.

34. GTI, *Phase 1 Report*, vol. 4, §29.1, 635.
35. GTI, *Phase 1 Report*, vol. 2, §13.103, 251.
36. GTI, *Phase 2 Report*, vol. 6, §97.39, 166.
37. GTI, *Phase 1 Report*, vol. 4, §29:45f, §29:54c, 648, 650; GTI, *Phase 2 Report*, vol. 5, §78.43. September 2024: 110.
38. GTI, *Phase 2 Report*, vol. 5, §78.56, §78.88, 114, 121.
39. GTI, *Phase 1 Report*, vol. 1, §1.14. October 2019: 6.
40. GTI, *Phase 2 Report*, vol. 5, §83.1, §82.10, 207, 203.
41. GTI, *Phase 1 Report*, vol. 2, §10.290, 158.
42. Betty Kasote, GTI witness statement, 27 June 2018: 8; Gitiara Pahlavani, GTI witness statement, 29 June 2018: 8; Florentyna Sobieszczak, GTI witness statement, 29 June 2018: 3; Hoang Khanh Quang, GTI witness statement, 1 May 2018: 8–9; Munira Mahmud, GTI witness statement, 6 June 2018: 5–6; Youssef Khalloud, GTI witness statement, 23 June 2018: 12; Mohammed Rasoul, GTI witness statement, 6 June 2018: 5; Paul Menacer, GTI witness statement, 17 August 2018: 8.
43. CM Jamal Stern, GTI witness statement. 14 February 2018: 11; CM Guy Tillotson, GTI witness statement. 4 December 2017: 6; CM Chris Secrett, GTI witness statement. 6 February 2018: 8; FF Harry Bettinson, GTI witness statement. 27 November 2017: 10.
44. Sharon Laci, GTI witness statement, 28 June 2018: 7–8; Rebin Sabir, GTI witness statement, 11 January 2019: 10; Fadumo Ahmed, GTI witness statement, 11 May 2018: 6–7; Roy Smith, GTI witness statement, 25 June 2018: 14; Rebecca Ross, GTI witness statement, 22 August 2018: 14–15; Ethiopia Assefa, GTI witness statement, 8 June 2018: 13; Christos Fairbairn, GTI witness statement, 17 August 2018: 7; Lina Hamide, GTI witness statement, 18 October 2018: 9; Ann Chance, GTI witness statement, 28 June 2018: 8; Natasha Elcock, GTI witness statement, 15 May 2018: 7; Antonio Roncolato, GTI witness statement, 3 July 2018: 15; Elpidio Bonifacio, GTI witness statement, 18 September 2018: 7.
45. FF Martin Gillam, GTI witness statement, 21 December 2017: 15.
46. GTI, *Phase 1 Report*, vol. 3, §20.13, October 2019: 469.
47. GTI, *Phase 1 Report*, vol. 4, §28.5, 596.
48. Home Office, Detailed analysis of fires attended by fire and rescue services, England, April 2017 to March 2018, 6 September 2018: 9.
49. Lane, *Phase 1 Report*, Section 20, 12 April 2018: 13.
50. GTI, *Phase 2 Report*, vol. 6, §85.43, 19.
51. GTI, *Phase 1 Report*, vol. 2, §11.34, 178.

52. Metropolitan Police, CAD 533: Transcript of emergency call received by MPS, 14 June 2017: 1.
53. Ann Chance, GTI witness statement, 28 June 2018: 4.
54. SM Daniel Egan, GTI Phase 1: Transcript Day 16, 4 July 2018: 49/15–19.
55. GTI, *Phase 1 Report*, vol. 4, §28.5, §28.18, §28.34, §28.63, 596, 599, 603, 610.
56. GTI, *Phase 2 Report*, vol. 5, §75.29, §75.32, 73–5.
57. Marcio Gomes, GTI witness statement, 4 June 2018: 38.
58. Helen Gebremeskel, GTI witness statement, 20 May 2018: 9.
59. Yehualashet Enyew, GTI witness statement, 17 July 2017: 3.
60. Alemishet Demissie, GTI witness statement, 30 June 2018: 6.
61. Ethiopia Assefa, GTI witness statement, 8 June 2018: 18.
62. Sharon Laci, GTI witness statement, 28 June 2018: 8–9.
63. Edward Daffarn, GTI witness statement, 15 May 2018: 16.

Chapter 9 Deregulation never stopped

1. Luke Barratt, 'Government's "one in, two out" deregulation rule suspended for Grenfell response', *Inside Housing*, 26 February 2019.
2. BEIS, Regulation for the Fourth Industrial Revolution, white paper, June 2019: 8.
3. Prime Minister's Office, Taskforce on Innovation, Growth and Regulatory Reform (TIGRR) Terms of Reference, 2 February 2021; Iain Duncan Smith, Theresa Villiers and George Freeman, Taskforce on Innovation, Growth and Regulatory Reform, May 2021: 118.
4. BEIS, Reforming the Framework for Better Regulation. July 2021: 3–4.
5. FBU, Reforming the Framework for Better Regulation submission, 1 October 2021.
6. Boris Johnson, *The Benefits of Brexit: How the UK is taking advantage of leaving the EU*. January 2022: 22, 27.
7. Nick Gutteridge, 'Rishi Sunak drops plans for war on Whitehall red tape', *Telegraph*, 3 January 2023.
8. Tom Clougherty and Robert Colvile, *The Future of Regulation*. Centre for Policy Studies. April 2024: 12.
9. Judith Hackitt, *Independent Review of Building Regulations and Fire Safety: Interim report*. 18 December 2017: 5; FBU, Independent review of building regulations and fire safety submission, October 2017.

10. Hackitt, *Independent Review of Building Regulations and Fire Safety: Final report.* 17 May 2018: 3; FBU, 'Statement on the Hackitt report into building regulations', press release, 17 May 2018.
11. FBU, MHCLG consultation, Banning the use of combustible materials in the external walls of high-rise residential buildings submission, August 2018.
12. FBU, MHCLG consultation, Review of the ban on the use of combustible materials in and on the external walls of buildings submission, April 2020.
13. DLUHC, Government response: review of the ban on the use of combustible materials in and on the external walls of buildings, 1 June 2022.
14. FBU, MHCLG consultation Building a Safer Future Proposals for reform of the building safety regulatory system submission, July 2019.
15. FBU, Housing, Communities and Local Government Committee inquiry into the draft Building Safety Bill submission, 11 September 2020.
16. FBU, Building Safety Bill: Second Reading briefing, 19 July 2021; 'Wrack tells MPs that "governments for decades" at fault on fire safety', press release, 16 September 2021; FBU, House of Commons Committee stage of the Building Safety Bill submission, 14 October 2021.
17. FBU, Building Safety and Social Housing, six years since the Grenfell Tower tragedy briefing, 6 July 2023.
18. FBU, Northern Ireland Department of Finance Consultation on amendments to The Building Regulations (Northern Ireland) 2012 (as amended) and associated technical guidance submission, October 2020; FBU, Welsh government consultation, Safer Buildings in Wales submission, April 2021.
19. FBU, Consultation on the proposed clarification of building regulations guidance on fire safety (Approved Document B) submission, October 2018.
20. FBU, MHCLG consultation, Technical Review of Approved Document B of the Building Regulations: Call for Evidence submission, 1 March 2019.
21. FBU, Home Office consultation, Regulatory Reform (Fire Safety) Order 2005 call for evidence submission, 31 July 2019.
22. FBU, Fire Safety Bill – second reading briefing, 29 April 2020; FBU, Fire Safety Bill: Public Bill Committee submission, 10 June 2020;

FBU, Fire Safety Bill – second reading House of Lords briefing, 1 October 2020.

23. FBU, Home Office consultation on fire safety submission, 12 October 2020.
24. HMICFRS, *State of Fire and Rescue report*, January 2020; FBU, 'Fire chief inspector's unwarranted attack on firefighters and their union', *FRS Matters*, March 2020.
25. Home Office, Reforming Our Fire and Rescue Service, White Paper, May 2022; FBU, Home Office consultation White Paper, Reforming Our Fire and Rescue Service submission, 7 July 2022; FBU, Fire White Paper: Empty, undemocratic and hostile to firefighters, *FRS Matters*, July 2022.
26. Home Office, 'A profession we can all be proud of', Response to White Paper consultation, 12 December 2023; FBU, Minimum Service Levels – unnecessary and unworkable, *FRS Matters*, February 2024.
27. Home Office, Fire and Rescue National Framework for England, May 2018: 14.
28. Peter Murphy and Katarzyna Lakoma, 'The (mis)interpretation of Section 25 of the Fire and Rescue Services Act 2004', *FIRE*, September 2020; Home Office, Report by the Home Secretary on fire and rescue authorities' compliance with the fire and rescue national framework for England, 29 June 2023.
29. FBU, Home Office consultation on Personal Emergency Evacuation Plans in High-Rise Residential Buildings submission, 19 July 2021.
30. HL Deb 4 April 2022, vol. 820, c1845.
31. FBU, Home Office consultation on Emergency Evacuation Information Sharing submission, 27 July 2022.
32. NFCC, Guidance to support a temporary change to a simultaneous evacuation strategy in purpose-built block of flats, October 2017; FBU, NFCC review of the guide: Guidance to support a temporary change to a simultaneous evacuation strategy in purpose-built block of flats submission, 30 April 2020.
33. Peter Apps and Nathaniel Barker, 'Dangerous buildings protected by "waking watches" have seen 300 fires since Grenfell, new figures reveal', *Inside Housing*, 3 April 2020.
34. HC Deb 21 July 2021 vol. 699 cc80–84WS; DLUHC, Waking Watch Replacement Fund 2023, 25 May 2023.
35. NFCC, *Fires in Tall Buildings and Fires in Buildings that Fail*, National Operational Guidance, 2021: 105.
36. FBU, *High Rise Buildings: Breathing Apparatus Safety Campaign*, June 2022.

37. Michael Spearpoint et al., *Means of Escape in Residential Buildings. Objective A3: Develop Method to Quantify Effectiveness of Evacuation Strategies*, 17 July 2023: 57–59, 64, 92.
38. Matt Wrack, Letter to James Cleverly, evacuation guidelines and research, 1 March 2024.
39. Prime Minister's Office, 'Statement from the Prime Minister on Grenfell Tower', press release, 17 June 2017; GTI, 'Sir Martin Moore-Bick appointed Chairman of Grenfell Tower public inquiry', press release, 29 June 2017; Theresa May, Letter to Martin Moore-Bick, 15 August 2017.
40. Martin Moore-Bick, GTI Phase 1: Transcript Day 88. 12 December 2018: 111/12–21.
41. Martin Moore-Bick, Letter to the Prime Minister, 10 February 2025.
42. 'Britain's boom in public inquiries into past disasters', *The Economist*, 19 August 2024: 21; GTI, Financial Report to 31 January 2025, 10 February 2025.
43. Imran Khan, GTI Phase 2: Transcript Day 309, 7 November 2022: 78/7–15, 94/115–22.
44. GTI, *Phase 2 Report*, vol. 1, §2.4, §2.13, September 2024: 9, 11.
45. Ibid., §4.23, §6.20, §10.4, §7.30, 43, 72, 146, 89.
46. Eric Pickles, GTI Phase 2: Transcript Day 262, 7 April 2022: 28/7–13; 104/15–20; 148/16–18; GTI, *Phase 2 Report*, vol. 1, §10.49, §10.50, 158–9.
47. GTI, *Phase 2 Report*, vol. 1, §12.49, 12.53.
48. Ibid., §2.43, 15.
49. GTI, *Phase 2 Report*, vol. 5, §83.1, §83.3, September 2024: 207.
50. GTI, *Phase 2 Report*, vol. 6, §85.39, September 2024: 18; GTI, *Phase 2 Report*, vol. 5, chapter 81; Matt Wrack, 'The provision and use of water for firefighting', brigade secretaries circular, 13 February 2024; Matt Wrack, 'Rescue from fire – prioritising children', brigade secretaries circular, 13 February 2024.
51. FBU, 'Firefighters demand no cover up on Grenfell Tower – justice for victims', press release, 19 June 2017.
52. FBU, Submission to Grenfell Tower inquiry terms of reference consultation, 20 July 2017: 3.
53. Martin Moore-Bick, Grenfell Tower Inquiry – Terms of Reference, 10 August 2017; FBU, 'Narrow Grenfell Inquiry too limited, says firefighters' union', press release, 16 August 2017.
54. Martin Moore-Bick, Formal Opening of the Inquiry: Transcript. 14 September 2017: 13/13–25; 14/1–8; GTI, *Phase 2 Report*, vol. 6 §84.4, 7.

55. Luke Bisby, *Grenfell Tower Inquiry: Regulatory Testing and the Path to Grenfell*. 2022: 127.
56. GTI, *Phase 2 Report*, vol. 1, §7.44, 93–94.
57. CS Todd and Associates Ltd, *Legislation, Guidance and Enforcing Authorities Relevant to Fire Safety Measures at Grenfell Tower*. March 2018; LGA, *Fire Safety in Purpose Built Blocks*. 7 July 2021: 120 (with redactions); Apps, 'Peer questions appointment of firm to write fire guidance citing director's comments about disabled residents', *Inside Housing*, 4 February 2022; GTI, *Phase 2 Report*, vol. 1, §14.17, 222; CS Todd and Associates Ltd, *Phase 2 Recommendations*. June 2023: 7, 15, 28.
58. Matt Wrack, Letter to the GTI, 12 October 2017; FBU, 'Firefighters' fury at Grenfell Inquiry panel appointment', press release, 11 December 2017; Steve McGuirk, *Report for the Grenfell Tower Inquiry*. January 2021; McGuirk, *Proposed Recommendations – Grenfell Tower Fire Inquiry*. 2023.
59. GTI, *Phase 2 Report*, vol. 5, §83.12, 209.
60. GTI, *Phase 2 Report*, vol. 3, §44.40, §44.44, §44.45, §44.46, §44.59, September 2024: 173–76.
61. Ibid., §113.5, 232.
62. Ibid., §113.12, §113.13, 234.
63. Ibid., §113.37, §113.38, 239.
64. Ibid., §113.8, 233.
65. Ibid., §113.41, 240.
66. Ibid., §113.51, §113.52, §113.53, 242–3.
67. Ibid., §§113.46–8, September 2024: 241.
68. Ibid., §112.4, 220.
69. HC Deb 4 September 2024, vol. 753, cc311–13, 324, 329–30.
70. HC Deb 13 February 2025, vol. 762, c36WS; 'FBU welcomes transfer of fire from Home Office to MHCLG', press release, 13 February 2025.
71. HC Deb 26 February 2025, vol. 762, cc777, 793.
72. UK Government Response to the Grenfell Tower Inquiry Phase 2 Report, February 2025: 19–20.
73. FBU, A good start – but still a long way to go, *FRS Matters*, March 2025.
74. FBU, *Executive Council's Annual Report*. 2018: 51, 53; FBU, 'Firefighters 100 Lottery and Grenfell survivors', *Firefighter*, December 2017–January 2018: 8.
75. FBU, 'One year on: Justice for Grenfell Solidarity March', press release, 31 May 2018; FBU, 'TUC 18: Fire safety failed at Grenfell Tower long

before fire broke out', press release, 10 September 2018; FBU, *The Grenfell Tower Fire: Background to an Atrocity*. 5 September 2018.

76. FBU, 'Residents must not pay for Grenfell-style cladding removal, union says', press release, 26 April 2019.
77. FBU, 'Firefighters launch Grenfell: Never Again campaign', press release, 14 June 2019; Tam McFarlane, 'Grenfell Never Again', *Firefighter*, August-September 2019: 16–17.
78. FBU, *The Grenfell Tower Fire: A Crime Caused by Profit and Deregulation*, September 2019; FBU, 'Government deregulation responsible for Grenfell, new report says', press release, 23 September 2019; *FBU response to the Grenfell Tower Inquiry phase 1 report*. January 2020.
79. Nicholas Burton, 'Forever in our hearts', *Firefighter*, April-May 2020: 16–19FBU, 'NAO cladding investigation "should shame this government", firefighters say', press release, 19 June 2020.
80. FBU, 'Firefighters call for Grenfell Inquiry to investigate "revolving door" between manufacturers and regulators', press release, 5 November 2020; FBU, 'Grenfell cladding lobbyists "aren't fit to lace the boots" of firefighters', press release, 9 December 2020.
81. FBU, 'Fire Brigades Union responds to Labour's demands for government action to fix building safety crisis', press release, 18 May 2021; FBU, 'Cladding scandal protest', *Firefighter*, June–July 2021: 5; FBU, 'New high rise fire highlights need for action on flammable cladding', *Firefighter*, June–July 2021: 7; FBU, 'Four years on – fighting the building safety crisis', press release, 14 June 2021; FBU, 'Labour conference agrees to FBU motion to fight cladding scandal', press release, 28 September 2021.
82. 'FBU slams government rejection of key Grenfell inquiry recommendation for disabled people', press release, 7 June 2022; Matt Wrack, Letter to Lord Greenhalgh, 6 June 2022.
83. FBU, 'Firefighters marking Grenfell fifth anniversary', press release, 14 June 2022; Helen Hague, 'Grenfell justice #Demand charges', *Firefighter*, June–July 2022: 12–13.
84. FBU, 'Grenfell firefighters settle for £20m in High Court', *Firefighter*, February–March 2024.

Chapter 10 Justice delayed, lessons unlearned

1. Pippa Crerar, 'Angela Rayner defends handling of meeting with Grenfell survivors and families', *Guardian*, 9 February 2025.

2. LFB, Flat fire – Dagenham, 26 August 2024; James Riding, 'Dagenham fire: what happened and what we know about the building', *Inside Housing*, 27 August 2024.
3. Timothy Edgley, 'Mosaic Apartments, Slough fire caused by balcony light fitting', *Slough and South Bucks Observer*, 20 February 2025.
4. 'Firefighters' union worried over reduced crew cover', *BBC*, 17 September 2024.
5. Robert Booth and Emine Sinmaz, 'Police under pressure to accelerate criminal investigation into Grenfell fire', *Guardian*, 4 September 2024; Martina Lees, 'We will seek manslaughter charges,' *The Times*, 7 September 2024: 13.
6. DLUHC, Building Safety Programme: monthly data release – September 2023, table 6, 19 October 2023.
7. MHCLG, Building Safety Remediation: monthly data release – January 2025, 20 February 2025; National Audit Office, Dangerous cladding: the government's remediation portfolio. November 2024.
8. Scottish government, Cladding replacement funding: FOI release, 9 September 2024; Charlotte Banks, 'One Scottish building remediated in four years under UK grant', 10 September 2024; Jayne Bryant, Statement by the Cabinet Secretary for Housing and Local Government: Building safety, 12 November 2024; Peter Roberts, *Improving Safety in High Rise Residential Buildings in Northern Ireland. Report of the Expert Panel for the Building Safety Programme Northern Ireland.* 7 December 2023: 18, 35.
9. Martina Lees, 'Scandal of the cladding victims left homeless', *Sunday Times*, 28 April 2024; End Our Cladding Scandal, 'The building safety crisis: still no end in sight', 4 July 2024.
10. GTI, *Phase 2 Report*, vol. 4, §67.16, September 2024: 322.
11. FBU, Phase 2 Written Submission on Recommendations, 31 October 2022: 8.
12. Ibid., 8–9.
13. Labour Party, *Change: Labour Party Manifesto 2024*, 13 June 2024: 58, 80.
14. GTI, *Phase 2 Report*, vol. 1, §2.13, September 2024: 11.
15. James Tapper, Roya Shahidi and Jon Ungoed-Thomas, 'Grenfell survivors furious over David Cameron's claim that inquiry backed him over red-tape drive', *Observer*, 8 September 2024.
16. Emily Dugan, 'Tony Blair told to "take responsibility" after Grenfell criticism', *Guardian*, 6 September 2024; FBU, 'Blair's "despicable" Grenfell remarks are out of touch, says firefighter union leader', press release, 6 September 2024.

17. Kemi Badenoch, *Conservatism in Crisis Rise of the Bureaucratic Class*, October 2024: 19.
18. Nigel Farage, 'Five years, we still haven't taken back control', *Telegraph*, 31 January 2025: 14; Chris Smyth, 'Keir Starmer invokes Margaret Thatcher as he goes for growth', *The Times*, 29 January 2025: 6.
19. Transparency International UK, *House of Cards: Exploring Access and Influence in UK Housing Policy*, 2021: 5; Autonomy, *Politics for Sale: Analysing Twenty-One Years of UK Political Donations*, 2024: 35, 47.
20. Mark Townsend, 'Grenfell families want inquiry to look at role of "race and class" in tragedy', *Guardian*, 26 July 2020.
21. GTI, *Phase 2 Report*, vol. 1, §1.25, §1.21, 6–7.
22. Imran Khan, GTI Phase 2: Transcript Day 309, 7 November 2022: 84/9–18.
23. Mario Ledwith, 'Sunaks are wealthier than Charles', *The Times*, 18 May 2024; 'Rich List 2017', *Sunday Times Magazine*, May 2017: 5.

Index

FBU refers to Fire Brigades Union; GT to Grenfell Tower